# LOST IN HOLLYWOOD

# LOST IN HOLLYWOOD

The Fast Times and Short LIfe
of River Phoenix

## JOHN GLATT

Primus

DONALD I. FINE, INC.

*New York*

Library of Congress Catalogue Card Number: 94-68094
Hardcover ISBN: 1-55611-426-5
Primus Paperback ISBN: 1-55611-440-0
Manufactured in the United States of America

10 9 8 7 6 5 4 3 2 1

Designed by Irving Perkins Associates, Inc.

*Grateful acknowledgment is made to the following to reprint previously published material:*

Henry Miller, *The Time of the Assassins,* Copyright © 1956 by New Directions Publishing Corp. Reprinted by permission of New Directions Publishing Corp. and Canadian Rights.

Grace Catalano, *River Phoenix: Hero & Heartthrob,* Copyright © 1986 by Ultra Communications, Inc. Used by permission of Bantam Books, a division of Bantam Doubleday Dell Publishing Group, Inc.

*Brief quotations in this work originally appeared in articles and stories in the following British publications:*

The Guardian, July 27, 1989, The Mail on Sunday, September 24, 1988, The Independent on Sunday Magazine, December 5, 1993, The Sunday Mirror, January 9, 1994, Today, March 24, 1994.

To Vicky

# CONTENTS

*He embraced the darkness* and *the light*

—THE TIME OF THE ASSASSINS,
*a study of Rimbaud by Henry Miller*

# AUTHOR'S NOTE

THIS BIOGRAPHY OF River Phoenix is the result of more than sixty-five interviews, including ones with Phoenix family members, close friends, fellow actors and directors; Phoenix family friends from the Children of God and experts on the cult; fellow band members; and drug companions. The author has also made use of magazine and newspaper articles as well as a taped interview by River Phoenix with Bill DeYoung of the Gainesville *Sun* in March, 1989; much of this interview was not published. Of particular help has been Tad Friend's April 1994 feature on River Phoenix in Esquire magazine and Premiere magazine's tribute to Phoenix the same month. All quotes taken from sources other than the author's own interviews have been credited to those sources. Where no source is identified, the quote was made directly to the author. The author made every possible attempt to interview River's parents, John and Arlyn, including writing a four-page letter on recycled paper explaining this project. At this writing they have declined to be interviewed.

The author would like to thank River's grandmother Margaret Dunetz for her background help and his great-aunt Frances Beck for her recollections of the Bottom family and the Phoenixes' first days in Los Angeles. Deep-felt thanks and gratitude must also go to the Phoenix family tutor Dirk Drake, whose advice and insight added another dimension to this book. The author also extends his gratitude to Josh Greenbaum for providing a unique insight into his "brother" and showing the author around the Gainesville music scene where River Phoenix had some of his happiest times. The author is also indebted to Mike Parker, Bob Pitchlynn, Wade Evans and Scott Green for their help in understanding how the making of *My Own Private Idaho* influenced Phoenix. Thanks are also due to Jonathan Sherman, Hap Wotilla and Dr. Sam Ajamian for their rare insight into the Children of God and the crucial part it played in River's life.

I am grateful to all those who agreed to be interviewed for this book, including: Dr. Sam Ajamian, Lt. Col. Bobby Bottom, Melanie Barr, Frances Beck, Deborah Berg, Pat Brewer, Bill Bryson, Anthony Campanaro, Joe Dante, Ron Davis, Aix Djelai, Lala Delude, Bill DeYoung, Jim Dobson, Joe Dolce, Dirk Drake, Margaret Dunetz, Wade Evans, Mali Finn, Tad Friend, Robert Fuller, David Gerber, George Gordon, Scott Green, Josh Greenbaum, Kenny Greenbaum, Rachel Guinan, Scott Green, Waris Hussein, Holly Jensen, David Jones, Jim Kesl, Adam Khan, Judy Knapp, Pat Koch, Det. Sgt. Mike Lee, Heidi Lopez, Pam and Paul Maneeratama, Susan Methany, Conrad "Bud" Montgomery, Diana Moran, Nigel Morris, Alan Moyle, Roy Nance, Mike Parker, Bill Perry, Paul Petersen, Mark Pinske, Bob Pitchlynn, Sasa Raphael, Michelle Rey, Nick Richert, William Richert, Abby Rude, Charlie Scales, Jonathan Sherman, George Sluizer, Dave Smadbeck, Lanny Swerdlow, Terri Treas, Steve Viens, Steven Ward, and Hap Wotilla.

The author would also like to thank his agent Susan Lee Cohen for her unstinting support and encouragement as well as Larry Bernstein and Don Fine for his belief in the project. Much thanks must also go to David Hayes for his early editing of the book as well as his invaluable advice and insight throughout the project.

Thanks also to: Yasmin Brennan, Lightning Slim, Roger Hitts, Shelley Marquart, Denise Childs, Susan and Peggy Comegys,

Mary-Beth Buckhout, Christopher Bowen, Daphna Inbar, Laurette Ziemer, Robert Sites, Geri Chark, Stuart Krichevsky, Pamela Dorman, Chris Comegys, Kate Caldwell, Wensley Clarkson, Mary Morrison, Tim Noad and Philip and Debbie Noble, Rosemarie Lennon, Paul Thorp, Danny Trachtenberg, Carl Pokrassa, Dave LaFontaine and Marion Collins.

RIVER PHOENIX STRUGGLED against his demons for most of his short life. And on Halloween 1993 he lost his battle, dying on a cold sidewalk outside a Hollywood nightclub called the Viper Room from a massive drug overdose. This tragic end to a brief, brilliant career brought the curtain down on one of the most unusual of show business stories. It also marked the end of the long, strange trip that River's parents had begun nearly a quarter of a century earlier.

The son of hippie runaways John Lee Bottom and Arlyn Dunetz, baby River was shuttled around ramshackle communes until his parents gave up drugs to hitch their wagon to the Children of God, a California-based Christian cult. The gifted child was taught from his earliest days that he was on a divine mission to save the world. He ended by losing himself to sexual abuse, half-formed philosophy and lethal drugs.

Apparently in line with Children of God teachings, River was initiated into sex with other cult members when he was four years old. Cult leaders taught that such behavior liberated the children from supposedly outdated mores while promoting a loving life; for River it seemed to lead to a lifetime of sexual confusion and pain.

The boy's parents, who had adopted the name Phoenix to symbolize rising from the ashes of a society they had rejected, and that had rejected them, were eventually dispatched to Venezuela to promote the gospel according to the Children of God. With his sister Rain and brother Yoaquin, River panhandled on the streets of Caracas, receiving an early lesson that he was to be the family provider. Denied the most basic education, the children were also isolated, which prevented their developing social skills. By the time the Phoenix family made their way back to the United States, the children were ridiculed as freaks and outcasts by other children their own age.

In California the Phoenix children earned a pittance panhandling on the streets of Westwood as John and Arlyn pushed ahead with their seemingly impossible dream—to make their children show-business luminaries. The notion was to take on Hollywood and win, to swim with the sharks and come out intact. Their sworn mission was to use the power of stardom to deliver their so-called hippie message and thereby save the world. Instead, the movie industry devoured River, who soon was supporting the entire Phoenix family as well as various hangers-on.

Celebrity and stardom never, it seems, brought River Phoenix happiness. The boy was still afflicted by early abusive sexual experiences. While other children were just starting to discover their first awkward feelings of attraction to the opposite sex, ten-year-old River declared a second virginity. Apparently it was his attempt at negating his past, but even going into deep denial did not exorcise the nightmares.

John and Arlyn had little awareness of the problems tearing at their eldest son. Indeed, they aided him five years later when he announced he wanted to make love to an older female friend of the family. River was merely seeking parental blessing, but his parents insisted on preparing a love tent in the backyard where the consummation was to take place.

By his mid-teens River Phoenix was a movie idol, especially for teenagers, but he had no love for his fame. He had realized, it seems, that his supposedly God-given mission was futile—perhaps bogus?—and found it difficult to reconcile himself to this unwanted enlightenment. He was also still struggling under the felt obligation to support his family, which meant rarely being able to take time off from his work. River could not share his doubts with his parents: Arlyn's idealistic flame still burned too bright, John's was burned out. The Phoenix patriarch had come to despise Hollywood, now deciding that it would only corrupt and destroy his family. But his was mostly an unheard voice, and he increasingly sought relief in alcohol, alienating himself from his family.

Feeling abandoned by his father, River sought for a replacement he could look up to. On each of his movies it seemed he would select his own father-figure and develop a friendship. This long line of actors included Harrison Ford, Sidney Poitier and Dan Aykroyd, as well as directors Joe Dante and Rob Reiner.

In River's mid-teens, his parents selected a young man called Larry McHale to be, in effect, his "nanny." McHale proceeded to introduce the young actor to partying through people who gave River his first taste of cocaine.

River now started turning toward alcohol and drugs to anesthetize his pain. And as he grew older he became increasingly dependent on a variety of stimulants. He did struggle to live a normal life while pursuing his acting career, but the destructive seeds, more or less dormant since his Children of God days, now began to take foot and flourish. *Fleurs de mal.*

The more River indulged himself in the so-called rock 'n' roll lifestyle, the harder it was to reconcile it to his public stance as a clean-living, nature-loving vegan. Time and again John Phoenix would get drunk and beg his son to quit the industry and save himself. But the bearded hippie, who alone in the family had clung to his sixties' beliefs, seemed to know he had lost the battle for River's soul. Eventually John would drop out a second time, becoming a recluse in Costa Rica and severing all ties to the town and industry that had claimed his family.

Father and son did eventually reconcile on River's twenty-third birthday as River promised John to make a concerted effort to stay straight and sober.

It would last just two months.

Tension on the Utah desert set of River's last film, *Dark Blood*, seemingly were too much for him. River headed to Los Angeles to find relief with his "friends." It was on the devil's own night that he was given the fatal Persian brown heroin by a friend in the Viper Room. It became apparent immediately that something had gone very wrong.

But in River Phoenix's death, as in his life, what help there was came too little and too late.

## Chapter One

# TAKE THE HIGHWAY

IN THE SUMMER of 1968, a twenty-three-year-old secretary called Arlyn Sharon Dunetz decided to turn on, tune in and drop out of her workaday life to pursue a hippie dream. One day she came home from the office and told her husband she was leaving him to find the truth. She told him that their marriage and their dreams no longer made sense; she wanted out, to find a new and more meaningful life.

Born on New Year's Eve, 1944, Arlyn was Meyer and Margaret Dunetz's third daughter. The Dunetzes were a typical Jewish middle-class family living on Faile Street in the East Bronx neighborhood of Hunts Point, New York. Meyer was a hardworking Chevrolet car salesman and a good provider for the family. Following her two eldest sisters, Merle and Rhoda, Arlyn went to the nearby Joseph Redman Drake School. Dark-haired, pixie-faced, she was an average student, and when the family moved to a bigger house on Valentine Avenue, thirteen-year-old Arlyn was sent to the Edgar Allan Poe Junior High School, considered by some a cut below the prestigious Hunter Junior High School, where her sister Merle was a student.

The Dunetzes were a close, loving family. There was always humor in the air. The girls' friends liked hanging out in the Dunetzes' apartment, where they could always share a joke in the genial atmosphere. Arlyn loved to organize her sisters to perform their carefully rehearsed singing routines that were the highlight of frequent family gatherings.

Soon after graduating from school Arlyn married a computer operator and found a job as a secretary in a Manhattan office. Like thousands of other young women, she got on the nine-to-five treadmill, catching the subway each morning to her office in midtown, shopping at Saks Fifth Avenue, coming home at night to prepare dinner for her new husband.

"I was just a clone, totally unconscious," said Arlyn much later. "I didn't know that the air was polluted and I didn't care. I just went to work and thought that everything the government told me was right and true. It took some time before I awakened. I became aware."

Resentment was building. She began to hate her humdrum existence, seemed to have nothing more to look forward to than being a housewife and mother. The late sixties were, of course, a time of intense change, social revolution was in the air. Arlyn dreamed of being in the front line, breaking free from drudgery to become a hippie flower child. She confided her intentions to her sister Merle's young friend Kenny Greenbaum, who shared her fascination with the new counterculture.

"She was unsettled," remembers Greenbaum, who would himself drop out to Woodstock a year later with his new wife and join a commune. "She wanted to go the hippie way and do her thing. It was as simple as that."

One day, to the astonishment of her husband and family, Arlyn stuffed some clothes into her backpack, took a few dollars of savings and left the Bronx to hitchhike to California with a friend.

"I knew she was going to become a hippie," said Arlyn's mother, Margaret Dunetz. "I wasn't thrilled, but what could I do? I didn't try to stop her because she was a grown woman already."

Arlyn would later sum up her decision: "It was difficult because my parents weren't seeing the same things, but I knew I had to change my life. It was a time of dimension and conflict in the nation. We were seeking an answer."

Three thousand miles away in Fontana, California, a steel town fifty miles east of Los Angeles where the Hell's Angels were founded in 1950, a young man called John Lee Bottom also dreamed of something other than his life as a gardener. The youngest of two sons, John, who was born in 1947, had virtually raised himself. His father, Eli, who had changed his name to Robert when he had joined the navy, was always too involved with building his glass business to spend time with his son.

"John was a wild boy," says his aunt Frances Beck, who used to visit the family. "They had problems and I don't think his parents were that good to the children. They had to root for themselves."

When Beck and her husband moved to nearby Long Beach they took pity on the dreamy young boy and invited him to stay for a week.

"We took him to Disneyland," she remembers. "He really loved it. His dad never took him places like other boys because he was too busy working."

John's life was devastated when his mother was seriously injured in a car crash that caused irreversible brain damage. After many months of hospitalization she was allowed to go home but would never again be considered normal. And soon after the accident John's parents divorced and his father moved to San Francisco and remarried before emigrating to Perth, Australia, where he died in 1993.

By the age of thirteen, John was sick of the strict private Methodist school he had been sent to and had started drinking heavily and smoking marijuana.

"I ran away from home to become a songwriter in Hollywood," John would recall years later. Eventually he was found and sent back to Fontana to finish his schooling, but when he was sixteen a serious back injury in a motorcycle accident left him permanently disabled. Depressed and disillusioned, he started drifting about California, eking out a living from odd jobs gardening and refinishing furniture. A brief relationship produced a daughter,

Jodean, but John Bottom was too restless to settle down and soon left to go his own way.


It was while John was driving in Los Angeles in his battered VW bus that he saw Arlyn, recently arrived from the Bronx.

"I was hitchhiking on Santa Monica Boulevard and John picked me up," said Arlyn. "He invited me up to his place and we went [there] two nights later. We talked and talked till early morning. We just knew we had similar desires."

Similar desires included an alternative to the materialistic world neither of them was comfortable in. They discussed the Vietnam War, the antiwar movement, how peace and love were the solution to the world's madness. Soon after, they fell in love and decided to stay together and become what they would later call "seekers."

Taking to the road now, Arlyn and John commenced wandering about the West Coast from commune to commune, experimenting with LSD and other psychedelic drugs and experiencing what they would describe as a "religious awakening."

"I just instantly saw that I was living in a pit," said John some twenty years later. "There were a lot of lost people and the president wasn't necessarily the nicest guy in the world."

An instant acid convert, Arlyn believed that LSD was nothing less than a "gift from God."

"We'd heard that acid was the truth serum," explained Arlyn. "It was the thing that was going to get you above the world, to a level of consciousness where you could feel the power of God. That was the only reason we took it."

John and Arlyn were eventually married in a hippie ceremony in 1969 and headed north to Oregon in their VW bus to work their way cross-country to Florida in a mobile commune. WHAT?

"We were flower children," said John. "We were full of faith and we loved everybody."

In the early summer of 1970 John and Arlyn Bottom and a dozen fellow-travelers they had met on the road drove over the breathtakingly beautiful Mount Hood with its lush, panoramic views into the flat brown desert country of Madras, Oregon—the peppermint capital of the world, where Bottom knew there was seasonal work to be had harvesting mint, and since his new bride was pregnant the commune would decide to settle for the summer until the birth.

At the main crossroads in Madras Bottom turned right and drove the four miles to the rural wilderness of the Nance Farm and offered their services.

"They were just traveling through here and I gave them a job for the summer," remembers owner Roy Nance, who let the commune move into a tiny old two-story house on his property. "I was the first one around here to employ hippies."

Nance, who raised peppermint for chewing gum and tooth-paste, put them to work changing sprinklers and hoeing mint but soon found that the hippie band marched to their own drum.

"Hippies were funny people and they had their own ideas of working," remembers Nance. "They'd work so long and then they'd take their break. They'd just sit down in the field regardless of what else was happening. We might be picking rocks and we'd look round and they'd be sitting in the field. I'd have to go back and ask them just what was going on."

There were more surprises for Nance, who wasn't prepared for the hippies' uninhibited lifestyle.

"They didn't have the morals that the rest of us had. They just didn't," said Nance. "When we'd be out doing mint they'd all be out skinny-dipping in the pond. It made no difference whether I was there or not. I was a young man at the time too."

Nance said he was often embarrassed by the hippie girls who never wore pants while they were working in the fields and de-lighted in sending their long skirts flying up over their waists.

"They thought it was funny," said Nance. "The guys would look at me and laugh and I'd shake my head. I'm sure they were on drugs most of the time."

Bottom's commune also tried to plant marijuana by the side of

the road, but their hopes of a crop were ruined when Nance
sprayed weed-killing chemicals over the seeds to protect his mint.

After a hard day's work in the intense heat of the fields the
hippies would retreat to their communal house where they
smoked marijuana by candlelight, listened to music and read
aloud to each other. Mostly they kept to themselves but they were
polite and well-liked by the other workers on the farm.

Lala Delude, who rented a small house from Nance, remembers
John and Arlyn fondly:

"They seemed so in love with each other," said Delude. "They
were so young but they had an amazing maturity. They left their
mark on everyone they met."

As Arlyn came nearer to giving birth she made it clear it would be
a natural one at home and she refused to go into the nearby
hospital in Madras.

"It just scared me to death," said Nance. "I said, 'Good God,
that's dangerous. We've gotta have a doctor.' I even said I'd pay
for it. Arlyn wanted the whole community in on helping with the
birth. I didn't want anything to do with it."

Worried about what he perceived as unhygenic conditions in
the commune house, Nance persuaded the Bottoms to move into
the somewhat better conditions of a rundown shack on Dover
Lane next to his house. Right up to her ninth month, Arlyn
worked in the fields hoeing down in the mud next to John.

When Arlyn did go into labor the whole commune rallied
around to help. Her labor lasted three long days, a difficult birth,
but Arlyn resisted calling for professional help. Finally at 12:03 P.M.
on Sunday, August 23, 1970, to a roar of applause by Arlyn's
friends, River Jude Bottom came into the world. His joyous parents named him River after the river of life in Hermann Hesse's
*Siddhartha,* which the commune had been reading together, and
Jude, after their favorite Beatles' song, "Hey Jude."

Judy Knapp remembers John Bottom running excitedly into the

general store where she worked to buy up her complete stock of candles for the naming ceremony.

"He was exuberant," remembers Knapp. "He told me they'd named him River Bottom and that they needed candles for a ceremony they were having. I remember thinking that River Bottom was a very unusual name."

Roy Nance held River when he was just an hour old after Arlyn proudly carried him across the drive to his house to show him off.

"River was just a cute little stinker," said Nance. "I couldn't believe they had named him River Bottom."

The arduous pregnancy had taken its toll on Arlyn. It would be months before she fully regained her health, and Nance tried to persuade her to see a doctor. Pale and sickly-looking, she steadfastly refused, saying medical treatment went against her philosophy.

As winter approached and the work on the farm ran out, John Bottom decided to move on and head south to the warmth of California so that his wife could better recuperate. The weather had turned cold and Bottom's VW bus, which had no heater, refused to start.

"I didn't want them to go," said Nance. "I knew it was pretty dangerous to be traveling in those conditions with a young baby, and his mother looked real sick to me. I didn't know what was to become of them."

Finally, Nance ended up towing the bus forty-five miles to the nearest big town, Bend, and left the Bottoms by the roadside with some groceries and provisions.

Over the next year John Bottom drove his young wife and baby on a psychedelic voyage east, going from commune to commune in the blossoming peace-and-free-love hippie culture. They faced hostility everywhere they went in the straight world, but when they met a fellow traveler there was an instant bonding. They drifted from group to group, staying a few days or weeks before it was time to move on. Hallucinogenic drugs and marijuana were plentiful and cheap, and John and Arlyn took them as an essential part of what they considered their inner journey. But their love affair with LSD abruptly ended when they both had some frighteningly mystical experiences:

"I had a vision," recalled Arlyn in 1979. "I was in total darkness when a golden hand seemed to rip away the darkness . . ."

John's presumed epiphany came while he was lying in the middle of a field and started to hear an unearthly voice saying, "Why don't you receive me?" John asked the voice to prove it was real and suddenly a "tall fellow" appeared and announced, "I'm a Christian."

"He had two Bibles," said John. "One was an antique. I was a history student. I felt God knew what would interest me. At first I cried. Then I quit drugs and smoking."

## Chapter Two

# THE CHILDREN OF GOD

IN 1972 ARLYN AND John turned from psychedelic drugs to religion in the form of the radical cult, Children of God—which survives under the new name, The Family, based in Los Angeles. The Bottoms were one of hundreds of families flocking to the controversial group, then popularily known as "Hookers for Jesus."

Founded in 1968 by charismatic traveling preacher David Brandt Berg, also known as Moses David, the cult was initially based in a coffeehouse in bohemian Huntington Beach, California, where it witnessed to hippies. Prospective converts were brought to the coffee house to hear Berg's antichurch, antiestablishment sermons. Soon the cult flourished, leading hippies away from drugs and then indoctrinating them with Berg's own brand of Christianity. Members became a common sight on the streets of Los Angeles in their striking red sackcloth robes, covered in ashes and carrying signs forecasting the end of the world.

A year later, fleeing "religious persecution" in Huntington Beach, Berg, then forty-nine, organized fifty hard-core disciples to split into teams to crisscross the country in convoys of trailers to recruit new members. They staged doomsday vigils outside high schools and college campuses as well as attending rock concerts and antiwar rallies where easily influenced young people tripping on LSD might be converted. The early cult members specialized in walking into Sunday church services en masse to disrupt and cause chaos. It was pure theater with the blood-red-cloaked cultists periodically hammering long wooden staffs against the ground to the communal shout of "Woe."

One of the Children of God convoys was led by twenty-three-year-old Hap Wotilla, who on orders from David Berg led thirty followers out of the cult's Crockett, Texas, headquarters, in an old converted school bus to start a commune in an abandoned resort near Colorado Springs. Set high up in the scenic Pike's Peak mountains, the new commune was comprised of a lodge and five outbuildings that served as dormitories. In less than six months Wotilla's commune was thriving with 150 converts—including the Bottom family.

Said Wotilla, who became the commune's shepherd, or leader: "These people were drug addicts, prostitutes and runaways who were totally lost and throwing their lives away. They were coming and joining the group and finding their lives rehabilitated."

After disillusionment with LSD, John and Arlyn saw the Children of God as the next step in their spiritual search. To the applause of the whole commune they were officially "saved" as they renounced their old lives and accepted Jesus as their savior. John, Arlyn and River were then given their new Bible name of Phoenix, which symbolized rising from the ashes of their old lives to be born again. They then enthusiastically turned over their valuables and possessions to the group and declared their undying allegiance to Jesus and the Children of God.

Known as "babs"—the group's name for new converts—the Phoenixes were first instructed in a special letter-writing class to ask their parents for cash and supplies that would be needed to run the commune. Then the newly named Phoenix family began regular "witnessing" expeditions to recruit new members around Denver, Colorado Springs and Boulder. They joined their new brothers and sisters in handing out cult literature and singing religious songs to people on the street to attract their attention for a possible "witnessing."

While his parents were on their conversion trips River stayed in the nursery with the other children learning the Bible and how to be a good cult member. From infancy River was subjected to fire-and-brimstone sermons from cult leaders about the evils of drugs, telling how cocaine was the devil's dandruff and that rock legend Janis Joplin had shot airplane glue into her veins the night she died. Berg also taught his followers that America would soon be destroyed by the Comet Kohoutek and prophesied the imminent coming of the anti-Christ and what he called the "End Times."

John and Arlyn were typical recruits for the eccentric Berg, who described himself as a "toilet" to catch the "damned hippies" and other "waste products of society. We flush them, channel them, filter them, cleanse them, distill them and cause them to be recycled that they actually vanish into thin air, they evaporate," wrote Berg the year the Phoenixes joined.

Berg's self-styled religion mixed the hippie doctrines of free love and antiestablishment rebelliousness to encourage adults as well as children to experiment with "God's gift of sex." New members received this 1973 edict from Berg: "Come on Ma Burn Your Bra. We have a sexy God and a sexy religion with a very sexy leader with an extremely sexy young following! So if you don't like sex you'd better get out while you can still save your bra! Salvation sets us free from the curse of clothing and the shame of nakedness!"

From their first days in the commune Arlyn became close friends with a vivacious, dark-haired woman called Bithia Sherman who had joined the group in Ohio two years earlier. She had an infant son Jonathan, the same age as River, whose father was commune shepherd Hap Wotilla.

"I was just like a lot of other kids," said Bithia, twenty-two at the time. "There was no real direction in my life. I needed somebody to love me. I needed to be accepted. I needed to have a purpose. And then I met the cult and they provided all that for me. I had never known a purpose before, and what more of a purpose could you have than to go out and save the world?"

According to Bithia, a large number of the cult practiced sexual freedom in the name of God, taking multiple partners, swapping husbands and wives and participating in orgies and pornography. "You could do anything in God's name if you did it in love," said Bithia. "That included sharing sexually with other people. We were taught that the ultimate sacrifice that a man could make to God was to share his wife with another man."

Shepherd Wotilla, who has since left the Children of God, now describes it as a "Christian sex cult."

"We built that group with converted hippies and rebellious youth who were already into the whole hippie trip with its promiscuity and sexual freedom. They came into the group to dedicate their lives to the Lord, but then Moses David came up with this doctrine of God saying it's okay for us to have sex with each other outside of marriage, explained Wotilla."

Birth control was discouraged by cult leaders and the swapping of partners soon led to women, becoming pregnant by men other than their husbands.

In 1974 the Phoenixes moved to the main Children of God commune in Crockett, Texas, with Bithia and Jonathan Sherman. Soon after arriving in the commune Arlyn gave birth to a little girl she named Rain Joan of Arc—it happened to be raining during the birth.

"I delivered Rain myself," John Phoenix said proudly. "We wanted to give her a Godly name."


During the next few years the Phoenixes were rewarded for their loyalty to the cult by rising through the Children of God hierarchy to be given extra responsibilities. As River reached his formative years he accompanied his parents on a neverending trek from commune to commune, helping them to recruit new members. He was a thoughtful little boy but already seemed guarded and withdrawn, not as animated as his playmates.

At four, in line with Berg's teachings, River began to experience sex regularly with the other young people of the group in the nurseries at night. Years later he would acknowledge in an interview with Joe Dolce of Details magazine losing his virginity as a young child:

"I'm glad I did it when I was young," he said. "But I didn't want those young vaginas and different body parts that were in my face to make me perverse when I'm older, so I blocked it out. I was completely celibate from ten to fourteen. You're just born into that reality and you accept it."

Jonathan Sherman, who grew up with River in both communes, says he too was initiated into sex at four years of age:

"Sex was part of our upbringing," he remembers. "It was part of the lifestyle and seemed quite natural as we didn't know anything else. They involved the kids in all aspects of sexual activity from a very young age. I was put together with other young girls and we played around. It was part of that whole post-hippie genre in the early seventies of free love, free sex, free everything. We're all God's children."

It wasn't, apparently, only the children that Jonathan was expected to have sex with:

"My mother's older friends would take me to bed with them and do a little experimentation. I was like four or five years old at the time. They'd just fool around and have me touch them and they'd touch me. I suckled until I was eight. They did basically everything."

Jonathan says the cult also physically beat children to keep them under its tight control:

"Children were community property and we were raised to be submissive. We were beaten and put in isolation and seclusion. You can't be rebellious at all. You're brainwashed."

In October 1974, an eighteen-month charity-fraud investigation into the Children of God by New York State Attorney General Louis Lefkowitz shone a spotlight on the cult for the first time. The sixty-five-page report accused the by-then worldwide organization of sexually abusing young members, of rape, kidnapping, brainwashing and virtual enslavement of converts. It also revealed that Berg, known to his followers as Moses David or Mo, lived in

Europe, from where he ruled his 120 American colonies and estimated eight thousand members through his "Mo Letters"—written edicts, often bizarre, which covered all aspects of cult life. The report, for example, described the "metamorphosis of the Children of God from a religious, Bible-oriented group to a cult subservient to the whims and desires" of its leaders. It also revealed that leaders and converts regularly "engaged in unorthodox sexual rites" and that Berg encouraged "incestuous behavior, youthful intercourse and the non-sanctity of marriage and family."

One witness described a "mass betrothal" in which Berg announced he would immediately marry a pretty young follower who had taken his fancy. Then, with his wife Jane and other adult and child cult members watching, he had sex with his new bride.

Although highly damning, the report concluded that the Children of God were constitutionally protected by the First Amendment and no direct legal action could be taken.

Former Children of God member Dr. Sam Ajamian, who was a member from 1969 to 1979 and as of this writing actively campaigns against the cult, says free sex and group orgies started as far back as 1971—a year before the Phoenixes joined.

"River Phoenix said once that he had lost his virginity at the age of four and that was reported as a joke," said Dr. Ajamian. "But he was not joking. I know that the group was into that when the Phoenix family were members. There were all kinds of sexual wrongdoings in the group at that time. It's very possible that River Phoenix did lose his virginity when he was four."

The group operated on a strict secrecy system within its communes so husbands and wives were often unaware of each other's sexual partners. Explained Dr. Ajamian: "A number of wives could have been involved in all kinds of things and I wouldn't know about it. That's how tight they were. David Berg even encouraged his disciples to molest their own children. He believed that one of the best ways for kids to learn about sex was by having it with their own parents. There was a memorandum about this sent out. People were supposed to read it and burn it."

In 1974 the Phoenixes were ordered to South America to become traveling missionaries for the cult. John, who now held the exalted position of Archbishop of Venezuela and the Caribbean, converted an old step-van into a rough-and-ready mobile home for his family to live in.

"We moved around a lot," River remembered many years later. "When I was four years old I heard [James Taylor's] 'Fire and Rain' a lot. So we were in Mexico and I was playing with a flashlight that was going dead, and we couldn't afford any more batteries. My father asked me to please stop, but I wanted to see how far I could push someone so I kept turning it on and off. He said, 'Could you please stop this?' with a stern voice and took it out of my hand, put it in the glove box and slammed it. The song was playing the whole time and it's something that stuck with me. I felt this tremble, this fear of authority and I felt I understood that you have to respect people. That there was a reason behind it. That was the first concept of reality as far as relationships go. I saw that there is not just this world of vagueness that you can just bounce off of."

From Mexico, the Phoenixes went to Puerto Rico, where their son Toaquin Rafael, later to be called Leaf, was born on the road in 1974. The family then spent almost two years in Puerto Rico witnessing to new converts and enjoying a brief stability in their nomadic lives.

But when John and Arlyn found themselves increasingly deep in debt they decided to move on and head toward South America, where they lived in various cities before settling in Caracas, Venezuela.

River, now five, and Rain, three, were coached by their parents to sing Children of God songs so they could panhandle on street corners to feed the family. For the family's first modest venture into show business they took the name *Los Ninos Rubios Qui Canta* —the blond children who sing.

"We sang in hospitals, jails and on the streets," said Arlyn in

1979. "We wanted them to realize how to love God and that God loved them."

Passing out Children of God literature, the family, all of whom spoke fluent Spanish, witnessed to hundreds of young people during the next few years.

Jonathan Sherman said Children of God missionaries were encouraged to use their children to sing on street corners to support themselves: "They used the kids because the kids are cute and they're harder to resist." Sherman traveled through Europe singing with his brothers for the cult at the same time the Phoenixes were in South America. "That's how you survived."

Slowly River and Rain were to become more professional in their singing act. For Christmas 1975 River was given a guitar by Spanish singer Alfonso Sainz, who had become a close friend of the Phoenixes. Sainz taught the little boy his first few chords and within months River was sufficiently skilled to strum along a simple accompaniment for their songs. Indeed, Sainz was apparently so impressed with River's talent that he issued an open invitation for the family to come to his recording studio in Orlando, Florida, and do some recording; they could never afford to go there.

One of River's earliest memories was of singing hymns and songs with Rain in the main plaza in Caracas when he was five and she was three:

"A lot of people would gather and listen to us," recalled River. "It was really a novelty. We had a whole act together. I'd be strumming on a guitar that was taller than me at about a hundred miles an hour. I knew about five chords—for my age I was one of the better guitarists around. We drew hundreds to the plaza who were delighted and charmed by us. That's where I learned to give a lot of joy and happiness from singing."

Ambitious for her children even then, Arlyn entered River and Rain in talent contests, but without much success. The children's street performances were about the only positive aspect of the Phoenixes' lives at that time. Poverty-stricken, the family were now existing in deplorable conditions in Caracas, never knowing where their next meal would come from. "It was disgusting," recalled River. "It was a shack. It had no toilet and was rat-infested."

The family received no help from their Children of God superiors, who often left their pioneering missionaries to fend for themselves if there were no established communes in the area.

"My children were often on the streets," says Bithia Sherman. "They went hungry. They were not well taken care of. They were undernourished and they were exposed to life-threatening diseases. It was just not a proper place for children to be." Bithia adds that from the cradle the Children of God told infants that their purpose on earth was to help save the world.

"There's an awful amount of stress placed on children's shoulders of having to save the world," said Bithia. "That's an awesome responsibility to place on a child."

The only contact between the Phoenixes and the Children of God was the constant stream of "Mo Letters" that arrived by mail every few days. Over the years these letters became increasingly bizarre with cartoon drawings showing infants making love.

In 1976 Berg issued an official edict ordering his female followers to become prostitutes for Jesus and use sex as part of their witnessing. Berg called it "Flirty Fishing," telling his followers: "If some of these guys are going to come all the way with the Lord, you may have to go all the way with them."

Arlyn said: "The guy running it got crazy. He sought to attract rich disciples through sex. No way."

By now Arlyn and John had become disillusioned with the Children of God; the final straw came after seeing pictures of a grinning Berg, in black robes and long beard, surrounded by beautiful nubile girls.

"The group was being distorted by a leader who was getting very full of power and wealthy," said Arlyn in 1989. "We were serving God; we weren't serving our leader. We sort of snuck out. It took several years to get over our pain and loneliness."

River Phoenix, who once proudly boasted that his dad "kicked ass as a missionary," told interviewer Michael Angeli a more intriguing version of why they quit the cult.

"What happened was, my dad started finding out stuff, getting into top secret categories, like that the leader was a big hypocrite, and this group wasn't as wholesome as they led people to believe. One day my parents just said, 'We're outta here.' "

Now, looking back at his experiences with the Children of God, John Phoenix still has some admiration left for David Berg, who is today wanted by the police in Argentina and has gone into hiding.

"He may have been a sexual pervert, but he is still a better man than a lot of people," says John Phoenix.

Desperate, penniless, the Phoenixes moved into a hut on the beach outside Caracas and prayed for guidance from what they called "the Universal being." They were so poor that John and Arlyn often went without food so the children could eat. Every night the family would huddle together in the hut and pray for deliverance from their nightmare. Arlyn was pregnant again and getting out of Venezuela to safety was fast becoming a matter of life and death. Although they were in such a desperate state, Arlyn refused to admit defeat and call her parents for help.

On August 23, 1977, River spent his seventh birthday sitting in the filthy hut eating coconuts and mangoes that had fallen from the trees. His parents could afford nothing better.

"I was never frightened," said River. "When you're raised on the road you don't fear these things, you don't question them. We had faith, a lot of faith."

When times got really bad Arlyn would cradle River, Rain and Leaf in her arms and gently rock them to sleep singing Carole King's "You've Got a Friend." Help finally came in the form of a priest who arranged for the family to escape back to the United States on a freighter taking a shipment of Tonka toys to Florida.

"We were stowaways," said River. "The crew discovered us halfway home. My mom was pregnant."

The crew were so charmed by the ragged stowaways that they treated them like V.I.P.'s, even throwing a huge birthday party for Yoaquin and giving the kids damaged Tonka toys as presents . . . "It was a blast," River would recall.

The Phoenix family landed in Florida without personal possessions; there had been no time to pack them. Their only souvenir of the past five years as missionaries was the old guitar that Alfonso Sainz had given River.

## Chapter Three

# THE ROAD TO HOLLYWOOD

WHEN THE PHOENIX family arrived back in the United States at the end of 1978 they found themselves totally out of step with the world around them. River, now eight, had never received any formal education or normal social conditioning, and his only worldly knowledge came from his parents and his early years with the Children of God. With his unique upbringing, River was in some ways far more advanced than other children his age. He was bilingual, could recite whole chapters of the Bible in Spanish. In other ways he was educationally stunted, with little basic knowledge of history or geography and no notion of traditional American culture. It was as if the three Phoenix children had just landed on an alien planet for which they were ill-equipped and totally unprepared.

"When we arrived, we were very naive and sheltered in many ways," River would say. "And then suddenly we were exposed to all this information. It was like a brainstorm."

In December of 1978 Arlyn gave birth to her fourth child, a girl she named Summer Joy, representing the family's hopes for a time of warmth and happiness after their nightmare in Venezuela.

But back now in America, and penniless, there was little joy as they faced the indignity of having to rely on the hospitality of

Arlyn's parents, Meyer and Margaret, recently retired to Winter Park, Florida. John Phoenix hated living on the goodwill of his in-laws and tried to get his family back on its feet by starting a land-scaping business. "I worked fourteen to fifteen hours a day," said John. "And Riv and the kids would help me out, carrying sod and things like that."

Life in America was a true culture shock for the Phoenix chil-dren, who had never even seen a movie or watched television. When they saw first glimpsed their grandparents' TV set they sat mesmerized, much to the alarm of their parents, who worried that they would be corrupted by the temptations of the media.

"Before I came back to America I thought features [films] were Kellogg's commercials and cartoons," recalled River, who said his first movie hero was Tony the Tiger. "Then I saw a western and I thought that companies paid people's families money to kill them. I just believed it."

Like a dry sponge River soaked up movies and TV and the more he watched the more fascinated he became with this exciting new way of portraying life which often blurred the edges between real-ity and fantasy.

"Woody Allen was the first time I really could not figure how something could be so real," said River many years later. "I was like, 'How can anything be this real yet contrived?' That question is what makes you want to find out."

At his grandparents' insistence River was sent to a local school but had a difficult time being accepted by his new schoolmates . . . he was so *different* from everyone else.

"When I was in first grade everyone made fun of my name, of course," he said. "I think it's kind of a big name to hold up when you're nine years old. It seemed goofy. I used to tell people I wanted to change the world and they used to think, 'This kid's really weird.' "

John and Arlyn distrusted the American educational system af-ter their own unhappy scholastic experiences and did not want their children to be a part of it. And during the next few years the family moved around so much that the children never spent more than a semester at a time in one school. Most of the learning took place in the kitchen, with John and Arlyn going through a home-study program.

"Their education was on the streets of the world," said Dirk Drake, who would later be hired by Arlyn to tutor River and the rest of the Phoenix children. "These kids had Ph.D.'s before they were ten. What would be taken as hard knocks by the rest of us were transformed into beautiful hippie knocks by their parents."

In March of 1979, while Arlyn was nursing three-month-old Summer, John Phoenix was forced to give up physical work when an old back injury recurred and left him a semi-invalid. It was at this low point in their lives that Arlyn was forced to take control—and she experienced an epiphany that would change their lives forever.

"We had the vision that our kids could captivate the world," said Arlyn. And deciding that the way to do it was through show business, Arlyn set out on an orchestrated campaign to transform River and Rain into musical entertainers. First she moved the family out of her parents' house to relocate in Brooksville in central Florida, where she started writing to producers and networking friends.

"We need a complete sponsor, an investor to help us get into the field," John said at the time.

To support the family Arlyn was forced to go back to work as executive secretary for the Hernando-Sumter Community Action Agency in Brooksville, and John did some light carpentry. But the family was finding it hard to pay the bills and could not afford to buy the children clothes.

"Rich kids gave us their old clothes," said River. "They were the best clothes we had ever had. We were these very pure, naive, poor children. The rich kids called us a lot of names but it never bothered us because we didn't know what the words meant."

During their free time River and Rain were busy developing a new musical act featuring popular songs instead of their old repertoire of hymns. River was also beginning to write his own songs for the act and Team Phoenix, as Arlyn now called the family, was totally focused on achieving success.

"We wanted to make it," River told writer Michael Angeli. "We all wanted to be entertainers and our parents did whatever they could to help us."

Some interest in the children was shown by Alvin Ross, who produced the rock band Kiss and liked their "natural abilities." But like so many other potential leads at the time it didn't go anywhere. "When the door didn't open, we didn't press it," said Arlyn.

In spring, 1979, River and Rain began entering local talent contests and performing at fairs around central Florida. They were a contrast in appearance. River was the all-American blue-eyed blond; Rain was much darker, more ethnic-looking.

Many years later River would describe how the Phoenix children were all very different in looks and personality. "We all have our distinct things," he told writer Dan Yakur. "Leaf was the family clown, very witty, very smart. Mom had to work a lot, so Rainbow was the mother and the older sister and trendsetter. Liberty was always the most physical, like an acrobat, very nimble and strong, a really beautiful girl. And Summer was the youngest, the baby of the family with big brown eyes and blond hair, more American-looking. Liberty and Rainbow have more of an ethnic look. Rainbow definitely looks Israeli or Italian. Summer is more WASPy."

In May, the family created a stir locally at the Hernando Fiesta. Reviewer Gayle Guthman in the St. Petersburg *Times,* wrote: "The children brought the audience to its feet when they finished singing 'You Gotta Be a Baby to Get to Heaven' in five languages—French, Spanish, Japanese, German and English."

In the rave review Guthman profiled the Phoenixes, who re-counted their history in print for the first time. With "a rural section of the county near US 98N" as his address, John Phoenix provided a version of the family's past that omitted any connection to the Children of God and described himself as an "independent missionary." John showed a skill in creative public relations with his description of River's first public appearance. He was managing and playing with a band in Venezuela, John said, when he lost his voice before going on stage and River and Rain stepped into the breach to give a triumphant performance in his place. "The kids just knocked the audience out," he said.

When asked about the possibility of him ever becoming rich and famous, seven-year-old River answered: "I hope I am famous some day, not to be proud of myself because I thank God for giving me my powers."

To the same question, five-year-old Rain said, "I don't want to get rich. I want to give money to poor people and some for us. I'd like to give to people who need help."

River and Rain's showstopping performance of "You Gotta Be a Baby to Get to Heaven" was also seen by a young man called Sky Sworski, who would soon play a vital role in the Phoenixes' life by becoming their benefactor.

"I fell in love with River when I saw him playing guitar at seven and singing," recalled Sworski. "River was definitely somebody who was a grownup at seven. You could have a conversation with him like you could with a thirty- or forty-year-old person."

Arlyn used the St. Petersburg *Times* as a platform for her beliefs, announcing that her family had become strict vegetarians as the next step to enlightenment after not managing to get there with drugs and religion.

"When we left the Children of God we thought, 'What next?' And vegetarianism was obvious, oh yes," Arlyn declared. "River actually took it one step further. He insisted we eliminate cheese, eggs and milk from our diets. He is a sensitive child. He cannot tolerate the slightest form of abuse."

Many years later River would explain his decision to give up meat: "When I was old enough to realize all meat was killed, I saw it as an irrational way of using our power, to take a weaker thing and mutilate it. It was like the way bullies would take control of younger kids in the schoolyard."

As part of their new ethical lifestyle, the family became vegans, radical vegetarians who in addition to not eating meat also eschew any products involving the perceived exploitation of animals in any form, including dairy products, leather, honey and even some soaps. "It's based on a philosophy of harmlessness," said Arlyn. "We don't harm animals in any way—that includes fish. We don't take from them either. Which means no milk or milk products. We even have trouble taking honey from bees. We also refuse to use soaps that use animal products in their ingredients. We just eat vegetables and lots of fruit and soy stuff. Once you meet all my kids, though, you'll understand how healthy our diet is."

And Arlyn still refused to have anything to do with modern medicine, never allowing her children to see a doctor. "I've refused to have them inoculated. I've never given them an aspirin. If some awful illness happened in our family, then I'd look at it as a challenge to heal ourselves with herbs and spiritual enlightenment."

The article in the St. Petersburg *Times* drew much local attention to this hippie family with its musical child prodigies. Arlyn was thrilled with it and sent a copy to her old Bronx school friend Penny Marshall, who was now a successful actress. Arlyn had long ago lost touch with Ms. Marshall but had recently seen her on television in the hit comedy series "Laverne and Shirley" and thought she would be a good networking connection. Marshall, now a top film director, says she has no recollection of Arlyn, though the letter did find its way to the casting department at Paramount Pictures.

A few weeks later Arlyn received a form letter from Paramount, inviting the children to an interview if ever they happened to be in Hollywood. Team Phoenix was delighted and saw it as a sign from God. Bankrolled by their independently rich new friend Sky Sworski, who had decided to invest in the family, John and Arlyn loaded up their nine-year-old VW station wagon for the yellow brick road to Hollywood.

Inspired by Arlyn's ambition, John Phoenix, who had no prospects of supporting his family in Florida, would later explain their decision to go Hollywood this way: "I said to myself, 'What a crazy person you are.' But the stars were so bright. I just felt that it was right."

The three-thousand-mile journey to Los Angeles was full of adventures. The van, which John had converted into a camper, was hardly suitable for two adults, four young children and the family dog, and trouble was their constant passenger.

"Things went wrong for us all the time," said Arlyn. "One night it was freezing but we didn't have a back window in the camper. It got so cold, we stuffed Pampers in the window."

Along the way they kept up their spirits by daydreaming about how they would take Hollywood by storm and River decided he would concentrate on acting and put music on hold. "I remember we'd roll into gas stations in our beat-up van and I'd tell the attendant, 'I'm going to be an actor.' "

When the Phoenixes finally reached California they were, once again, destitute. Out of desperation John Phoenix first drove to his aunt Frances Beck's house in Orange County to ask for help.

"It was a real surprise when John turned up on my doorstep after all these years with his new wife and children," said Frances. "I was just thrilled to see them and we all hugged each other. They didn't have anything to live on and they were awfully hard-up. Arlyn was odd in her way. They were strict vegetarians and when they came out here I had to fix either a vegetable platter or a fruit platter. And they would not eat the two together. It was either one or the other. We managed to feed them all and then they spent the night in their old camper before leaving for Hollywood."

But when the Phoenix family arrived at Paramount for their audition the studio didn't want to know them and sent them on their way.

"We were really naive," said River. "I figured I'd play guitar and sing with my sister and we would be on television the next day."

Arlyn took control of the situation by taking a secretarial job at NBC-TV while John did odd jobs and was Mr. Mom during the day. They lived wherever they could, renting cheap apartments in Los Angeles that they furnished with old mattresses and furniture Frances Beck managed to scrounge up for them.

Arlyn's job at NBC's casting department turned out to be a good place for a would-be stage mother to find out where and when auditions were being held for TV commercials, and soon River was a regular at the auditions, accompanied by his father. Of course, the competition for jobs was intense with hundreds of children turning up at each one. It was a hard dose of reality as River suffered a stream of rejections.

"We had no money whatsoever," River would tell journalist Michael Angeli many years later. "It was just day to day. I was terrible for commercials. I couldn't smile on cue."

Outside of show business, life in L.A. was still tough for the family, evicted every couple of months for late payment of rent or being too noisy. "We had a shitty little apartment in North Hollywood," said River. "No kids were allowed so we had to hide in the closet when the landlady came round."

Each time they were evicted John was obliged to drive back to his Aunt Frances with, in effect, his tail between his legs until the family could regroup for another try at Hollywood. The constant moving, the insecurity would not surprisingly have a lasting effect on River and the other Phoenix children, who had never known the stability of a permanent home. "Moving calls for adjusting to a new place and learning not to get attached," River said.

Trying for another source of income, River, Rain and Leaf regularly sang and played guitar on street corners in the villagelike surburb of Westwood alongside the Hari Krishnas and jugglers, with John passing round the hat for coins.

"The Phoenix family were just part of the street-musician scene in Westwood," said Wade Evans, who lived in Westwood at the time and would later become a good friend of River. "They all had Western-style matching outfits with fringes and they had a whole act together."

Arlyn's ambitious plans for her children seemed to take a giant step forward when she made an appointment to see Hollywood's leading children's agent, Iris Burton. A tough, seasoned professional, Burton was an agent of the old school who had been in show business all her life. In 1952 she had made her own bid for stardom in a stage version of *Gentlemen Prefer Blondes* at the Brighton Theater in Brooklyn. Eventually she moved over to the business side of the profession, specializing in children and handling some of the top young names in Hollywood.

"Don't call me an agent, honey," says Burton. "I'm a groomer. A talent scout. I watch their weight. Hair. Nails. And most of all I watch their parents. By the time a kid walks through the door I know if he or she's a winner or a loser. If they jump in or slouch in, if they're biting their nails or rocking back and forth I don't want 'em. If I don't see the hidden strength, feel the energy, then the magic isn't there. I can smell it like a rat."

Burton apparently smelled talent in River Phoenix and offered to sign him up on the spot. "River was the most beautiful child you've ever seen, like a little Elvis," she said.

Burton in turn impressed Arlyn with her no-nonsense approach. She was pragmatic enough to know that the Phoenix family needed an inside guide to the world of show business. If philosophical compromises with family ideals had to be made for the sake of River's career, well, so be it, that was the price they would have to pay. At first John Phoenix was suspicious of playing the Hollywood game, but Arlyn assured him that they would never compromise their ideals.

So only a year after leaving Venezuela, River, who had never even known what the word *competition* meant, was thrown into the show-business jungle, where an inch of growth could kill a career and there was, it seemed, always a newer, cuter child waiting in the wings. The pressures to succeed were immense, and River would soon be carrying the financial burden of his whole family on his very slender shoulders.

"This is a fantasy world," explained Hollywood casting agent Sheila Manning. "We're turning children into little adults, asking them to do an adult job for adult money. But they're kids."

Four years later Iris Burton would sum up in Time: "I hate to say it but kids are pieces of meat. I've never had anything but filet mignon. I've never had hamburger. My kids are the choice meat."

The standard day's pay for a commercial in the early 1980s was $317.40, which was huge money to the Phoenixes. Soon Burton managed to get River booked for his first commercial and soon after that she had established him as one of the hottest young stars in the business. He was the angelic-looking, all-American kid in ads for Mitsubishi, Ocean Spray and even Saks Fifth Avenue, where Arlyn had liked to shop at lunchtime during her days as a Manhattan secretary.

Then, abruptly, River suddenly announced he did not want to have anything more to do with commercials . . . they were "phony," he didn't believe in the products. And Burton, who had never encountered anything like the Phoenix family and their hippie idealism, was understandably stunned by River's decision, one which his parents fully supported.

"They said they wouldn't do commercials because they were vegans," she would say some years later. "I said, 'What the hell's a vegan?' I thought it was an alien. I said, 'So I guess you don't do Kellogg's commercials. I guess you won't do McDonald's.' "

River and the family had laid down ground rules for their career in show business, determining that fame and fortune should take a backseat to their divine mission of trying to save the world. John Phoenix wanted his family to continue their work as missionaries, except this time using Hollywood's global reach. Any success that River might have would be used to better the world, and with those ideals in mind he almost ended his show-business career before it began.

"Commercials were too phony for me," River would say. "It was selling a product, and who owns the product? I mean, are they supporting apartheid? I just didn't like the whole thing, even though it helped us pay the rent. How could I tell anybody to drink canned cranberry juice? *I* didn't drink it. I didn't believe in what I was saying. I guess what I was zeroing in on was that performing was more about telling the truth through a different character's eyes. I felt that the constant lying, the smiling on cue and the product-naming was going to drive me crazy or numb me to a not-yet-developed craft that I was beginning to feel staring me in the face."

The family did hold fast to their ideals for the next year as they launched River into the L.A. audition circuit, and powered by prayer, Team Phoenix never stopped believing that the "Universal Force," which they felt had seen them safely out of the jungles of South America, would see them through Hollywood too.

"Whatever that connection was that kept us through that time is still keeping us through this time," explained Arlyn, summing up her ambitions for River and the family to Premiere magazine in 1988. "Because of that the success and the money and the fame and all of that aren't really important to us. Aren't as important as accomplishing the mission of *doing* it, because we felt this is what God was leading us to do. And the children have the talent and everything to go with it. I mean, River has his own drive to do what has to be done, and God willing, he will come out unspoiled.

"And maybe by some other miracle we can use whatever we've gained to enlighten and help the whole world, not just our family . . ."

## Chapter Four

# CLIMBING THE LADDER

IN EARLY 1982 RIVER Phoenix finally got the big break he was praying for through his music. After his retirement from commercials there had been a long period of inactivity during which his confidence had been shaken by continuous rejections as Iris Burton sent him to auditions playing cutish kids in large families. During the lean times River and Rain concentrated on their music in the streets of Westwood to hone their act, hoping that they might be spotted by some record producer.

One day Iris Burton called with news that she had arranged for River to audition for the popular television show "Fantasy," which was looking for a talented child who could sing. Each week "Fantasy" gave three guests the chance to live out their dream on television, and the producers agreed to showcase River and Rain's singing talents. Brother and sister were a great success on the show, which led to River being called to audition for a new CBS-TV series, "Seven Brides for Seven Brothers." The show, which resurrected the 1954 MGM musical and updated it to 1982, was the first spin-off from a musical into a television series, and the producers needed actors who could sing and dance as well as act. The show's executive producer, David Gerber, was struck by River at his audition for the youngest brother, Guthrie McFadden.

"He came in with that wonderful ingenue look," said Gerber. "He had that clean, fresh, wholesome young look and a really ingratiating smile. He was a natural. I always thought he was the peach-fuzz kid." Gerber was also impressed by the boy's talent as a singer and guitarist and gave him the part on the spot.

Recalled River, who was then eleven: "I just leaped five feet into the air. I got all red and freaked out. It was my first television show. Real exciting. A glorious moment. It was something I just waited for, and it's such a rare thing, being at the right place at the right time and just fitting the part. It seems like repetitive crap now, but then a series was big."

Delighted that River was to be a TV star, the Phoenix family moved to the northern California town of Murphys to be with River for the filming, but from the first day there the Phoenixes' strict veganism would cause trouble on the set.

"There were conflicts around his family's ideology," recalled cast member Terri Treas, who starred as Hannah, a bride in the show. "His parents didn't want River to wear leather, and when you're doing a western you have to wear cowboy boots made of leather. That wasn't ideologically acceptable to them. It put River in a very uncomfortable position as a kid, but what could he do except obey his parents?"

In spite of the crew's attempts to persuade the Phoenix family at least to allow River to wear a leather belt, Arlyn and John refused to give in and executive producer Gerber had to be called in to settle the matter.

"He said they had a problem," recalled Gerber. "I said, 'What's wrong?' and the director told me that River doesn't want to wear a belt, he's a big environmentalist. I was used to bigger problems than that. I said, 'We're up here in the country so give him a bit of rope or something to wear.' "

After the belt episode River became a scapegoat for the other cast members who teased him about his beliefs, several times reducing him to tears. With no experience at social interaction, River was just bewildered and powerless to defend himself.

"I felt very sorry for him," said Treas, who would later go on to star in the hit TV series "Alien Nation." "His feelings were getting hurt a lot. He wasn't used to being treated that way and he'd burst out crying, which only made things worse. River had been really isolated and he didn't have the social skills to know how to be with other boys. He had never had to go out and defend himself in the playground and make his way in the world. I think being in a macho environment where boys are always competing with each other, whether to get attention or just kidding on the set, was very hard on him. He wanted to be a part of it. Very much. But he didn't really know how to be."

Terri Treas would often see River sitting by himself between takes, his guitar his only company. "River always had a guitar in his hand and was always playing," said Treas. "That was a constant for him."

The boy's musical skills became a pivotal part of the show, which ran every Wednesday night on CBS, and River soon impressed Gerber with his professionalism and acting ability. Viewers seemed to love River's good looks and, to his astonishment, he began getting fan mail from adoring young female fans.

"We got heavy fan mail for River," said Gerber. "The young girls really liked him and we started giving him a bigger role in the show because he was so popular."

Flattered by the attention, River, who was shy with girls, answered each letter personally. Now, as one of the stars of a network TV series, River even had his own press agent Joe Santley, of ICPR Public Relations who gave interviews on his behalf. Santley told the St. Petersburg *Times,* whose story had first lit the spark that had brought them to Hollywood, that the Phoenix children's duets were now "as slick as Vegas." He added that River and Rain had entertained the show's cast at its 1982 New Year's Eve party. Referring to the Phoenix family as "self-styled ex-hippies," he said there was "no pressure on the kids to do anything but be kids and to enjoy what they're doing. River is a very intelligent, quiet, resourceful, polite kid."

Still, even from the beginning, River tended to shun the limelight, apparently uncomfortable being the center of attention. As

Treas said: "He didn't like the burden of being the star. He didn't really like the attention he was getting. He liked being an actor but he didn't strike me as somebody who wanted to be a star."

While River was filming the show in Murphy, the six-strong Phoenix family lived in a motor home and invited their relatives to visit them and watch River filming.

Great-aunt Frances Beck, who came out on several occasions, said: "We were just so proud of River. He was such a talented little kid and we all knew he was going places."

But River's success was short-lived when CBS canceled "Seven Brides for Seven Brothers" after just one season of twenty-two episodes, leaving the Phoenixes broke yet again. For the next few months River and his father were back in the auditioning line with the young boy's brush with stardom a distant memory. John Phoenix, now relegated to a role of a housebound Mr. Mom because of his painful back problems, increasingly turned to alcohol and marijuana to relieve his frustrations. With little money coming in, the pressures were mounting on River at each audition to get the part and keep the family afloat.

Said director Joe Dante, who often auditioned child actors for his movies and would soon give River his first starring role in a feature film: "All you have to do is be a director and watch a kid's face if he doesn't get a part. When a kid comes in to read you want to make it seem like a game and lighten things up a bit. But when that kid leaves the mother always has that look . . . 'You'd better have gotten that part.' And there's a real feeling of failure if you don't get the part.

"Many parents have the attitude of 'you have a job to do. Your job is to go out and get these parts. We want you to have a career in the movies. We want you to win, win, win. And if they don't win they lose. So what does it do to a kid to lose every day at auditions?"

River's lifelong friend Jonathan Sherman, whose mother Bithia had now left the Children of God and renewed her friendship with Arlyn, saw the kinds of pressures he was under:

"His mother was a stage mother," said Sherman. "She was dominant. She was strict. She was the promoter. She realized that her kids had potential at an early age and just went out and harnessed the system. She met the right people, made the right contacts and promoted her kids. I don't know how that affected River. I think at the beginning he was happy. He liked the attention. But at the same time he wasn't doing it for himself."

Meanwhile John Phoenix worried about how the frequent rejections were affecting his eldest son, and began directing his growing fears inward.

Arlyn's persistence and River's hard work finally paid off with a succession of minor guest appearances on TV shows such as "Hotel," "Family Ties" and "It's Your Move." But his breakthrough came with key roles in two well-received television miniseries. In *Robert Kennedy: The Man and His Times,* River played Robert Kennedy as a boy and attracted much attention among Hollywood casting directors. In his next TV movie, *Celebrity,* River played the role of a young boy having to come to terms with his father's homosexuality. At the climax of the controversial film River's character surprised his father in bed with another man.

"It was a big dramatic scene," River would characterize it.

In March 1984, River starred in a one-hour TV special called "Backwards: The Riddle of Dyslexia," in which he played a young boy with a reading disorder. River's evocative performance as Brian Ellsworth was singled out for attention by the critics, and he was invited to audition for a major role in a new ABC-TV movie, *Surviving: A Family in Crisis.*

*Surviving*'s English director Waris Hussein recalls: "River was very much a part of the Hollywood auditioning scene at the time but he stood out from the others. I remember his parents took him to the audition and I think his father was instrumental in coaching him for the reading.

"This film was an important event for River, who had done a few TV parts before but this was his first really big role in terms of dramatic characterization," says Hussein.

Loosely based on a spate of teenage suicides in Plano, Texas, *Surviving,* which starred Ellen Burstyn, Marsha Mason and Paul Sorvino, cast River as the young brother of a suicide victim, played by actor Zach Galligan. River's character tried to copy his brother's suicide with a drug overdose but was saved by his mother.

Throughout the five-week shoot in Oklahoma City Hussein was distinctly aware of John Phoenix's constant presence on the set. "I thought his father supervised him quite heavily," said Hussein.

Hussein says he found River an instinctively good actor who always knew his lines when he came to work in the morning. Everything went well until a key scene during a barbecue when River's character needed to reminisce about his dead brother. For some reason the young actor was having trouble concentrating and could not get it right. With the daylight fading, Hussein became increasingly impatient with River as he botched take after take.

"Finally I said to him, 'Well, you'd better pull your finger out because you're letting the side down,'" says Hussein. "I was determined to get it right. Finally his father took him aside and talked to him. Coming back, John apologized: 'River's not usually like this and I've told him to get the scene right because it's holding up everybody.' It was almost like I'd challenged his father directly. Parents live through their children in these circumstances."

Halfway through the *Surviving* shooting Iris Burton called with news that a Paramount casting director wanted River to fly back to Los Angeles to test for a big-budget science-fiction feature called *Explorers* to be directed by Joe Dante, who had just had a hit with *Gremlins.* This was the break the Phoenixes had long hoped for, but unfortunately the proposed screen test clashed with *Surviving*'s filming schedule.

"River's father came and asked permission for him to go to test for *Explorers,*" remembers Hussein. "At one point it didn't look as if it was going to be possible because of the way we were shooting and the locations available. But I said we really ought to let him go because he was so anxious to audition. I changed things around so we could free him.''

River was clearly excited at the chance to star in a space fantasy, describing his opportunity as "a movie kid's dream.''

"I got a thrill just from reading the script," he said later.

River originally tested for the role of Darren Woods, a kid from the other side of the tracks much like the part he would go on to play in *Stand By Me,* but Dante would cast him as the nerdy, be-spectacled boy-scientist Wolfgang Muller.

"One thing River did not consider himself was a geek. It was quite a stretch for him to do because he was so unlike that character in real life," says director Dante.

"I was immediately impressed by River's fresh and natural acting ability which is a rarity in Hollywood, where parents encourage their stage kids to be phony to win parts. We liked his acting and his personality so much that we ended up offering him the part that was the furthest away from his real persona.''

After flying back to Oklahoma City to complete *Surviving,* John and River Phoenix returned to Hollywood to prepare for *Explorers.* The film was about three young friends with very different personalities who build a spaceship out of junk. River played Wolfgang, who invented the spaceship. Ethan Hawke, in his debut film, played the dreamer Ben Crandall and Jason Presson was the streetwise mechanic, Darren Woods—the part River initially had tested for.

"We've got the combination of the right kids who work well together," said the film's producer, Edward S. Feldman. "We were very careful. It's hard to find three kids that the audience will want to look at for two hours.''

Once on the set River soon became fast friends with his co-stars and for the first time began socializing with other kids his own age outside the Phoenix clan. But from the beginning River stood out on the set because of special meals brought in daily by his ever-watchful parents, always in the background to monitor his work. This time, though, John Phoenix agreed to relax his vegan restrictions on River wearing leather to make things easier for the wardrobe department.

"There was always an outsider quality to River," said Dante. "I think he must have felt that way because his family was unusual. River, I think of all the kids, wanted to grow up fast. He didn't like the idea of being a kid."

Dante says that although fourteen-year-old River was extremely bright, his lack of education and inexperience with life soon became apparent on the set. "They'd be a lot of times when reference would be made to things River didn't understand or know about," said Dante. "Things that other kids might take for granted. Commonly used words. Historical events and figures. Past presidents. Famous writers. Famous actors or singers. River didn't have a lot of material knowledge of the world because of the way he had been brought up. The meaning of things often had to be explained to him and it put him in a difficult position."

It became a standing joke on the set when River, who often didn't understand words in the script, would guess at their pronunciation rather than risk looking foolish in front of the other children: "River would get stupid on-screen if he didn't understand the dialogue," said Dante. "He didn't want anybody to know that he didn't understand and sometimes he would mispronounce words hoping it would be right. Considering River had been somewhat deprived of an education he was a very bright kid and very smart and knowledgeable about things. He just didn't have a lot of facts at his command because he'd never been walked through history and literature."

For the first time in his life River found himself being challenged about his beliefs and would go on the defensive when he was forced into justifying them: "River had a very doctrinaire set of ideas that he had been taught by his parents," said Dante, who would often eavesdrop on the children's conversations through his headphones between takes. "Ethan, who was a far more worldly boy, would often challenge River and I don't think he was used to that. He was suddenly confronted with a whole lifetime of thinking one way and finding out that it wasn't the way the mainstream of the world thought.

"It was probably the first time that River had spent time with people who weren't necessarily agreeing with everything that he had heard at home. It was a great experience for him and very mind-expanding."

As shooting progressed River and Ethan bonded and started becoming rambunctious on the set, which forced Dante to step in. Later River would explain his behavior saying: "It's been hard because when we get hyper on the set, sometimes we get on the adults' nerves. And there were times that we just got tired of hanging around the set."

*Explorers* was the first movie for both young River and Ethan, but neither seemed too impressed by the experience. Dante wanted the film to be as realistic as possible and much of the kids' dialogue was adlibbed. It turned out that River excelled at improvisation, and it was as Wolfgang Muller in *Explorers* that he would first reach deep into himself to try to become the character he was creating.

"You have to do that if you're really going to create the role and put all you have into it," said River, who actually developed a keen interest in physics after playing the young scientist. "You must try to figure out how Wolfgang would live. So I thought about his financial situation. Like are his parents middle class, upper class or lower class. What kind of clothes he wears. If he likes girls or school."

Dante believes that River pulled a lot of his character for Wolfgang right out of himself.

"He did become the character," says the director. "River reacted and improvised with the character but in doing so he brought the character back to what he was really like. And although River liked to be cool and act cool, there was a geek inside him that would come out and embarrass him. He did not enjoy watching himself in that part. I think that he saw a lot of things about himself that he wished he didn't have. There were childish things that he was trying to change . . ."

During the five months of filming River entered puberty. He seemed confused about sex, trying to overcome the guilt and emotional baggage he still carried after his early experiences of sex in the Children of God. Having stopped having sex at the age of ten and declaring a second virginity, River had tried to block out all his early sexual memories.

"Getting laid was a major goal in his life," said Dante, who did not know about River's early sexual experiences. "It was one of the things that was most important to him."

River, self-conscious about wearing the big thick nerdy glasses for his character, would always take them off whenever there were girls around, much to Dante's amusement. River also developed a crush on the actress Amanda Petersen, but she preferred Ethan, much to River's disappointment.

During the making of *Explorers* River became attached to Ethan and Jay, discovering what it was like to be a more-or-less normal kid for the first time in his life. By law the kids could work only four hours a day so there was time to play after they finished their daily studies with their tutor. One day River walked in and found MTV playing on a studio monitor. He was spellbound and sat for hours as though mesmerized by the high-gloss videos.

But River, who had been taught to keep Hollywood at a distance by his father, was determined to keep his feet on the ground and not become a spoiled movie kid. "There are some Hollywood kids who are really brats and it's just hard to deal with them," he would say. "I've been lucky that I haven't been such a brat. I'm trying my best not to be."

While making *Explorers,* Dante and his three young actors developed a lasting friendship. The most exciting part for River was going up to Lucasfilm's Industrial Light and Magic studios in San Rafael to film the complicated blue-screen special effects on a huge set the young actors called Funhouse.

"We were up there for a long time and there wasn't much to do," said the director. "I got to know River and the other kids really well and felt like their older brother. It was kind of like a family, as much as movies are. You work with people that intensely for a short period of time."

After the end of filming River was upset to have to say goodbye to Ethan, with whom he had grown so close during the previous five months.

"River was weeping and crying when Ethan got the bus to leave to go home to New Jersey," remembers Dante. "He was broken-hearted. River was from a very tight-knit family and I don't think it was that simple for him to transfer his affections from one place to another. I think he genuinely felt liked in this group and now it was all ending."

## Chapter Five

# RIVER CATCHES FIRE

BACK HOME IN Los Angeles in the spring of 1985 River fell back into his routine of auditions and helping out with the family chores. He had no friends outside the family and it was anticlimactic to be back home with no further projects on the horizon. *Explorers* had a July release date and although River was surely excited about the film that could change his life, he refused to admit it, pretending that his movie debut was nothing out of the ordinary. Meanwhile Iris Burton, who had just cast Leaf in another children's sci-fi movie *Space Camp,* as the little boy Max who befriends a robot, was now in daily contact with Arlyn plotting River's further career.

One day Arlyn called River in from a game of yard football excited by the news that Burton wanted him to test for a role in a new film with the working title of *Stand By Me.* River was one of three hundred young people that director Rob Reiner had tested and the first actor to be cast. Best known as Archie Bunker's "meathead" son-in-law in the seventies hit comedy "All in the Family," Reiner had moved on to become a successful film director with comedies *This Is Spinal Tap* and *The Sure Thing. Stand By Me* was a labor of love for Reiner, who hoped it could "find a small audience to enjoy it."

The story of four twelve-year-old boys on the cusp of adolescence in a small Oregon town in 1959, *Stand By Me* was a difficult sell for Reiner, who warned his scriptwriters: "There's no way this

46

picture is going to do business, because no one who went to see *Rambo* will go to see our film.''

Based on the Stephen King novella *The Body,* the film tells the story of the boy's four-day odyssey to find the body of a young boy who has been struck by a train. After overhearing an older boy talk about the accident, they decide they will be hailed as heroes if they can discover the body first. The film shows their rites of passage to manhood during their journey. Reiner knew that the key to the film's success was in finding the right actors:

''The characters were very strong and very well drawn,'' said Reiner. ''For me it became more than just four boys searching the woods for a body.''

In June River flew to Eugene, Oregon, with his father to meet his three young co-stars—Wil Wheaton, Corey Feldman and Jerry O'Connell. They gathered in a hotel suite to spend a week playing games based on Viola Spolin's *Improvisations for the Theater.* Reiner wanted the boys, who were strangers outside of the auditions, to get to know each other as friends through role-playing.

''Theater games develop trust among people,'' said Reiner. ''Her [Spolin's] book is the bible.''

In his first acting class River pretended to be a mirror while the other boys mimed his gestures; continued telling a story; was led around the hotel lobby blindfolded; and tried to remember imaginary items that had been packed in a trunk.

Reiner says that he deliberately chose River to play the pivotal role of Chris Chambers, the boys' leader and peacemaker, because he was so close to the character in real life:

''River has all the strength the character has,'' said Reiner. ''It's clear he's been loved by his parents, who are people who have been able to maintain what was good and pure about sixties' morality without the garbage.''

The four boys soon bonded, discovering that they had much in common as stage children. Production began in Eugene on June 17 and the whole Phoenix clan drove up from Los Angeles so they could be with River and provide support. To help his young actors get a feeling for the movie's 1959 time period Reiner gave them a cassette tape of the film's soundtrack on the first day of shooting. Made up of many of the popular hits of the late fifties such as Ben E. King's "Stand By Me," it would prove to be highly effective in the completed film.

"We listened to the music over and over," remembered River, who learned all the songs by heart. "We even learned all the slang language they used back then."

If the set of *Explorers* had been disciplined and well-behaved, Reiner deliberately encouraged his cast to run wild in order to develop the right on-screen chemistry. Taking the boys to carnivals and on white-water rafting trips, Reiner molded the four young actors into a real-life friendship that would outlast the making of the film.

The two months of shooting *Stand By Me* would be special for River. The fourteen-year-old would not only catch up on some of the childhood fun he had missed out on during his years as a missionary but would also start drinking beer and smoking cigarettes—and have his first introduction to drugs.

"The first three weeks were the most fun," said River. "We took all the hotel pool chairs and threw them into the pool. We soaked Corey's clothes in beer and they dried and he smelled like a wino."

With the nonjudgmental acceptance of the group, River's confidence seemed to grow and he became their ringleader, encouraging Wheaton to doctor the video machine in the hotel so they could get free games . . . "I took the blame," said River. "I said, 'You do it for me and I'll take the blame.' "

River smoked marijuana for the first time during the making of the film. Corey Feldman remembers going into River's dressing room one day and found him getting high.

"I went into his room and I saw a joint and he said, 'Oh, it was someone else's . . .' I had been doing it too, but it was one of those things where we really didn't want to let each other know what we were doing," said Feldman.

The four boys, their adolescent hormones raging, were obsessed with sex and talked about little else. During the making of the film River was smitten by an eighteen-year-old friend of his parents who offered to initiate him. He was delighted but insisted that they first ask his parents for their blessing! When they did, John and Arlyn were so delighted that they decided to transform the event into a sort of family celebration and decorated a love tent in their backyard for the act to take place.

"It was a beautiful experience," remembered Arlyn many years later.

"A very strange experience," was how River would describe it, adding that he didn't want just a one-night stand. "I got through that, thank God."

The next day River turned up on set with a big grin, recounting his exploits to the other boys and anyone else who would listen.

"This may be the greatest story of lost virginity I've ever heard," said Rob Reiner. "He said, 'She was so patient with me and told me what to do.' I did get the sense he was searching and confused about things and insecure."

River also told Joe Dante the news in a letter he signed *Rio* (the Spanish translation of River that he increasingly liked to be known as), writing in capital letters, "WELL IT HAPPENED. IT FINALLY HAPPENED."

Despite off-set distractions, River kept strongly focused on his role, meticulously studying his lines and trying to understand every aspect of Chris Chambers' life to become the character.

"When I first start working on a role I really go overboard," said River. "For about a week I guess you could say I overact. Then for about three days I just think about my lines . . . every single word. Once I start filming, I let everything go and try to be as natural as possible."

Looking back at the film three years later, River would say that there was a lot of himself in Chris Chambers:

"I just went on a lot of instinct and my own emotions," he told Peter Keough of the Chicago *Sun-Times*. "I was very young and they were appropriate for the part. *Stand By Me* was a weird time for me as a person. I was going through a lot of doubt, a lot of insecurity, coming of age growing up. A lot of sexual frustrations and things like that you go through at age fourteen.''

On set Reiner would first act out each character before a scene so the cast could hear what the part should sound like. He also worked very closely with River and the other boys to help them make their characters as natural as possible.

"I talked about the whole history of Chris with Rob," said River. "I decided he was older, thirteen, and he had flunked one grade. I'm a lot different from Chris. Chris never got out of the small town he grew up in, and he didn't have a family who loved him, like me. And though at his age I was as poor as Chris, I was rich in that I'd already seen a lot of places. But like Chris I'm the peace-maker and diplomat in my family.''

At the climax of the film, River had to play a crucial scene when "that no-good Chambers kid" finally confronts the town's contempt for him and his blue-collar family after being publicly branded a thief for stealing milk money which his teacher had really taken.

"He had to cry," said Reiner. "It was not as good as I knew he could do and I said to him, 'River, think about somebody in your life who you looked up to and disappointed you. You don't have to tell me who it is, just think about it.' And the next scene he did was the take that's in the film, where he cries like that. All his emotions came out. After we did that take he was really shaken. He was crying and I came up to him and I held him. He didn't have a lot of technique—you just saw this kind of raw naturalism. You just turned the camera on and he would tell the truth. I've seen the movie a thousand times and every time I see that scene I cry," said Reiner.

Later, looking back at his performance in *Stand By Me,* River all but disowned it, saying it made him cringe to watch himself on the big screen:

"It's not easy watching yourself so vulnerable," he said at the time. "I was going through puberty and I was hurting real bad. "Personally I didn't think my work was up to my own standards. I have a tendency to be supercritical of myself."

When *Stand By Me* was released in the summer of 1986 it did not do great business, but over the next months, as word slowly spread about the film's power, it became the sleeper hit of the year, outgrossing all other movies at the box office for that September and taking over the number-one position from Tom Cruise's *Top Gun.*

Writing in the New York *Times,* Aljean Harmetz called the film "a small, inexpensive, throwaway movie that has become an unexpected hit. In particular audiences are responding to what a number of critics have called extraordinary ensemble acting on the part of four eleven-to-fourteen-year-old actors."

River's portrayal of the chain-smoking leader of the gang was singled out as "particularly outstanding" by the trade paper *The Hollywood Reporter,* and the Washington *Post* said that River's performance gave the film its "center of gravity."

People magazine called River "One of the most exciting young actors on the screen," describing his "quiet intensity" as being reminiscent of Steve McQueen and Montgomery Clift.

The success of *Stand By Me* would change the Phoenix family's lives forever, launching River into stardom and giving the family financial security for the first time. It also presented a whole new set of problems as River began trying to cope with being a celebrity in Hollywood.

Over that summer, River had become recognizable wherever he went. His face started to turn up on the covers of teen magazines, and each day brought thousands of requests for fan letters and autographs. It was scary stuff for the shy, introverted fifteen-year-old who was determined not to be sucked into the so-called Hollywood Babylon and let success change him.

"After *Stand By Me* came out people were telling me, 'You're so good,' 'You're going to be a star,' and things like that," recalled River. "You can't think about it. If you take the wrong way you can get really high on yourself. People get so lost when that happens to them. They may think they have everything under control, but everything is really out of control. Their lives are totally in pieces.''


Over the next months Arlyn used River's earnings to establish a new stability for the family, which had moved at least forty times during the last thirteen years. On the advice of Iris Burton, the family incorporated as Phoenix In Flight Productions. Arlyn also hired a bearded man in his early twenties named Larry McHale, as a housekeeper with special responsibilities to look after River and be his friend. Given the affectionate title of NANNY (New Age Non-Nuclear Youth), Larry, who had met Arlyn through mutual friends and in part had been invited to join the family because he seemed lonely himself, handled everything from logistics to the laundry. Arlyn also hired a young man, Ed Squires, to tutor the children at home. Since River had such difficulty reading and was so far behind other children his age, Squires decided that River was suffering from dyslexia, a disease in which the brain distorts the written word. Arlyn and John refused to believe anything was wrong and refused to seek help, which, according to Dirk Drake, went against their beliefs.

Arlyn's main priority was finding River's next movie role, which would be the vital next rung in his career. There was no shortage of offers. It seemed that every producer in Hollywood was now beating a path to Iris Burton's door with movie projects. But on Rob Reiner's advice they were holding out for the right opportunity.

River was now Iris Burton's most successful client, whom she had started referring to as "my baby" and calling herself his second mother. She found time to accompany River to Tokyo for the premiere of *Stand By Me*. Burton, now in her sixties, and the good-looking young teenager made an incongruous pair at Frank Lloyd Wright's luxurious Imperial Hotel, where he met his new fans.

"He'd tell them, 'Come up, come up to the room,' " recalled Burton. And that room was filled with kids from the park. He would play guitar for them and give them fruit and juice.' "

Back in Los Angeles, River accepted a minor role in a two-hour CBS movie of the week, *Circle of Violence: A Family Drama,* about abuse of the elderly. River played Chris Benfield, a boy in a dysfunctional family whose mother, played by Tuesday Weld, physically and mentally abuses his grandmother, played by veteran actress Geraldine Fitzgerald. Years later River would, perhaps revealingly, cite the film as having the worst line of dialogue he'd ever had to deliver:

"It was something like, 'Mom, why can't we be like most families and get along?' Like most families get along."

Meanwhile River's own family tensions were threatening to engulf him. While his mother carefully plotted his career, growing ever closer to Iris Burton, his father was withdrawing, perhaps sensing the seeds of destruction for his family now taking root. River was confused. He found himself conflicted . . . between Arlyn's ambition for the future and John's wanting to keep his family dream intact by turning his back on worldly success.

Because of his unique upbringing, River had no real friends outside of his brother and sisters and very much wanted to have some companions his own age and outside of the Phoenix clan.

"I've always felt somewhat out of place with other kids my own age," he said at the time. "I was constantly reminded by people's reaction to our names and our diet that we seemed weird to them."

River now started hanging out with his "nanny" Larry, who began introducing him to his own friends around Los Angeles, many of whom were involved in drugs. One day in late summer McHale brought River to a day-long party at the Magic Mountain amusement park. Pat Brewer, then a twenty-five-year-old acting student, did not recognize the innocent-looking kid when he turned up with McHale.

"I thought what's this kid doing here," said Brewer. "He was only fifteen at the time and he looked younger. We partied all day with River becoming the butt of a lot of jokes because he was so young,'' remembered Brewer. "When we got back from Magic Mountain somebody brought out some cocaine and started cutting lines. River looked very unsure, it was something new to him. I remember saying, 'I wouldn't give any of that to the kid.' But then River insisted on having his share. I think he was trying to prove himself in the group and felt peer pressure. I don't think he really enjoyed it because after he snorted up the coke he started getting short of breath and went out in the garden by himself. I walked out to see if he was okay and I took him for a walk to Santa Monica Pier to clear his head. I didn't even realize he was River Phoenix until some little girls came up and asked him for his autograph.''

For the next few weeks River and Larry were regular visitors to Brewer's house and they became good friends, discovering a common interest in music.

"He'd play guitar and we'd talk music. He was not at all into the Hollywood life and he just wanted to be John Doe and anonymous. At first he was very self-conscious about doing drugs and didn't really know what to do. He soon picked it up, though.''

As River started experimenting with drink and drugs he was very careful about keeping it secret, especially from his parents. Since his earliest days in the Children of God, when he'd been taught how to speak to the outside world in a way to protect the cult, he had become something of an expert dissembler.

It was during this time that River first developed a moral stand in interviews in which he spoke out against drugs, playing down any of his own involvement:

"I've tried marijuana a few times but I don't like it," he told People magazine just after his sixteenth birthday. "I get really boring on marijuana. It makes me dull."

## Chapter Six

# BACK TO THE JUNGLE

AT THE END of 1986 River Phoenix and his father went back into the Central American jungle of Belize to make *The Mosquito Coast*—a film that uncannily mirrored the young actor's own nightmarish childhood in Venezuela. Australian director Peter Weir was looking for a young actor to play Harrison Ford's eldest son but had initially rejected River as too old at fifteen. When no suitable younger actors could be found, casting director Dianne Crittenden took another look at the test tapes and decided that River was right for the part. Crittenden went into Weir's office with the tape and made him watch it. Weir agreed River was good but still felt that at fifteen he was too old and turned him down again. He was also interested in Wil Wheaton, who had played opposite River in *Stand By Me*, but eventually Weir did decide to cast River in the role after reading his résumé and seeing the striking similarities between River's childhood and Charlie Fox's.

"I finally said to myself, 'What does it matter how old he is?'" said Weir. "He looks like Harrison's son. And I cast him."

The other leading roles went to British actress Helen Mirren, who played Charlie's mother, eleven-year-old Jadrien Steele, who was cast as his younger brother, and Hillary and Rebecca Jordan as his twin sisters.

Based on Paul Theroux's 1982 novel, *The Mosquito Coast*, the film tells the story of the Fox family, which like the Phoenix family, leaves America to find a new life in the jungles of South America. In an eerie parallel to River's own story, the film traces the Foxes' perilous survival in Mosquitia led by their obsessive father Allie Fox, played by Harrison Ford.

"It isn't so much that they took my story, it's like I mislaid it," said River, whose character Charlie Fox is the narrator of the movie. "In the movie I play this really sheltered kid—all I know is what my dad tells me. He gets sick of society and we go down to some subtropics area to live."

With a tight budget, Weir had just sixteen weeks to shoot the movie in Belize and left his actors in no doubt that he would not be wasting any time, stating his intention of treating the uncomfortably hot jungle sets like a Hollywood backlot. In the film, Allie is an inventor who drops out and leaves America with his family to fulfill his dream of bringing an ice machine he's invented to the jungle. He buys an abandoned town named Jeronimo and builds a settlement for the natives that will be his utopia. To expedite filming Weir had three separate versions of the town built at different stages of construction so that the cast could move from one to the other and save weeks of expensive filming.

During the long grueling hours on set River became close to Harrison Ford, who took him under his wing and taught him lessons in acting technique that would prove invaluable in his later movies.

"Harrison was very down to earth," River would say. "I've read that he's cold but he's actually very warm. It's just that in his position you have so many phony people trying to dig at you that you've got to have a shield up. Harrison is a great presence. He's very wise too."

River was not, though, artificially deferential to the superstar and the two developed a close rapport and a lasting friendship.

"I understood where he was coming from," said River. "And I think he understood where I was coming from. I don't think I nagged him. I didn't ask him all the time how Indiana Jones was. I learned a lot from him. The biggest thing about Harrison is that he makes acting look so easy, he's so casual and so sturdy.''

As River gravitated towards Harrison Ford, whom he tended to see as a strong father-figure, his real dad John was blaming himself for ever allowing River to go to Hollywood. Now away from Arlyn, John saw his beloved son slipping away from him as River became more and more successful. He was also bothered by the similarities between the plot of the film and his life as a missionary in Venezuela. Living rough with his son in a village near Belize City, John was always looking for ways to escape the set with his son and perhaps get closer to him. He kept trying to persuade River to take a trip to Guatemala. The boy would patiently sit his father down and explain that he could not be that irresponsible:

According to set publicist Reid Rosefelt: ''River would say, 'Listen, Dad, I know I'm fifteen years old and I should have fun. But I have to do my scene tomorrow and I have to learn my lines and I have a responsibility to be on set and be rested.''

River did, in his fashion, start to rebel by breaking his strict vegan code and sneaking junk food whenever his father's back was turned.

''He'd stuff himself with a Mars Bar and a Coke,'' said Weir, who witnessed River's mini-mutiny. ''It seemed a healthy steam valve.''

Weir did not realize that there was a harder edge to River's rebellion. High-grade cocaine and alcohol were freely available in that part of the world, and River, although discreet, was not shying away from the temptation of his self-proclaimed demons.

''It was like living in the drug capital of the northern hemisphere,'' said River several years later. ''I know drugs were rampant everywhere in town. I've been so much more exposed than my folks think.''

River seemed to have long recognized the darker forces within him and even discussed them with Reid Rosefelt, the unit publicist on *The Mosquito Coast:*

"I was a curious kid when I was younger," he told Rosefelt. "I wouldn't be satisfied unless I had experienced everything I had a question about. I always wondered what it would be like if I cut myself with a razor blade. So I did it, when I was eleven, and realized this pain stuff isn't the way to go."

Peter Weir was well aware of the tensions between River and his father although he kept a distance and didn't get involved:

"With a young person who suddenly becomes the key breadwinner of the family there's an incredible amount of rearranging things in the family hierarchy," Weir said. "Sometimes a tension develops, particularly with the father."

While making the film River started dating his fifteen-year-old co-star Martha Plimpton, who became his first girlfriend. In their first scene together Plimpton, who played a missionary daughter called Emily Spellgood, tells Charlie: "I could be your girlfriend if you like. I think about you when I go to the bathroom."

When River first met Martha, the beautiful, petite blond daughter of actor Keith Carradine and Broadway actress Shelley Plimpton, seven months earlier they had not liked each other. Now, maturer and more confident, River started courting her on the set. "We grew up and realized we both had changed a lot," said River.

Most of River's scenes, though, were played with Harrison Ford, who was impressed with the young actor's technique:

"What he has is some manner of natural talent," said Ford. "There are a lot of people who have that, but River is also very serious about his work, very workmanlike and professional, far beyond what you'd expect from a fifteen-year-old boy . . . I don't like to talk to other actors about acting. I think it's a real mistake. But River asks a lot of questions that require answers, none of which I can really supply but they're interesting questions."

Director Weir also recognized River's screen presence:

"River Phoenix was born to movies," said the director. "He has the look of someone who has secrets. The last time I remember seeing it in someone unknown was with Mel Gibson."

Since Belize was totally isolated in the jungle the daily rushes had to be sent to the United States for processing and then flown back again. As Weir and Ford watched River's performance develop on the dailies they couldn't believe the natural alchemy he had with film:

"It's something apart from the acting ability," said Weir at the time. "Laurence Olivier never had what River had."

Cut off from civilization, the only entertainment for the actors and crew were videos flown in from the States. Halfway through filming, rock star Frank Zappa's children Dweezil and Moon Unit, who knew River from Los Angeles, flew down to the set for a long weekend. But there were few distractions. During the day, when they were not filming, River, Martha and the other young actors studied three hours a day with the set tutor. River, who disliked the formality of any kind of classroom experience, often was a truant, preferring to play his guitar. And to escape the pressures, which would grow geometrically with his career, River increasingly turned to his music and drugs, inhabiting his private world.

"He wanted to be a rock musician like Sting," recalled photographer Nancy Ellison, who was the still photographer for *The Mosquito Coast*. "He was talking about changing his name to Rio, a single name, like Sting. He didn't think River Phoenix was an interesting name."

Still shy and self-conscious, River hated being photographed and often played practical jokes to unsettle the photographer:

"Sometimes it would be silly dangerous," says Ellison who remembers River once pretending to set his tongue on fire with a cigarette lighter during a photo session on *The Mosquito Coast*.

It seems Charlie Fox was the character River most admired in his career. After finishing the film and going back to Los Angeles he found it difficult to revert to being the lonely and friendless River Phoenix who felt like a stranger wherever he went:

"I had a kind of identity crisis," River would say. "I liked Charlie Fox's character a lot and it was a great experience for me. I knew that character so well because I *was* the character. I knew his whole past."

It was in *The Mosquito Coast* that River first discovered he could use a movie role like a drug to lose himself and become somebody else:

"It just feels so good, it's such a great escape, you know, it really is," River told Bill DeYoung of the Gainesville *Sun* in 1989. "It's a great fantasy. It has nothing to do with the idea of movies, it's just getting lost. Having an excuse to get that far out of your head is just a really good feeling."

The studio's publicity machine was not shy, exploiting the newsworthiness of the Phoenix story, leading to headlines such as the one in Life: *One Big Hippy Family—River Phoenix and Company Move into Hollywood.*

River, it seemed, arrived at just the right time to provide Hollywood with a clean-cut role model to offset such as Sean Penn and Rob Lowe.

"One of the brightest of kid actors, the tow-headed sixteen-year-old also displays the new generation's best qualities," said Jack Curry in *USA TODAY*, adding that River could be expected to win a best-supporting Oscar nomination for either *Stand By Me* or *The Mosquito Coast.* "He's polite, articulate, clean-living and good to his mom. If there's a Teen Angel Pack, Phoenix may be its ace player."

Recounting his rags-to-riches story for Curry, Phoenix charmed the writer, saying, "I'm glad I wasn't born with parents who had a big farm or a big house. That wouldn't be me. I learned a lot from it all and I'm not going to forget it. Those experiences make me a better person for knowing both sides of the tennis court."

In reality, River was feeling the pressures from never knowing a traditional childhood and finding himself with the heavy adult responsibilities of being a successful actor *and* supporting his family while still in his mid-teens:

"When your parents are also your business managers, the training to excel takes on a whole different angle," he would say. "See, what I'd really like to do is have fun all the time, just mess around. That's the thing, see? I really want to get good as an actor. I want to grow in the profession. And that goal doesn't leave room for fooling around much."

After their filming in Belize, River and Martha Plimpton continued to see each other and their relationship deepened. From the beginning he tried to convert his new girlfriend to his vegan way of life with his usual but charming flair for the dramatic.

Remembered Plimpton: "Once when we were fifteen, River and I went out for this fancy dinner in Manhattan and I ordered soft-shell crabs. He left the restaurant and walked around on Park Avenue, crying. I went out and he said, 'I love you so much, why?' He had such a pain that I was eating an animal, that he hadn't impressed on me what was right. I loved him for that, for his dramatic desire that we share every belief, that I be with him all the way."

When *The Mosquito Coast* was finally released it was panned by the critics, who criticized its shift in focus from the Charlie Fox character to his unlikable father. River's performance, though, was praised:

"[River] Phoenix is as good as the screenplay and direction allow him to be," said New York *Times* film critic Vincent Canby. David Robinson writing in the London *Times* praised River's performance for its "insights" and "depths of secret anxieties."

River said he was "shocked" at the movie's critical and financial failure at the box office:

"I thought Harrison did a great job," he would tell the *Hollywood Reporter*. "Most people expected another Indiana Jones-type hero. They didn't want to see an antihero. I felt much better about my work than I did about my performance in *Stand By Me.*"

*   *   *

On their return to Los Angeles John Phoenix decided to move the
family away from Hollywood to a twenty-acre ranch in San Diego
where they presumably could go back to nature. The elder Phoenix was becoming more and more apprehensive about the dangers of fame and success to the family and whether the ends
justified the means. Now that River's acting career was taking off,
offers were coming in for the other kids, and John thought he saw
everything spinning out of control. Iris Burton, with Arlyn's support, was fast turning the Phoenix family into an acting dynasty—
Rain making her film debut with Ally Sheedy in *Maid to Order,* and
Leaf and Summer acting together in the movie *Russkies* about a
Soviet sailor washed ashore in Key West and the three teenagers
who helped him.

When Interview magazine's Kevin Sessums visited the so-called
Hollywood Nomads on location in Key West for *Russkies* in early
1987, it all seemed a bit too good to be true. Nanny Larry McHale
was firmly in charge of getting the kids to their calls on time while
Arlyn was on hand to explain veganism and the family's divine
mission in Hollywood. Now aged forty, her closer-cropped hair
going gray, Arlyn had evolved into a mature, striking beauty.

Waving the Phoenix banner, the matriarch told Sessums: "I
really think there is a purpose why all this has happened to us. We
just have to be patient and let it find us. The world's in such an
awful shape right now that maybe somehow we can make a difference. Life is all about finding reasons. All you have to do is open
your heart."

With, in retrospect, chilling foresight, Sessums sensed a darkness in the Phoenix utopia, wondering "if the perfection these
children present to the world is but a patina over some deep-
seated pain. They've been through a lot in their short lives. When
will these kids rebel? Or will they *ever,* since they've been raised by
rebels themselves? Their life together has been lived in such a
primal way that there must be the same sort of scream scraping

around inside each of them, one that is growing along with their bodies.''

The only other person who seemed to recognize this on the horizon was John Phoenix, but by now he was a man receding into the background more and more, until, finally, he left once and for all.

## Chapter Seven

# JIMMY REARDON

AT SIXTEEN RIVER Phoenix faced the difficult transition to adult leading-man. In just two years he had finished three motion pictures, grown four inches and dropped twenty pounds to become a lithe and remarkably handsome young man. He was a bona-fide teen movie idol with a rock-star following of young girls, but although he goodnaturedly posed for beefcake shots and did interviews, he very much wanted to be accepted as a serious adult actor.

As Hollywood's most successful children's agent, Iris Burton was well aware of the problem of young actors making the transition to grownup roles. Asked about River's chances of continued success Burton had only confidence: "River is a strong, intense young actor with great longevity." Unfortunately, his next film cast him as a sexually precocious high school Casanova who beds every female in sight. It would prove an embarrassment for River and his family.

*A Night in the Life of Jimmy Reardon* was directed by William Richert. It was based on a semi-autobiographical story he had written about growing up in Chicago in the early sixties:

"Jimmy Reardon was a satire on aspects of myself," said Richert, who would become one of River's closest confidantes. "I used to walk around bars and drink anything anybody handed me when I was growing up. That was partly about what Jimmy Reardon was about.''

The first time Richert saw Phoenix was when the young actor arrived to audition for the lead role:

"I walked in from lunch and I saw this young kid waiting for me next to a potted plant. He stood up and he was luminous. He had a light surrounding him like a medieval icon. He said, 'I'm River Phoenix.' I said to him, 'You're going to be great in this movie.' He said, 'How do you know?' I said, 'I just know.' "

After a five-minute talk with Phoenix, Richert gave him the script to show his mother and within days he had signed a contract. The movie follows seventeen-year-old Reardon's life during several days as he tries to get eighty-five dollars to fly to Hawaii with his girlfriend Lisa, played by Meredith Salenger, after one of his conquests cheats him out of his college tuition money for an abortion. River would have to play a string of risqué love scenes, including a Jack the Ripper sex fantasy with his best friend's girl, played by Ione Skye; the seduction of his mother's friend, Joyce Fickett, played by Ann Magnuson; and pimping for his friend Fred Roberts, played by Matthew L. Perry.

John Phoenix was strongly against his son doing the film, but he was overruled, with Arlyn and Iris Burton apparently feeling it would be a necessary career move to establish River as a more rounded actor. Soon Phoenix was eagerly preparing for the film, which he was enthusiastically describing as a cross between *Catcher in the Rye* and *Risky Business,* which had launched Tom Cruise's adult film career three years earlier.

"When I started working with River he was so intense," said Richert. "He wanted to look a bit older for the part and decided that if he worked out and became more muscular it would make him look like he was eighteen. So he was always doing push-ups. Most kids aren't like that.''

The project, though, soon ran into trouble when it was bounced from Island Films to Twentieth Century Fox in pre-production and Richert was told to turn it into a teenage morality tale.

"Jimmy Reardon was something like two or three notches ahead of his own [River's] experiences with women," said Richert, who had to coach the shy and sensitive Phoenix in his first-ever love scene. "It was funny. He'd approach Ann Magnuson like a puppy sniffing at some weird plant. He knew he liked it but he didn't know what to do about it. So he'd touch her and move back. I just told him, 'Now get on here and put your leg here and your arm here.' And he said, 'Is my mother going to be upset about this?' "

For the first time River's parents were *not* on the set supervising, as they were in Key West chaperoning Leaf and Summer on the set of *Russkies*. Instead they asked River's grandfather Meyer Dunetz to go to Chicago to look after the boy. Bill Richert's son Nick, who became close friends with River on the set of *Jimmy Reardon*, says it didn't quite pan out that way:

"River was definitely calling the shots with his grandfather," remembers Nick, who had a small part in the film. "He had the least supervision of any of the kids on the set."

Looking back at his time in Chicago a couple of years later, River would acknowledge, "I could get away with a lot, because he didn't know me, so he didn't know how I acted. So I could not be River, and there wasn't my mom around to say, 'Hey come on, what's going on, you're losing yourself.' "

Meredith Salenger, who played River's girlfriend Lisa Bentwright, remembers how all the young actors played hooky from the set tutor:

"When you're under eighteen you have to have three hours of school every day. "We would tell the social worker on the set that we were going to school, and then we'd go into River's trailer and talk and play, and when she'd come in we'd pick up the books and read."

Salenger recalls once catching the dyslexic Phoenix reading Hermann Hesse's *Siddhartha*—which had inspired his name—upside-down just to see if he could do it.

"That was just like River," said Bill Richert. "He read life upside-down too . . . I didn't know there were people like River out there. He was so natural and completely open."

Phoenix and Nick soon became close friends with Meredith Salenger and Ione Skye, and since there was little to do in Evanston, Illinois, they all socialized in their hotel rooms at night:

"River definitely made use of the available stimulants when he was on his own," said Nick, who also said the young star was very secretive even to his friends about his use of marijuana and cocaine.

During the filming the two teenagers became very close and one night River confided how unhappy he was about his father's drinking.

"There was definitely something going on with River about his father," said Nick. "He used to say that one of the things we had in common was that we didn't really have fathers. They were both absent."

Jim Dobson, who worked as Phoenix's publicist on *Stand By Me* and *A Night in the Life of Jimmy Reardon,* said the young star disliked having his picture taken and giving interviews. The top Hollywood publicist says that he often had to treat Phoenix like a child and make interviews fun or he was liable to lose interest and walk out in the middle of them.

"I could only get River to do things if I made it fun for him," remembers Dobson. "I would arrange for his friends like Ione Skye or Martha Plimpton to be there and it would make him feel more comfortable.

"He would tell me after we'd do shoots that he was like an Indian chief and every time he had his picture taken it would take away part of his soul. I remember once the only way I could persuade him to cooperate was to have him pose like a rock star. I had to say, 'Well, River, let's play the guitar. We're going to shoot you and the guitar.' " And Phoenix enjoyed playing a rock star so much that he refused to leave until the photographer had fired off forty-two rolls of film.

One day during filming Richert was talking to River about an upcoming scene in his trailer when the conversation turned to James Dean and River admitted he had never seen any of his movies.

"I was amazed," remembered the director. "River had, of course, heard of James Dean but he had never even seen a picture of him. I showed him a photograph and told him, 'That's the guy they're going to compare you to.' It was obvious. River looks a little like James Dean. When he saw the picture he had no reaction. He was not interested in him at all. River didn't give a shit about James Dean."

As Phoenix immersed himself in *Jimmy Reardon* he started changing some from the shy sensitive introvert into more of a typical male. Bill Richert remembers once coming out of a trailer while they were shooting in the countryside around Evanston to be greeted by a field full of schoolgirls on a trip.

Richert said: "River just looked across this field and said to me, 'How many blowjobs do you think are lying out there?' "

On the other hand, Richert said, River "could have had his pick of women because they all wanted him. But he never acted on that. He didn't jump after women."

Playing Jimmy Reardon, River discovered his sexual attraction for women and was propositioned by most of the female cast.

"He resisted temptation," says Nick Richert. "All the women in the cast wanted River and they were throwing themselves at him. He was going out with Martha Plimpton at the time and he stayed faithful."

After the sexual experience of his early years Phoenix was, not surprisingly, confused about handling a conventional sexual relationship. He would talk loftily about sex, taking the high ground, but there were also his "demons." And playing the promiscuous Jimmy Reardon character only added to his internal conflict.

"I'm the monogamous type," he would say. "I believe romance is important in sex. Doing it just for sensation and immediate gratification is selfish. We all have these kinds of urges and feelings inside us and we can't always suppress them."

Whatever, or in spite of, his moral outlook, Phoenix was secretly giving in to the temptations around him. Actress Jane Hallaren, who played his mother, once caught him with a girl in a hallway while they were making the film:

"He said, 'Don't tell anybody, okay?,' Like, yeah, I'm going to call his girlfriend," remembers Hallaren. "But that was River. Whenever you thought you had him pigeonholed, he was someone else."

When Martha Plimpton visited the set River played the dutiful boyfriend and the two seemed inseparable. Director Richert thought they looked like "two little Tinkerbells," but his son, who was much closer to the couple, saw first-hand how the strong-minded actress dominated River, who played the role of naughty little boy.

"She seemed to be in charge," said Nick, who would later socialize with them in New York, where Martha lived. "She was upset with him a lot of the time. I was never sure exactly what he'd done but she probably had good reason. River was always apologizing to her for something. He was always in the dog house."

During the making of *A Night in the Life of Jimmy Reardon*, River became increasingly moody and difficult to be with, feeling he was being possessed by the character of Jimmy Reardon:

"Acting is like a Halloween mask that you put on," he said later. "I like to pretend. I was probably better off the set than I was on film. I always feel closer to whatever I'm playing, even if it's that fucking Jimmy Reardon. That was such a downer. A real roller-coaster trip," he said in 1989.

Bill Richert would say that Phoenix was totally vulnerable in the Reardon role because it was so close to himself: "I don't think River liked the kid's morals," said Richert. "I think he felt that he was showing people a side of him that he didn't want them to see. There were lines in there about drunkenness that he made me take out. He would not say, 'Let's get drunk,' because he felt it would influence kids that way."

Josh Greenbaum, whose parents knew Arlyn when she was growing up in the Bronx and who would soon enter River's life as his best friend and musical collaborator, believes Jimmy Reardon and River Phoenix were one and the same person:

"You could definitely see Jimmy Reardon in his personality," says Greenbaum. "Jimmy Reardon was this daring young vivacious sneaky kid who was going to do what he wanted regardless of the consequences." Greenbaum believes River was exploring his inner self and pulling out real emotions buried deep inside to shade in the Jimmy Reardon character. "And these are things that he may not have dealt with before," says Greenbaum. "In order to be a character in a film and make it believable you have to bring things out of yourself."

Later Phoenix would bitterly attack Jimmy Reardon as if he were a real person: "The character was abusive to people, only out for himself, walking aimlessly through life. He was a jerk. Jimmy Reardon was one big mistake. I was very naïve and didn't know that I was misusing my talents in a major way. I was exploiting something special."

Just how much Phoenix had somehow assimilated the character of Jimmy Reardon was illustrated when he insisted on driving his motor home back to Los Angeles from Chicago after filming was completed. Larry McHale, now acting as his "guardian", was asleep in the back when River got stopped for speeding in New Mexico and in true Jimmy Reardon style jokingly called highway patrolman "ossifer" instead of officer:

"He was a kind of hard-ass New Mexican cop," recalled Phoenix. "And he went to phone some other guy to do a check. They can't believe a sixteen-year-old kid in a motor home . . . what the hell? Did I just steal it or something? So I get down on the floor and start to do push-ups. It was like two in the morning and I'm doing push-ups there. The guy comes out and I don't stop for him, and it's like, What do you think you are, you clown? Anyway, they search the whole motor home for drugs and narcotics. They went through everything. The [speeding]ticket said you had to pay it or end up in jail, and I didn't mail it in for three months."

When River finally joined the rest of the family on the *Russkies'* location in Key West he was no longer River Phoenix:

"I thought I was just a kid from Chicago. It was weird. I don't know. It was strange," Phoenix told Premiere magazine, adding that without his family to take care of him, he would have required psychiatric help.

*A Night in the Life of Jimmy Reardon* was released with an *R* rating, so many of Phoenix's younger fans could not see it. Receiving mixed reviews, the film did not set the box office on fire but Phoenix was once again praised by the critics for his performance:

"River Phoenix deserves credit for making something of his cocky, chip-on-the-shoulder part," wrote the *Hollywood Reporter*. "He bounds around like a well-scrubbed Cagney, fitting his wrong-side-of-the-tracks nature."

Looking back at the film, Phoenix blamed himself for the movie's failure, saying he wasn't macho enough to carry off the Jimmy Reardon role.

"It didn't turn out the way I thought it would," he said. "I'm not sure I was even the right person for the role. The whole plot revolves around the guy's sexual exploits that one night, and for it to work properly, I think you want to see someone a little bit more masculine, like Tom Cruise. He'd have done it much better than me."

Director Bill Richert loved River's music and invited him to write the *Jimmy Reardon* theme song. River wrote a song called "Heart to Get" that he recorded as a sixteen-track demo but it was never included in the film. The demo did attract the attention of Chris Blackwell, who, as head of Island Records, was one of the most powerful men in the record business. Blackwell, whose affiliate Island Films had distributed *A Night in the Life of Jimmy Reardon,* almost singlehandedly popularized reggae and launched U2 in America. He heard something special in the young actor's music and offered him a development deal.

"I was Chris Blackwell's pet project," Phoenix would tell Bill DeYoung in the Gainesville *Sun* interview in 1989. "It's an open-ended contract and works entirely around the career in films I've established."

Blackwell agreed to put up seed money so Phoenix could get a band together and write some songs without any definite commitment on either side.

"Chris is very patient and is happy to let it brew away and see what it turns into," River added.

When River's aunt Merle heard that he was trying to start a band she put him in contact with Josh Greenbaum, who was playing drums with a Ft. Lauderdale band called Toy Soldier, which later would change its name to Saigon Kick and enjoy some success.

The Phoenixes invited Josh to spend Christmas, 1986, with them in Royal West Palm Beach.

"River and I had always known about each other and it was only a matter of time before we'd meet," said Greenbaum, whose father Kenny had grown up with Arlyn Phoenix in the Bronx.

Greenbaum, who was then working as a pizza delivery boy, drove over to the Phoenixes' in his dad's old blue Chevy van and they instantly hit it off:

"He was really excited to meet me," remembered Greenbaum, who was thirteen days older than River. "He knew I was family and he also knew I was a drummer. River felt he could instantly trust me, which was unusual for him to feel about anybody. The Phoenixes are very family-oriented and outsiders are outsiders until they prove themselves."

During this first meeting Greenbaum spent a week hanging out with River and listening to his "progressive ethereal folk-rock" songs and getting to know him. The two found they had an excellent musical rapport, and Greenbaum was impressed with River's songwriting and his musical originality. He also got to know the Phoenix family and realized how much in common he had with

River; he also was a child of hippies and had spent much of his childhood in a commune in Woodstock.

"River moved around a lot as a child and I think that made him question normalcy more than usual," said Josh. "He didn't have that sense of suburban stability, he had a lot of different homes. We were both not from the typical nuclear family of four, living the all-American lifestyle."

Serendipitously, right after Christmas Phoenix flew back to Los Angeles to start work on a new film about an all-American teenager forced to question everything in his life when he finds out that his parents are longtime Soviet spies.

## Chapter Eight

# TROUBLED YOUTH

THERE WAS VERY little in River Phoenix's own life to prepare him for his next role—Jeff Grant, a patriotic young American whose life is turned upside down when he discovers that his parents are Communist agents. Billed as "a fast-paced suspense thriller in the tradition of classic Hitchcock," *Little Nikita* cast Phoenix alongside veteran star Sidney Poitier. The film was also a coming-of-age teen movie tailored to appeal to the young actor's growing number of female fans. Arlyn Phoenix, who was now officially managing her son's career, and Iris Burton decided that *Jimmy Reardon* and *Little Nikita* taken together would demonstrate Phoenix's acting range.

River Phoenix was now unquestionably the hottest young actor in Hollywood, and Paramount Studios had high hopes of a blockbuster, with one executive gushing: "It's the perfect story, great director, latest acting sensation around. We wanted it bad." But problems with the script descended on the project as a small army of writers tinkered with it almost up to the day shooting began.

In *Little Nikita* Phoenix played clean-cut teen hero Jeff Grant, whose application to join the Air Force Academy reveals his parents to be deep-cover KGB agents. Phoenix coasts through the first half hour with his acting skills barely stretched until Sidney Poitier, playing FBI agent Roy Parmenter, forces him to make the choice between his parents and his country.

"The biggest difficulty was selling myself the whole plot," said Phoenix, who found it "farfetched."

Nonetheless, he worked hard to try to save the film and, when shooting started in January of 1987 he had totally immersed himself in his character. Josh Greenbaum said Phoenix's method of preparing for all his movie roles by going into seclusion and cutting himself off from family and friends and everything else that made him River Phoenix.

"To get into a character he really had to live it, so he did not want any outside influences," said Greenbaum. "River would go two weeks early to wherever they would be making the film and set up and live there. After rehearsals he would just sit around, read the script, play guitar and think about the character. He'd try to live the reality of that character."

Greenbaum also said his friend could be hard to deal with when he changed characters and became somebody else: "It could be a problem at times. I just saw different personality traits and knew right away he's different."

In a later interview Phoenix tried to explain the transformations he would undergo to become his characters:

"You can't just wake up the next morning and be the character. It's a slow process. You have to neutralize yourself before you can become another character. I become non-opinionated, refusing to think from River's perspective and then, slowly, I add characteristics and start thinking the way the character would. I play a lot of mind games with myself."

During the filming Phoenix and director Richard Benjamin clashed on set. River felt he was being treated like a child by not being allowed to see the rushes of his performance each day and found it hard to maintain his performance:

"I felt so out of place with my acting," he complained, and later described Benjamin's style as "Method directing." "I just felt off. I feel like I gave a television performance, a combination of "Leave It to Beaver" and Kirk Cameron and Michael J. Fox."

Benjamin, who turned a deaf ear to Phoenix's criticism, had nothing but praise for his young star at the end of the movie:

"River has wonderful instincts," said Benjamin, adding that he had "one foot in childhood and one foot in adulthood. He is not only a superb actor but he is real. He cannot fake. That's not in River, only the truth is in him, and it's wonderful to see."

The one bright note in *Little Nikita* for Phoenix was working with Sidney Poitier, who had recently come out of a long retirement. The seventeen-year-old River, who hadn't been born when Poitier won an Oscar for *Lilies of the Field* in 1963, found he had much in common with the then sixty-four-year-old star, whom he adopted as a surrogate father. The half-century difference in their ages seemed to evaporate as River charmed Poitier with his passionate idealism and beliefs, even persuading him to become a vegetarian.

The worldly Poitier sensed Phoenix's growing problems in coping with the pressures of Hollywood during his formative years.

"He gave me tips about life," River would say. "I learned not to take everything personally. Not to take the negative things about your acting personally and not to take this fame personally. It's just a job and I'm trying to do it well."

Like Harrison Ford had done in *Mosquito Coast,* Poitier also gave River a master class in acting technique. And River, always a willing pupil, watched closely and listened to everything Poitier told him:

"I was so open to his advice and suggestions," said Phoenix. "He's a wonderful person and a really bright man."

Poitier was also highly impressed with Phoenix, and many feel their scenes together elevate the film out of the prosaic.

"River is so spontaneous and so quick, it charges my batteries," said Poitier, who would star with River four years later in *Sneakers.* "As an actor, River is so naturally gifted. You're not working against an actor who's relying on technique. You're working against raw talent and that's very invigorating to me. He sparkles."

By now River Phoenix, recently tagged Hollywood's hottest

teenage property by Playgirl magazine, was on his way to becoming a millionaire who could command $400,000 a film. He was the breadwinner of the family, which was now living on a rented ranch outside San Diego, and felt tremendous pressure for the responsibility of so many people's survival.

"His parents saw him as their savior," girlfriend Martha Plimpton said. "And treated him like the father."


River's biggest professional headache was finding new scripts. Given his dyslexia and limited education he found it difficult to judge the quality of new projects that Arlyn and Iris Burton were selecting for him. His lack of objectivity and questionable judgment would lead to big problems as he became Hollywood's brightest young talent.

"*Jimmy Reardon* is when we first had financial stability," River would say. "That's when we bought a car that wasn't used or old. I live pretty simply. I'm not into the whole clothes thing, although I have comforts that a lot of people don't have—a blender, a toilet, a shower," he added mischievously.

Although he was successful beyond his imaginings as an international star, instantly recognizable wherever he went, River became increasingly moody and depressed. He dreamed of leading a normal life with a stable home and family like any other kid his age. He was at once petrified and confused about suddenly finding himself a glossy teenage coverboy generating thirty-four thousand letters a week from young girls who thought they knew him.

"He found it abhorrent," said Josh Greenbaum. "He had to deal with it but it took a long time for him to put it in perspective and not let it affect him."

On the other hand, River was intrigued by the idea that so many girls he'd never even met fantasized about him:

"You mean there are hundreds of girls out there who *really* want to have a date with me?" he asked a journalist who had questioned him about being a sex symbol. "Wow. I mean, I've never really thought about that in those terms. It's like there's a football grandstand full of girls who think I'm the greatest without knowing anything about me personally. It makes me very nervous. It's as if everybody's getting all worked up over an image they don't know anything about. And if *you* are that image . . . I mean, don't they know I'm an actor?''

The teen magazines served up trite profiles of Phoenix for their readers, telling them everything they wanted to know about their hero, from his favorite color to his taste in girls. He was quoted in one magazine saying: "I like girls who are so natural because I'm natural in everything that I do." In another teenage publication the reluctant heartthrob told his fans, "It's a great feeling to think that I can be a friend to so many people through my movies."

Greenbaum believes River found it difficult to deal with the fantasy image that Hollywood's publicity machine was manufacturing and constantly questioned whether he was successful because of his acting talent or merely because he was a glamor boy.

"That was a big problem for River," said Greenbaum. "Is it because I make this kind of face in a film and look cute or because they saw my chest in a scene, or is it because of my acting skills? Do you like me because I'm a human being?"

Dirk Drake, whom Arlyn later hired as the children's tutor when the family moved to Florida, believes that River's coverboy good looks confused him:

"River hated being on the cover of Tiger Beat," said Drake. "Pulling a fancy T-shirt down and exposing a nipple. He was totally ashamed of doing it but he understood that was part of it all. The mission. The purpose. The job. But he also found it ridiculous at the same time. That's heavy pressure when you're a self-conscious lad of sixteen."

And John Phoenix's crisis apparently was deepening as River became more successful. He could already see that the family's "divine mission" was being diluted by Hollywood and that his idealistic principles could not survive in the hard-nosed movie business, where only success mattered. He urged River to leave

Hollywood and use the money they had made to start a new life away from the perceived corruption of civilization.

"My father is worried that we could be ruined by this business," said River at the time. "It's got a lot of pitfalls and temptations, and he doesn't want us to become materialistic and lose all the values we were brought up believing in.

"Yes, he's pleased we're doing well, but in a way he's almost reached a point where he could just drop out again like he did in the sixties and move to a farm and get close to the earth."

Arlyn argued that they could still work within the Hollywood system with Iris Burton as their business contact and keep the Phoenix dream intact. Although he would have happily walked away from the endless rounds of lunches, publicity parties and meetings that Hollywood stardom required, River loved acting and felt he needed to fulfill his considerable potential.

After long and intense family discussions it was decided that the family would move out of southern California and set up a new home far from the glitz of Hollywood. River also offered to buy his father his own retreat in South America, which he could escape to when things became too much for him.

The Phoenixes now decided that the ends did justify the means and that River should use his fame as a platform to deliver a positive message to change the world. At this point there was a definite split between River's parents, and John started spending more and more time away from Arlyn and his family to become, in effect, a recluse.

Where he had once shied away from interviews, River now welcomed them as an opportunity to air his views and beliefs, surprising many journalists accustomed to Hollywood celebrities heavily promoting their next film.

With his honest if at times simplistic black-and-white view of the world, River launched into a series of interviews that would brand him the Environmental Poster Child. The image would become painful as it became harder and harder for him to live up to it.

In an interview with the Boston *Globe*, "The Utopian View of

River Phoenix,'' the seventeen-year-old actor sounded like a New Age politician as he launched into a treatise on the world and his hopes for it, mixing missionary zeal with a dose of pop culture:

"I'm quite in love with the human race and this planet that we live on," River began. "I see life as very fresh and beautiful. People say to me, 'Oh, you have the world in your hands,' or 'You're young and you have all these opportunities.' But that's not why I feel the way I do. It's just reality. I've felt that way before, too. Still I get very frustrated with the pace of my life—I want so badly for people just to understand each other and communicate better. With all this technology, that's the best we can do? Pride so often gets in the way, in politics and everywhere else. It's depressing.

"But there's the optimistic side of me, too, which believes that we live in an incredible time and that if we all came together on the important issues and stand up for our rights, as Bob Marley said, we could really accomplish a lot. In my mind I have all these utopias and fantasies, but I believe they can work, I really do." Phoenix then used his family as an example of the goal to strive for:

"It's a pioneering effort. In our family parents and children are equal. We concentrate on a common goal. We want to contribute something to the world, not to take or to abuse the position we're lucky to be in. I feel blessed. I have a solid good background. I grew up without strife in the family, in an honest environment that had no manipulation, and with the ability to express myself."

After widening his sermon to call for more black actors in leading roles in movies and for people to accept themselves even if they don't have Robert Redford's looks, Phoenix concluded by pledging, "I can't on my own change the regime in South Africa or teach the Palestinians to learn to live with the Israelis, but I can start with me."

River Phoenix had felt the weight of the world on his shoulders since his days with the Children of God, when he had handed out cult literature and sung hymns telling astonished passers-by, "Hi, we love you."

"He grew up as a naive little kid saying, I want to save the world," said Josh Greenbaum. "As he got older he started to realize that it was impossible to do. Nobody can. A lot of people go nuts because they feel the pain and they want to do something about it and they can't. I think River felt that very intensely."

Martha Plimpton, who lived with the Phoenix family on and off during her relationship with River, saw as an outsider the damaging effects of his childhood and sensed trouble ahead:

"I love River's family. They brought him up to believe he was a pure soul who had a message to deliver to the world," Plimpton told Esquire writer Tad Friend. "But in moving around all the time, changing schools, keeping to themselves and distrusting America, they created this utopian bubble so that River was never socialized. He was never prepared for dealing with crowds and with Hollywood, for the world in which he'd have to deliver that message. And furthermore, when you're fifteen, to have to think of yourself as a prophet is unfair."

As River tried to balance his moral dilemma of being a "prophet" with the allure and temptations of Hollywood, he began an internal conflict between perceived good and evil that eventually would tear him apart. He was fearless in his pursuit of pleasure, and it was against his nature ever to play it safe. So now he was secretly using cocaine regularly and experimenting with hallucinogenic drugs such as peyote and magic mushrooms.

"Achieving success gets complicated," said River. "You find yourself hanging around with a different crowd. I probably would have shied away from it but after a while you can't help but get sucked in . . . all those parties and premieres and limos picking you up. And after a while if you hang in with this little group you lose your sense of reality completely."

When Pat Brewer, who had been with Phoenix at his cocaine initiation, saw him two years later he noticed a big change in his friend:

"He was no longer a little kid and he seemed to have adjusted to the lifestyle almost too easily," remembered Brewer. "He had his own supply of cocaine and he seemed very comfortable doing it. He had grown up and I no longer felt I was partying with a little boy."

It was during this period that River started peppering his conversation with references to the Antichrist and God, and his life started to be an ongoing struggle between absolute good and evil.

"I'm confused," River told Premiere writer Blanche McCrary Boyd in April of 1988, likening his success in Hollywood to "the Devil's bribe" he wanted to "use for God."

He then amazed Boyd by saying, "The Devil is so pretty and tempting. I go back and forth about success and wealth. Sometimes I wish I wasn't as conscious as I am. It would be so much easier."

In the summer of 1987 Phoenix traveled to New York City to be reunited with Martha Plimpton, who was to co-star with him in a film called *Running On Empty*. Directed by Sidney Lumet, the film paralleled Phoenix's own life and would bring him an Oscar nomination for best supporting actor. While River was making *Little Nikita,* Lumet had sent Iris Burton the script and asked to meet with Phoenix to discuss *Running on Empty*.

"I was really interested," said Phoenix. "There's a connection there . . . I think that's maybe why the *Running* script appealed to me from the start. The concerns of these parents are something I could see my own parents dealing with, having dealt with."

Phoenix was also anxious to work with Lumet, whom he deeply admired:

"I really enjoyed his work on films like *Dog Day Afternoon* and *Prince of the City*. I read the script and met with him in New York and we decided to do it."

Written by Naomi Foner, the film is about radical sixties activists Arthur and Annie Pope, played by Judd Hirsch and Christine Lahti, who have been on the run from the FBI for fifteen years since accidentally blinding a janitor when they blew up a napalm bomb. Phoenix played their seventeen-year-old son Danny, who has never known a stable homelife, the family having had to change identities every few months, constantly moving to keep one step ahead of the authorities. Phoenix related to Danny Pope, who like himself was trying to build a normal life and find stability. The similarities went ever deeper as Danny Pope falls in love with Lorna Philips, played by Plimpton, and is a gifted musician who wants to accept a scholarship to the Julliard School of Music.

Asked about the parallels with his own life, Phoenix would become defensive:

"My parents were never on the run. People think the Popes are like my family but they aren't."

Whatever, Sidney Lumet recognized Phoenix's talent. He had started his own career as a fifteen-year-old actor in 1939. After moving to the other side of the camera in 1957 to direct Henry Fonda in Reginald Rose's courtroom drama *Twelve Angry Men,* Lumet found success when his 1976 *Network,* written by Paddy Chayevsky and produced by Howard Gottfried, won four Academy Awards.

*Running on Empty* would examine the effects of the sixties on youth of the day, and the part of Danny Pope was pivotal. Discussing his decision to cast River Phoenix in the role, Lumet drew some interesting parallels between the raw young actor and Henry Fonda:

"The talent is original and the personality is original," said the director. "River doesn't know how to do anything falsely. Give him a false direction and he'll look up helplessly. Henry Fonda had that built-in barometer of truth.

"He has a surprising technique that he has developed on his own; he has never studied acting. He's one of those people who's so talented I don't know where he's going to go. The world is open to him."

Lumet's method of having his actors prepare for *Running on Empty* was unusual and proved effective in adding to the film's realism.

"On the two weeks' rehearsal," River said, "we memorized the complete script and would go through it as though it were a play. We kept going through it again and again, and then took all of that technical data and put it in our subconscious and lived the thing as though we *were* these people. Lumet's way of capturing everything on film spontaneously was really nice. There was nothing about it that felt worn out when we were actually filming."

Lumet's directorial skills utilized River's real-life vagabond experiences to make Danny Pope come alive on screen, River's own insecurity and uncertainty coming across in the film.

"He's a superb actor with real technique, despite his years," said Lumet. "He's never studied formally, but boy, does he know how to reach inside himself. I don't know what combination of things make a star. You have to have a very strong, clear persona and you have to be a very good actor. He is both, so he ought to have a brilliant career."

Screenwriter Naomi Foner, who co-produced the film, got to know River well during the filming and, like *Explorers'* director Joe Dante, was appalled at his lack of general knowledge:

"He was totally without education," said Foner, who bought River a collection of classic novels for his eighteenth birthday. "Education certainly wasn't, in the conventional sense, important to [the family]. I mean, he could read and write, and he had an appetite for it, but he had no deep roots into any kind of sense of history or literature.

"There was a line in the script—he was talking to Judd Hirsch—in which he said something like, 'Who do you think you are, General Patton?' And he turned to us and he said, 'Who's General Patton?' "

During the filming in New Jersey and New York City the film's plot and Phoenix's life seemed to merge into one. Now approaching his eighteenth birthday, River was becoming more and more independent from his family in the same way that Danny Pope was leaving his in the movie.

Naomi Foner agreed that her script accidentally reflected what was happening in the Phoenix family now that River was starting to strike out on his own and moving further away from his father:

"I was trying to write about what happens to every family when parents have to let their children go," said Foner. "She [Arlyn] knew that one day she would have to say goodbye to him. I think she was saying he was ready to move on."

The on-screen relationship between Phoenix and Plimpton paralleled their real one. On one occasion the film's producer, Griffin Dunne, caught the couple in the midst of a heated argument and couldn't tell if it was real or a rehearsal for an upcoming scene. Spending the summer together in New York filming only intensified their relationship. Nick Richert, who was living in New York at the time, became River's close confidant over this period:

"He was really in love with Martha," says Richert. "River used to talk about how wonderful she was and he'd get really torn up when he thought about other guys being with her."

Naomi Foner remembers seeing the couple in New York one night after they'd been filming on the Upper East Side:

"He was leaping and jumping, sort of like a young deer," said Foner. "He would hail taxis, leaping like Baryshnikov, and Martha would say, 'That taxi's taken, River. See, the light's off.' He didn't care. He danced down the street."

Chapter Nine

# PUTTING DOWN ROOTS

AFTER FINISHING *Running on Empty* in August 1987, his third film back-to-back, River Phoenix needed a break away from the cameras. As he turned seventeen he decided to focus on finding a new family base away from Hollywood where he could melt into a community and live a "normal" life. With no immediate movie commitments, *A Night in the Life of Jimmy Reardon* had been put on hold by the studio to rework the music, and *Little Nikita* had been pulled from its fall release slot and rescheduled for 1988, it was a perfect time to take a breather and recharge his batteries.

The Phoenix family at first considered settling in Mexico or Venezuela but in the end decided to base themselves in America for the sake of River's movie career, although at the moment River's priority was getting a group of musicians together and concentrating on his two-year development deal with Island Records.

The family decided the ideal place to settle would be a college town with a strong music scene and narrowed the choice to Austin, Texas, or Gainesville, Florida. After a reconnaissance of both towns they picked Gainesville as their headquarters but also bought a second home outside Austin.

Nestled in the swampy belt of central Florida, Gainesville was well off the beaten track, 70 miles west of Jacksonville and 109 miles northwest of Orlando. With no direct service to New York, the Gainesville airport moved at its own relatively slow pace with its small terminal and coffee bar.

Gainesville summers can be an ordeal with a relentless sun and high humidity sending temperatures soaring into the nineties and hundreds. What sets Gainesville apart from the other small towns in the crocodile-infested rural countryside is the University of Florida, with thirty-five thousand young men and women in their teens and early twenties. Gainesville is also one of the less expensive places to live in America, drawing young people from all over Florida whose parents can't afford the pricier tuition at the University of Miami.

Laid out on a grid extending out from the university campus, Gainesville has something of a reputation as a party town. As of this writing, at Joey's on most nights offers all the beer you can hold for five dollars, and the Market Street Pub brews strong English-style drafts like Gainesville Gold for a couple of dollars a pint. There is also a supply of locally grown marijuana called Gainesville Green around the town.

The sixties seem alive and well in Gainesville, which has developed a strong counterculture with its own cable TV show, head shops and alternative newspapers. Many young people come to Gainesville and never leave, lulled into its laid-back lifestyle.

So in the fall of 1987 the Phoenix family moved into Gainesville and rented a large white house hidden away behind Spanish-moss-covered oak trees until they could find a permanent place to settle down. Inside, the house was sparsely furnished and visitors often got the impression that the occupants were in transit. River's motor home was parked outside.

The Phoenix children were now growing up. Rainbow, who had reverted back to her original name, Rain, was fifteen; Leaf was thirteen; Liberty was twelve; and Summer was nine.

"We never treated them like children but like extra added friends," said Arlyn. "And they have always held up their part of the deal. It was never like, We know better because we're the parents. It was more like, This is the first time we've ever done this too. What do you think? And the children were so wise. If we made a mistake we made it together. But if you open yourself up, a way presents itself. You find the right path.''

In the Phoenix family everyone was equal and John Phoenix, who had suffered a childhood virtually ignored by his father, was careful not to repeat his parents' mistakes.

''Even when we were younger it was never, Well I'm the parent and you're the kid,'' River would say. ''You wouldn't be held back because of your age. Just the opposite. My father used to say, 'The youngest gets to yell the loudest because they're never listened to! My father talks to Summer, who is the youngest, the way he talks to my grandfather or anyone else.''

The children had all been brought up in their parents' sixties ideals. None had been allowed to attend school for more than half a semester, thereby avoiding possible contamination by the negative influences of peer pressure.

One of the first things that Arlyn did now was to find a new home tutor for River and his brother and sisters. Dirk Drake, a genial man in his early twenties sporting long blond hair and three dreadlocks, applied for the job. A self-confessed navy brat, Drake impressed Arlyn at his interview with his intelligence and quick wit. It also helped that before his move to Gainesville four years earlier, Drake had worked as an historical advisor in the film industry. John and Arlyn hired him with special responsibilities to act as River's guide in Gainesville and help him develop a more rounded education.

''John and Arlyn had a mistrust of formal education,'' said Drake. ''And I think that was because of their own bad experiences with public education as kids. I knew from the beginning how special these children were because they had been raised with such special ideals. Jodean [John's daughter from a teenage relationship] summed it up when she said, 'Those kids were raised in the stars. Most of us were raised on the floor.' The question was how would River deal with it?''

River immediately felt at home in Gainesville. At last he could lay down roots, find friends and belong somewhere instead of always having to move on to the next place as soon as he started feeling secure. Determined to be anonymous, River grew his hair into a long helmetlike fringe and combed it over his face whenever he went out.

Every day he went to town to explore, chatting to the young college kids he saw sitting outside the library or by the old clock downtown. After constantly being recognized on the streets of Los Angeles and New York, it was refreshing to be mistaken as just another college kid. To blend in he cultivated a grunge look, dressing down in torn jeans and dirty old T-shirts.

"I wanted to get away from being recognized," he told Joe Dolce in Details magazine, adding, "Please don't mention where I live."

As he wandered about town he also discovered the friendly college record stores and would go in searching for his favorite music, such as XTC, whose reclusive leader Andy Partridge was River's biggest hero and main musical influence.

"He came in one day and started talking about XTC," remembers Hyde & Zeke Records owner Charlie Scales. "I thought he was just another kid and he was so excited that I had a particular XTC bootleg that he'd never heard. I'm usually wary of lending people albums but he loved the band so much I let him have it. A week later he came back with the album and thanked me. I didn't realize he was River Phoenix until months later. I think he enjoyed the fact that I didn't know who he was."

Moving to Gainesville allowed Phoenix to live a normal life for the first time ever and he thrived on it:

"I was feeling very lonely for a while," he later told Joe Dolce. "I've never had friends before now. I was always moving and I never wrote postcards or letters. The only people I've known are Martha, Larry, who's a friend of the family, and my brother and my sisters. Because we traveled around so much, I never wanted to stand out like an awkward newcomer so I adopted a neutral attitude around people. I'm not that social a person anyway, and it takes a lot for me to get involved in a relationship."

In Gainesville Phoenix worked hard at making friends. For the first time he realized he could be part of a social scene with people liking him for himself and not just because he was a film star.

"I say this funnily," he told Dolce. "But I've never been so happy."

One of the first things Phoenix did was to call Josh Greenbaum and invite him to move into his Gainesville house and help him set up a band using the money from the Island Records development deal.

"I said I'd come out and visit for two weeks and jam," said Josh. "I wanted to see the town and how it would be living with his family."

River showed his new friend around Gainesville and played him some of the new songs he had written since they had last met. Greenbaum also spent a good deal of time with the Phoenix family, who welcomed him into the fold.

"They were hilarious," said Greenbaum. "The funniest people I'd ever met. I met the whole family and I loved them from the start. They were like the family I'd never had. I'd never known such warmth and love."

After two weeks with the Phoenixes, Greenbaum, then seventeen, moved out from his father Kenny's home in Ft. Lauderdale, quit his band Toy Soldier and moved up to Gainesville.

"It was one of the hardest decisions I've ever made," he said. "I thought it was a positive move in my life. It wasn't just the music, it was the whole thing. I found River's music very interesting, very different. I moved up here to play his music and change my life for the better."

The Phoenixes were delighted that River would have a new friend to share Gainesville with.

"They just added a brother," said Greenbaum. "John and Arlyn were like my parents, and the siblings were like my brothers and sisters. Right from the beginning my friendship with River was more than just a friendship. We were like soul brothers."

In their first few weeks together, River and Josh spent their time working out music in the Phoenix backyard, where they would sit on the trampoline and play for hours. They were also busy making the connections they would need to break into Gainesville's flourishing college music scene when they were ready.

"We got memberships to the Gainesville Health and Fitness Club and we'd work out and then go eat at Falafel King," said Greenbaum. "We started going to parties and checking out the town to see the new bands and find out what was going on."

After Josh had been living with the family for a few months, his father, who was working as a plumber in Ft. Lauderdale, called and Arlyn picked up the phone.

"I knew River's mom in the old days when we were growing up in the Bronx," said Kenny, a divorcé who had lost custody of his daughter and was now living alone. "Arlyn asked me about the reality of staying in Ft. Lauderdale without Josh and said it would be a good idea if I came up and moved in with them. I've been doing that all my life. Just give me five minutes to throw everything in my van and I'm off."

Kenny, a wiry, hyperactive man with white hair and a beard, felt at home with the Phoenixes and was soon accepted into their inner circle, which now included Sky Sworski, the man who had bankrolled their initial trip to Hollywood, Larry McHale and Dirk Drake.

"It was good vibrations," said Kenny. "They're my kind of folks and I loved them immediately. They weren't into Chryslers, carpeting, new couches. They were interested in what was taking place on the planet."

During the next few months River and Josh started recruiting musicians to join their as yet unnamed band. Chris Blackwell of Island Records had assigned a young A&R woman called Kim Buie to oversee the two-year project, which would be frozen every time River had to go off to do a film.

"We think he'll be around a long time so there's no need to rush him," she said at the time.

The Island deal provided funds for Phoenix to put a band together, rehearse and record some demos with Blackwell's promise to release an album on his label if the music was good enough. Once Phoenix was settled in Gainesville, Buie started helping River find the right musicians to play with. She suggested he meet Josh McKay, a twenty-two-year-old guitarist from Denton, Texas, who played with a band called Joshimisho; she thought they had similar tastes.

McKay's friends thought he was crazy when he said he was thinking about joining a band with a movie star and said it would never work. But when he received a cassette of the music River and Greenbaum had been recording he was impressed.

"I thought these tight jam-box garage tapes were really nice," said McKay to the Gainesville *Sun*. "This was about music and not just some movie star's hobby trip."

And the more he listened to River's music the more he liked the unusual melodies and quirky songs, with titles such as "Aleka Doozy Encircles" and "Dublin in Mardi Gras" (written for Dick Drake) and he found himself working out bass lines. As McKay spoke to River on the phone, he felt closer to him. They were both vegetarians and animal-rights advocates and were passionately dedicated to their music. Finally, deciding he had nothing to lose, McKay left for Gainesville as soon as he finished his final exams in anthropology.

"I just said this is a very unusual thing to fall down from nowhere," McKay told the Gainesville *Sun*.

Phoenix and Greenbaum met McKay at the airport, and he too moved in with the family. To round out the band Rain joined playing keyboards and singing harmony and they recruited a local classically trained viola player called Tim Hankins. Just seventeen years old, Hankins was a member of the Gainesville Chamber Orchestra and had never played pop music. He and Phoenix were total opposites and their often stormy relationship would almost sink the band.

In early 1988 River Phoenix was forced back into the spotlight as *Jimmy Reardon, Little Nikita* and *Running on Empty* were released one after another. Ironically none of the films made it to Gainesville's small movie house, to the considerable relief of the actor, who wanted to maintain as low a profile as possible. To promote the films Phoenix temporarily came out of seclusion to fly to Los Angeles for interviews or meet with the occasional reporter who ventured to the hinterlands of Gainesville.

In early 1988 novelist Blanche McCrary Boyd flew to Gainesville to profile River for Premiere magazine and found him having what seemed an identity crisis, trying to be a teenager while struggling to handle "the pressures of worldly success."

"It's hard to be a normally smart-assed teenager in such a permissive atmosphere," wrote Boyd in a revealing portrait of the Phoenix family that appeared in Premiere. "Hard to rebel against parents so rebellious themselves, and River Phoenix manages only patchily."

Blanche Boyd witnessed a family discussion about drugs in which River's parents discussed their "religious awakening" on LSD and their search for truth through drugs, to the consternation of their eldest son who asked, "Must it be through drugs?" At another point while Arlyn was describing the family's sacred mission to help the world, River interrupted, saying, "Mom, can I have $650 cash? I want to go down and buy a guitar."

River then took Boyd into town to buy the guitar, exposing his sense of deep conflict with the help of the padded dashboard of her rented car:

" 'If your mind's up here,' he said, his long fingers sliding up the blue padded dashboard, 'and you're really down *here* . . .'— he thumps the base of the vinyl hill—'then the guy down *here* isn't getting any attention.' "

In town, Phoenix first searched out a free vegan lunch that he had heard the Hare Krishnas gave every day before he bought the new guitar. He then took Boyd home and insisted on playing her some of his new songs, including one about his relationship with Martha Plimpton.

After spending a day with Phoenix, Boyd would write, "It's hard not to be touched by this beautiful boy struggling with grave moral issues. The impact of Phoenix's family situation on his ability to perform is difficult to overestimate. The Phoenixes are a team, a tribe, a set of beliefs. River can lose himself in a role because his family provides him with a physical, emotional and spiritual center. Somebody's home in his eyes because somebody's home at home too."

Family center notwithstanding, a few months later Phoenix would reveal to the Los Angeles *Times* how the intense pressures of his Hollywood career had got to him before his move to Gainesville:

"My parents are the main reason I'm still managing to have a life as a kid. 'I mean I could have just become paralyzed by all this attention and what I guess is a kind of invasion into my life. The temptations to rebel, and to not produce anymore, are always there; but the family makes them seem sort of ridiculous. I mean, it's not what we were brought up with."

In February of 1988 *A Night in the Life of Jimmy Reardon* finally came out and in spite of River's contempt for it became a minor hit. Complaining that the studio had turned it into a "sex comedy" by heavy editing, Phoenix told an interviewer in the New York *Daily News*, "I don't agree with that kind of film."

Asked about his next career move, River said: "I'll be reading scripts, playing my guitar and jumping on my trampoline. I think I want to take some college courses." He also said he wanted to get away from the heartthrob image of his movies and take on grittier, more realistic roles. "I'm not trying to build an image," he said.

"I just want to shed the old skin and work on real stuff about real people. Something significant—not just another blah movie."

River, though, found it hard to judge scripts objectively. After potential scripts were vetted by Iris Burton and his mother, River would secretly ask friends to read them and tell him what they thought and if they would be "cool" for him to do:

"River would bring scripts into our tutor sessions for me to read," remembers Dirk Drake. "I sensed that there was a problem that he wasn't getting the right scripts."

Drake also realized that his pupil might be dyslexic, noting how River was also struggling to read his home-study course books. For his first tutorial semester Drake started River and his brother and sisters on a library reading list that included J. D. Salinger's *Catcher in the Rye* and a child's introduction to physics called *Physics for the 21st Century*.

"I remember one day we were reading the book and we got to nuclear bombs," remembers Drake. "Suddenly River became very serious. He asked me what it would be like walking down the street in Hiroshima or Nagasaki when the bomb went off. I described the point of detonation and the terrible effects of radiation on people. River was horrified. He asked me how many bombs there were, and when I told him that President Reagan had enough nuclear power to blow up the world twenty times he was astounded. It was a magical moment and something clicked inside him."

Soon the Phoenix children's home-study lessons became ongoing letter-writing campaigns to protest to various heads of state about human-rights violations and the environment. Drake would then Xerox the letters and send a copy to the home-study center, where they would count as credits.

"River had his own way of writing and structuring paragraphs," said Drake. "He could understand the rules of grammar but when he wrote things down it was all very freeform like e. e. cummings. But when River had to sit down to sign publicity photos for fans he could write fluently and always found nice things to write."

Realizing his educational gaps, River started talking about taking noncredit courses in literature at the University of Florida, but it never went any further than talk.

Meanwhile, on the heels of *Jimmy Reardon*, *Little Nikita* was released in March to bad reviews. The New York *Times* called it "farfetched stuff designed for the nearsighted." The film soon dropped out of sight but it did generate a fresh new publicity blitz on River Phoenix, who just could not shake off his teen-heartthrob image.

"If I see my face on the cover of a magazine I go into remission," he would say. "I shut myself out and freak. I don't like being out there."

Only in easy hindsight can one begin to realize how serious he was about not "being out there."

## Chapter Ten

# TAKING IT TO THE STREETS

In June of 1988 the expanded Phoenix tribe moved to a twenty-acre spread in Micanopy, twelve miles outside Gainesville. Named after Chief Micanopy, who in 1821 led the Seminole Indians in a futile bid to stop the United States government from seizing their lands, the town had been something of a backwater. In the late sixties bands of hippies moved into the town, setting up communes and selling arts and crafts to make a living. The young people loved the wildness of the rural jungle landscape and stayed, opening antique shops and stopping Micanopy's clock at 1967. They were also a shot in the arm for the slumberous town, bringing an economic recovery in their wake. The hippies would gain power and influence in the town, fiercely protecting Micanopy against attempts to disfigure the charm of the village with billboards or fast-food outlets.

Micanopy was also a natural place for the Phoenix family to lay down roots. They purchased a beautiful rambling ranch on land once owned by Chief Micanopy's wife. The center of the complex, which lay off Whiting Road, was a wooden three-bedroom house idyllically set in ten acres by a small stream. Known as "Camp Phoenix" to the locals, the house soon took on the look of a sixties' commune with brightly colored hanging tapestries and environmental posters. The bookshelves housed titles like *Confessions of an Eco Warrior* and *A Guide to Gaia*. One of the bedrooms

97

was shared by the parents, who also used it as an office; the second was Leaf's and River's room; and all three Phoenix girls slept in the third. The house was ecologically correct—to save energy they turned on the hot-water heater only ten minutes a day before showers; declined to have a dryer; used only recycled paper products and never threw away anything that could be reused.

In Micanopy, day-to-day life for the family was little changed from their days in Venezuela with the Children of God, except that now they had plenty of money and no worry about where their next meal was coming from.

"My parents are no longer missionaries," said River in 1988 to the *Hollywood Reporter.* "But they're still very loyal to their code of ethics and we all try to live the same way." And in a Playgirl 1988 interview: "They're very spiritual but it's not organized religion like it was before. My father still reads the Bible a lot and applies it to everyday life. He's a very practical, logical man, and then there's this other side of him that's completely way out."

In Micanopy John Phoenix could devote himself full-time to cultivating an organic garden to help make the family self-sufficient. But he was far from content, mostly internalizing his fears for the family. He would speak out about how Hollywood was corrupting his cherished dream mostly when he was drunk:

"Hollywood is the great Babylon," he would tell River and the other children. "They care for money and nothing else. It's an evil, bad place."

John's relationship with his wife, who was now known by the earth name Heart, was under strain as she urged River to stay in the movie business and ignore his father.

"We had our differences, let's put it that way," John would say. "Heart thought she could look after River, protect all his interests within the system. But our original idea was for him to make enough movies for us to be financially secure—milk the system, if you want—then stop. We had made enough money to keep all those closest to us, in-laws, outlaws, friends, environment groups, whatever, and I wanted us all to get out. Still, the pressure was there to keep going, make more.''

Many nights River would walk into the Hardback depressed and wanting to escape the tensions of his home life. Over pints of draft Guinness he would tell the friendly barmaid Rachel Guinan how he was being torn apart by his parents' arguments over whether or not he should quit Hollywood.

"His mother was definitely the queen," says Guinan. "She's got them all under her thumb. She's the big mama, she made all the decisions about money. I can't help but feel resentment in a way because they were all so much more on top of things than River was."

When River sided with his mother, John felt that he had truly lost the son he loved so much and was unable to cope with that reality. When he was at home he would consume quantities of port, vodka, beer and smoke the Gainesville Green with Arlyn. But however much he drank, John would always be the first one up the next morning, eating his tofu breakfast and scouring the newspapers for bad news, to remind himself of the evils of the world he ached to escape from.

On the morning Blanche Boyd visited she noticed he had eerily listed on the back of a photo of the Phoenix family:

> airplane crash
> radon leak-gas
> whites hacked to death
> garbage leak.

When Martha Plimpton came to stay that summer she was shocked by the disharmony in the family. River too was now a serious drinker as well as smoking Gainesville Green, snorting cocaine and tripping out on magic mushrooms. The troubled father and son had also started drinking together, as though trying to build bridges in their crumbling relationship and find a common bond;

"River and his father were *always* having breakthrough conversations where River would tell his father his feelings about alcohol, about their roles," remembered Plimpton in Esquire in March of 1994. "But the next day nothing would change. River would then say to me, 'Well, it's not *that* serious, it's not *that* bad.'"

Sky Sworski, who had first seen River and Rain singing in St. Petersburg more than ten years earlier, had moved into the Micanopy ranch and now looked after River's day-to-day affairs, screening him from the attention of the media and fans. With his long black beard and so-called Brooklyn accent, some saw the security-minded Sworski as the Phoenix family's Rasputin. Indeed, Sworski at times even represented himself as River's brother to protect River.

"He sort of runs interference," River told writer Michael Angeli. "I guess he is my brother, really. Anyway it works out well with him posing as my brother."

As they became accepted into the Gainesville scene, River and Josh Greenbaum also started becoming downtown regulars. Nights they would go drinking at the Market Street Bar, Club Demolition or the Hardback. On one occasion River and his tutor Dirk Drake were arrested in the street late at night for drinking in public.

"He was always a target," remembers Drake. "You have to remember that River had never seen alcohol when he was growing up, so when he finally started, he'd drink all-out. It wasn't like you or I would drink. He often became a fall-down drunk."

And he also found easy access to drugs through his new Gainesville friends, who steered him toward dealers who jumped at the chance to service the needs of a rich Hollywood star.

"He really liked getting drunk and high," said Martha Plimpton, "but he didn't really have a gauge for when to stop."

By the summer almost everyone in Gainesville had heard about their new Hollywood neighbors and River was starting to be asked for the occasional autograph on the street. He and his brother and sisters became regular sights on the streets as they shopped and hung out with friends. By now River Phoenix, with his long hair and unkempt appearance was almost unrecognizable from the fresh-faced youngster in *Stand By Me.*

He was also getting involved in local issues. He filmed a public-service announcement for Amnesty International and aligned himself with PETA—People for the Ethical Treatment of Animals. And, perhaps ironically, this almost uneducated young man even drew up an ambitious scheme to buy a bus and lead a group of college students in a tour of schools across America.

"I want to give educational seminars," he told the Los Angeles *Herald Examiner* in September of 1988. "All very unbiased, all very neutral, reporting on important issues that are overlooked—from political oppression to an awareness of what's going on with the environment and the atmosphere and trying to show them where America's priorities lie as of now."

One day Dirk Drake introduced his young pupil to his friend Anthony Campanaro, who was in his mid-twenties and was married with a young son Dante. The two became immediate friends and soon River was a frequent visitor at Campanaro's large two-story house, where they would take magic mushrooms and talk about art and music.

"I have this saying, *El Mato,* which means old soul," said Campanaro. "River was an old soul and I am an old soul and as soon as I met him I realized he was one of the souls. It comes from knowing about people and things that happen to them. I realized that this person had a lot to offer."

One night Phoenix and his band went to Campanaro's house to try out their material on a group of especially invited friends. They were eager to start playing in public and wanted feedback on how they actually sounded. After being the only one to take some hallucinogenic magic mushrooms, Phoenix walked around the whole house with his prized new twelve-string guitar trying to see which room had the best acoustics. After choosing the verandah,

Phoenix, Campanaro and another friend drove to a nearby convenience store to buy beer and cigarettes for the all-night session.

Campanaro remembers: "I was talking to the clerk and paying for the beer when River comes up behind me and goes, 'Hey, great to see you. I haven't seen you guys in a while.' And then he walks out the door. I didn't catch on at all and I thought he was off the wall because we'd all driven there together. When I got back to the car he looked really proud of himself and had a big grin. You see he was under age so he didn't want the clerk to know he was with us. That's when I clicked. This guy's an actor. He just took on another persona, as if he had just seen me for the first time. River's an actor and he can turn it on and he can turn it off."

That night at Campanaro's house Phoenix and the rest of the band got high and improvised intricate space music recorded on a small cassette recorder as the first public performance of the newly named Aleka's Attic.

River had recently come up with the name after waking up from a dream with the words *Aleka Dozy Encircles* in his head and he then made a mythical story around the name:

"Aleka is a poet philosopher," he later told Bill DeYoung of the Gainesville *Sun*. "The Attic is a meeting place where he lives and he has a secret society. They come and visit him and read his works. He then dies and they meet irregularly and continue the readings of his works, and from that learn their own, and become filled with this new passion for life. And they express it through music and form a band. We've put it in a fairytale setting."

Phoenix's lyrics for the song "Aleka Dozy Encircles," which tells the fairystory of the band, was his first collaboration with bassist Josh McKay. The words have a haunting, childlike lyrical quality.


Josh Greenbaum says that the band would practice acoustically in the attic of the Micanopy house before going to their outside studio to play electric. Encouraged by the success of the first performance of Aleka's Attic in Campanaro's house, River decided to rent a hall in Gainesville for their first public performance and then undertake an "underground tour of East Coast colleges."

But first Phoenix had to put the band on a hiatus for four months while he flew to Colorado to restart his movie career.


River Phoenix celebrated his eighteenth birthday by coming out of retirement to play a high-profile cameo role as young Indy in Steven Spielberg's *Indiana Jones and the Last Crusade*. In an action-packed ten-minute opening sequence, Phoenix plays the Harrison Ford role in a flashback that explains the hero's phobia about snakes and how he got his Stetson. Spielberg and his co-producer George Lucas saw Phoenix as their secret ingredient to give the movie youth appeal and help ensure good box office for the successor to their $100 million grossing *Indiana Jones and the Temple of Doom*. They tried to keep the young actor's involvement under wraps until the film's summer 1990 release, but the news leaked out. To throw reporters off the scent, the studio spread the false rumor that Phoenix would be playing Indiana Jones' brother.

"It's really a little cameo," said Phoenix modestly. "The part is listed as 'boy on train,' literally."

Happy to be reunited with his mentor Ford in Colorado, River delighted in his new action-hero persona:

"There's lots of mad escapes," he said. I did a lot of the stunts because I felt so much of the character and what he had to do was physical. It would have been lying to have someone else do the stunts."

Describing how he prepared for his role as Indiana Jones as a boy, River said he was careful not to mimic Harrison Ford and used him only as a reference:

"I would just look at Harrison. He would do stuff and I would not mimic it but interpret it younger. Mimicking is a *terrible* mistake that many people do when they play someone younger, or with an age difference. Mimicking doesn't interpret true, because you just can't edit it around.''

Asked if he might ever inherit the Indiana Jones role from Harrison Ford, River said he could never do it justice:

''A production without Harrison would never be that good,'' he said. ''I think it should remain the way he has done it.''

After finishing filming River went to Los Angeles to prepare for the September 9 release of *Running on Empty*. He gave a series of interviews in Hollywood's Bel Age Hotel and the penthouse suite of the Four Seasons, though his favorite torn jeans and ragged T-shirt seemed out of place in those proper settings.

Phoenix, though, had decided to rid himself of his ''goody-goody, sticky-sweet'' image once and for all, and so the River Phoenix who greeted reporters was almost unrecognizable from the fresh cherub-faced star they had once known—lank hair falling over the collar of an old gray thrift-shop shirt, jeans fashionably torn at the knees, sneakers full of holes. Playing the role of the antistar, River, who now referred to all interviews as ''propaganda,'' would often launch into a stream-of-consciousness monologue about his career, his beliefs and his family.

''Phoenix doesn't seem to give a hoot about his appearance,'' wrote Susan King of the Los Angeles *Herald Examiner*. ''His long dirty blonde hair is matted, his clothes have a distinct lived-in look.''

In an attempt to bury his sweet-teen image, Phoenix also lashed into a teen magazine that had run a contest offering readers a dinner date with him.

''That's such a lie,'' he would tell the Los Angeles *Examiner*. ''That's *really* awful. No one will *ever* win a dinner date with me because I'll *never* do it.'' He said he was being misrepresented by these magazines and was trying to break out from being a teenage heartthrob.

''I had some photos shot of me several years ago,'' he said. ''And they're still being used in those magazines. But they're not what I'm like, and it's created the kind of image for me that's the worst. And I hear from friends all these things said about me in those magazines that are so wrong."

Frustrated by his old image, River, rather naively, offered the editor of one magazine an interview and a photo session so he could set the record straight for his fans.

"I told them I was tired of being in the magazines, and how they made it sound like I love them and want girls so badly to buy them. I'm also doing a photo shoot in a couple of weeks, good, honest pictures. They're going to print these pictures anyway, so they might as well be pictures of what I'm really like."

Loosening up, Phoenix also told reporters about his new family home and how he had left Hollywood to "get a grip on things and unwind," but made them promise not to print that he was living in Gainesville.

"It feels so good to be home," he told the *Examiner*. "It feels good to settle down and live in a family and see what it really is like. Where we lived before revolved around the movie set. I never wanted the wealthy fantasies of limousines or the pride of arriving at school in nice clothes. I wanted money so we could buy a great piece of land and be self-contained. That impresses me, that really feels good. It feels like something's been accomplished."

Phoenix also talked openly about his problems with the business side of Hollywood and how he was trying to be more selective in his choice of scripts.

"This business can be very overpowering and can affect you in a very negative way if you're not careful," he told the Boston *Herald* in September of 1988. "I'm not afraid of rejection and I'm not afraid to quit while I'm ahead.

"I've become very choosy," he added a year later to the New York *Daily News*. "I've been reading scripts but nothing's given me a lot of inspiration. There was a period, between when I made *Mosquito Coast* and *Running on Empty*, that I did film work for work's sake. But that doesn't do much for your career." He tried hard to point out how his whole career had been about not getting typecast:

"I think of the roles I've played lately, the one in *Running on Empty* shows the direction I want to head in—on the leading edge *out* of the teenage years."

*Running on Empty* was acclaimed by the critics and River's performance was singled out for special mention. He was now a solid favorite to win a best supporting Oscar, but he seemed near-paralyzed in selecting any new script to commit to. The only project that had piqued his interest was a film adaptation of singer/poet Jim Carroll's best-selling book *Basketball Diaries* about his harrowing days as a heroin addict in New York's East Village.

"I'd like to do something that is significant without being blatant and corny," he told the *Hollywood Reporter*. "Something that's real candid and has a lot of form and strength."

## Chapter Eleven

# PARTYING WITH OSCAR

For Christmas, 1988, Aleka's Attic rented a small theater hall in Gainesville for sixty-five dollars to give their first concert for the band members' family and friends. The first sixty-five people paid a dollar each, and after that everyone got in free. The show was a well-kept secret in Gainesville, River being petrified that if his fans found out it would become a fiasco.

River proceeded to lead the band in a short set, playing the songs he'd been writing with Josh McKay, and got a standing ovation. But not everyone was bowled over by their first performance.

"I thought they were a little amateurish," said Charlie Scales from Hyde & Zeke Records. "The song writing had not yet developed and after the first couple of songs, which were pretty new and novel, it kind of stalled."

But River, who was the undisputed leader of the band, was so pleased by Aleka's performance he decided to take the band in his motor home on a six-week East Coast tour in January. Sky Sworski was appointed manager and Kenny Greenbaum, who was now working full-time for his son's band, was put in charge of the logistics of the first Aleka's Attic tour, during which they would be playing second and third on the bill.

"I wasn't only security, I was a roadie, I was a drum tech. I did whatever was necessary to aid and abet their success." said Kenny Greenbaum.

Few bands just starting off with such limited experience could have afforded to undertake such a tour and many critics questioned whether the whole thing wasn't just the whim of a rich movie star. Not surprisingly, band members were particularly sensitive about being called River Phoenix's band.

"Because River was famous we didn't have to take the typical route that a lot of bands have to," admitted Josh Greenbaum. River's fame also didn't hurt bookings, and local club owners fairly jumped at the chance to book Aleka's Attic, signing a rider forbidding them to promote the show using River Phoenix's name. But then they would quietly spread the word that River Phoenix would be appearing live. Soon the tour lunged out of control, with hundreds of young girls turning up at shows to mob Phoenix. His young fans would stand near the stage screaming and throwing their bras and panties at their embarrassed hero, who would do his best to ignore them by playing with his back to the audience.

When Aleka's Attic played CBGB's in New York City River was forced to hire a security force to control his fans. At the 9:30 Club in Washington, D.C., where they opened for an obscure group called Pussy Willow, River's own publicity agent took the unusual step of declaring an information blackout on the star.

"River's getting so much publicity that his appearances are taking on a Bruce Springsteen stature that is overshadowing the band," said the Washington *Post*.

While they were in New York, Aleka's Attic joined the B-52's and Go-Go's guitarist Jane Wiedlin in a benefit for PETA at the Palladium, where excited paparazzi caught Phoenix and Martha Plimpton in a tender shot that made all the New York newspapers the next day. Phoenix also found time to put on a white shirt to attend the D. W. Griffith Awards at the Lincoln Center Library, where he was named Best Supporting Actor for *Running on Empty*.

*   *   *

Back on the road, Kenny Greenbaum drove up to Boston, where respected Boston *Globe* music critic Jim Sullivan saw Aleka's Attic at the legendary Rathskeller club, known as the Rat, and was impressed:

"The hour-long set was modest, pleasant and serious," wrote Sullivan. "Aleka's Attic packed a lot of parts into their herky-jerky songs—a number of twists and turns, propelled by Phoenix's guitar. They're mining an exuberant, peppy art-rock field, reminiscent of early Talking Heads.

"Not all their material connected. Despite their abrupt sonic shifts, there seemed a limit to their overall range. Still, this was no lark; there's room to grow and, certainly, an enthusiasm on everyone's part."

After the show, Phoenix was careful to tell Sullivan that he was not just another egocentric actor flirting with rock 'n' roll:

"A lot of people expect a rock-star trip," said Phoenix, dressed in a plaid flannel shirt, jeans and sneakers, his blond hair hanging like a protective curtain across his face. "There's that kind of preconceived idea."

On a limited budget from the Island Records advance, Phoenix, Rain, Josh Greenbaum (who had now adopted the name Greene), Josh McKay, Tim Hankins and Kenny Greenbaum traveled from gig to gig in the motor home and stayed in cheap motels outside town. There was cocaine and Gainesville Green to help wind down after shows, but the use of drugs shocked viola player Tim Hankins, who refused to participate.

After one late night of partying in Philadelphia, River was awakened in the middle of the night by a phone call from Iris Burton with the news that he had been nominated for an Academy Award as Best Supporting Actor for *Running on Empty*.

"I was like completely out," said River. "We were on the road in a hotel room and Iris my agent is going, "Oh, my baby!" And it was like, Well, okay. And I went back to sleep."

By the next morning Phoenix had forgotten about the nomination.

"Later that night we were in a bar before we were due to go on stage at J. C. Dobbs," said Phoenix. "And I was watching television in between the sound checks and the story about me being nominated came on. It was like holy shit, did Iris call me this morning? It was no big thing."

Later he heard he had won the National Board of Review's Best Supporting Actor award for *Running on Empty*. His response was to ask what the society was, and to say he did not want to win the Oscar since it went against everything that he believed in.

"I'm praying that I don't win," said Phoenix. "I don't really want to get up there and accept it. It's not my thing to get up there at the altar and give myself praise and look good."

River Phoenix, one has to believe, sincerely felt that he had not yet paid his dues and did not deserve to be judged alongside such actors as Sir John Gielgud, Sir Alec Guinness and Kevin Kline:

"I don't think it's fair to these actors who have been around a lot longer than me," said Phoenix. "That's not courteous respect to them. My feeling is that if I win it'll be because of politics."


Back in Gainesville, River started feeling comfortable enough to raise his profile, both musically and to help his favorite environmental causes. He filmed a series of public-service announcements for the local branch of PETA and agreed to play a benefit for the Friends of the Whales.

"I know there's sort of a goody-goody image that goes along with that sort of thing," said Phoenix, "but there are some things that are just very important. Just using the notoriety and respect that I have amongst certain people, for some reason it works—as far as people saying, Oh, what does he have to say? I'd rather do that than fucking do a Pepsi commercial."

But River who secretly searched thrift shops with friends looking for leather belts and boots, conceded that there was a danger of his becoming an environmental crusader and spreading himself too thinly: "I can't let myself get turned into the poster child for every cause there is," he said.

Feeling confident after his East Coast tour, River announced a Major Aleka's Attic first public concert in March at the Sun Skate Center on Main Street in Gainesville. He even invited the local daily, the Gainesville *Sun,* to attend, granting an interview after the show to arts and entertainment editor Bill DeYoung, who had been chasing River for months.

"I first heard that River Phoenix was in Gainesville when a friend of mine recognized him in a music store buying a keyboard for his sister Rain," said DeYoung, noting that the only other celebrity who ever lived in Gainesville was Tom Petty, who was born there. "I remember thinking, What the hell's the kid in *Stand By Me* doing here? So it became a mission of mine to try to find him."

DeYoung told his contacts to call him whenever they saw Phoenix and soon he was getting "sightings like the Loch Ness Monster." One day DeYoung got a hot tip that the actor was in a downtown store and he rushed over to catch him.

"River passed me in the door as he was going out to his car," said DeYoung. "I told him that I wanted to do a story about his band now they were going to play around town. He said he didn't want people to know he was hanging around Gainesville and was painfully serious about it. I mean, in all the time I knew him he would never even admit to living here. He always had that cloud up there all the time. I finally convinced him that I didn't want to write a movie-star story and he agreed to speak to me."

When DeYoung met River backstage between sets, Martha Plimpton, newly shorn with a crewcut, was with him. They were busy going over an environmental speech they were writing for Phoenix to deliver to the audience during the second set, so DeYoung was left to observe them for a few minutes.

"River and Martha were sitting there arguing about what he was going to say," said DeYoung. "They had notes like Save the Ferrets or Weasels Forever. It was like watching two junior high school kids getting ready for debate class. They hadn't got a clue what they were talking about. I got the impression that he was doing what was expected of him.''

After finishing off the speech, Gainesville's only movie star was not happy when he began the interview.

''Tonight was the worst that we ever have been,'' a visibly disappointed Phoenix told DeYoung. ''We had the East Coast tour that gave us a lot of experience but it was just not there tonight.''

Trying to maintain his nonsmoking position, Phoenix, who had smoked since making *Stand By Me,* said that he needed a smoke to help him through a migraine headache:

''It just hit and I'm trying to trudge through,'' he explained. ''It was very weird. I feel very tense and I just want to do something like smoke because when I take a drag off a cigarette I get so high. I don't do it regularly, you see.''

Asked why he was in Gainesville, Phoenix told DeYoung it afforded him the opportunity to keep a low profile and forget his stardom.

''I really try to avoid thinking about it,'' he said. ''Unless I accidentally trip on the magazine stand at 7–Eleven, or unless someone reminds me or says, you know, Gasp. But otherwise, I'm just completely naïve to all of it. I'm really sheltered from it too. That's one of the big reasons I'm here in Gainesville, whenever I *can* be here.''

When DeYoung remarked on his appearance, it became obvious, DeYoung said, that Plimpton did not approve of Phoenix's grungy style.

''I usually dress cleaner,'' he said. ''I've just been moving shit all day long. I'm usually so much neater.'' At which point Plimpton said, ''He's always like this. He always dresses like this.''

When DeYoung asked River whether his movie career might start taking second place to his music, he answered, ''I'm not giving anything up. I have nothing to prove or hold onto. It's definitely not the fame or the finances that keep me going. It's what I get out of it."

Ten days before the Oscar ceremony, the Gainesville *Sun* laid out the red carpet to welcome officially the internationally famous actor to town with the headline RIVER PHOENIX, REGULAR GUY.

"River Phoenix likes Gainesville," DeYoung's Monday profile began. "Here he has everything an eighteen-year-old kid could want: friends, family, a decent car, places to hang out, a garage out back for his rock band to practice in."

Asked about his musical influences, River cited Elvis Costello, Velvet Underground, early Bowie and Roxy Music and the Smiths "before they were too indulgent."

The two-page article portrayed River as the boy next door who just happened to be a rich movie star living in Gainesville:

"On the street, he is virtually unrecognizable, favoring jeans, sneakers and flannel shirts," wrote DeYoung. "His hair is long and hangs lower on the left side, quite unlike the hip, sculptured locks he generally sports in his movies."

Soon after the article appeared in the Gainesville *Sun*, there was a backlash against River. Hostile members of a rival local rock band called the Smegmas launched a campaign to humiliate him by plastering one of his early beefcake shots all over town.

"River's feelings were badly hurt," said Dirk Drake. "He felt that now he had finally found somewhere to live that he liked, he wasn't going to be allowed to settle down peacefully. He couldn't understand the hostility."

As a counter, River arranged to have Aleka's Attic open for the Smegmas. And when hundreds of kids arrived and paid the cover charge to see River play he insisted on giving all the box-office proceeds to his persecutors. The campaign against him was halted.

But however much he tried to escape or deflect his stardom, River would always find himself a target wherever he went. Dirk Drake remembers him being taunted by a group of racist skinheads at a party in Gainesville:

"He smiled with an unbelievable innocence and said, 'If you really want to kick my ass, go ahead, just explain to me why you're doing it.' The skinheads were dumbfounded. One guy started to say, 'Ah, you wouldn't be worth it.' And River said, 'We're all worth it, man, we're all worth millions of planets and stars and galaxies and universes.' "


On March 29, 1989, a tuxedoed River Phoenix, with his escort Martha Plimpton, made a star entrance into the Dorothy Chandler Pavillion to attend the Sixty-first Academy Awards ceremony. Hair slicked back and wearing glasses, he escorted Plimpton and his mother Heart to their table. It would be Kevin Kline, co-star in River Phoenix's next film, who won the Best Supporting Actor Oscar for his role in the John Cleese comedy *A Fish Called Wanda.*

"I had to stop River from running to hug Kevin," said his mother. "It never crossed his mind that *he* hadn't won."

After the ceremony River was philosophical, saying that his nomination wouldn't change his direction as an actor:

"I guess many people would change after a nomination in the way they see things," he said. "In my case, it's really irrelevant in terms of what I do. Still, it was an incredible experience which I will put in my memories, like everything else."

Soon after the Oscars, Martha Plimpton decided to end her four-year relationship with Phoenix because, she told Esquire, she couldn't cope any longer with his drugs and drinking:

"When we split up, a lot of it was that I had learned that screaming, fighting and begging wasn't going to change him. He had to change himself and he didn't want to yet."

The breakup with Plimpton was a huge shock to Phoenix, who was deeply in love with her and had become emotionally dependent on her. Without Martha there was no one to rein him in.

"I think when he lost Martha he started going downhill," said Jim Dobson, who had stayed close to the Phoenix family. "Then he started playing alternative rock clubs at night, performing until three A.M., and he got heavily into the New York music scene where he was up all night and hardly sleeping."

Over the next few months River did seem to drown his sorrows in his music. Aleka's Attic began playing every weekend around Gainesville and got a residency at the Hardback, a small punk-rock no-frills club with a neverending supply of warm Guinness on tap. River seemed to like the dark recesses of the club, where he could hide himself with his friends and not be bothered by strangers.

"River drank his sorrows away many a night here just like everybody does," remembers Hardback barmaid Rachel Guinan. "He wasn't a punk rocker like most of the people here who are raw-edged. He couldn't relate to punk rock but at the same time he could hang out."

After playing late-night sets with Aleka's Attic, River and his regular entourage of Josh Greenbaum, Josh McKay and his brother Leaf would drink into the night. It was at the Hardback that he loosened up and relaxed, but even here he was different.

"River was comfortable with everybody but he didn't come from the same background as we all did," said Rachel Guinan. "It was like he was an insider and an outsider all in one. I think there's a parallel too with Hollywood, where he was an insider but he wasn't like the rest of them."

When Rachel Guinan found herself in trouble after destroying a wall outside the Hardback with her truck, River came to her rescue.

"I was breaking up with my husband and I was going nuts," she would say. "They wanted five hundred dollars to fix the wall and I was broke, I had a young baby to support. We're a very tightly knit community and River knew my predicament because he always took the trouble to ask about me. He had Aleka's Attic play a benefit gig so I could repay the money. He really cared and he didn't have to. He really touched me."

Later, when River developed a crush on her and started courting her, Rachel refused to go out with him because she did not want to be seen as a groupie.

"I tried to avoid him. I thought River was a decent person but I just didn't want to deal with that whole glamorized version of life. I never had any desire to know him in that way at all. I was just the bartender, you know."

Bill Perry, an employee of Hyde & Zeke Records, says Phoenix was testing people out in the beginning to see whom he could trust:

"The first time I ever met him I walked up to him and said, 'Hey, you're River Phoenix.' And he said, 'No. My name's Rio.' And I just laughed because Rio means River. I thought 'Funny, ha, ha.' He had to figure out which people were going to treat him like a friend and not like a star. I thought he was a bit standoffish but I knew that he didn't want to be bothered, so I said, 'Okay, I won't be in your face.' "

His friend Anthony Campanaro says River experimented with drugs as an entrée into the Gainesville music scene, which he wanted to be a part of:

"I would sometimes look at him when I saw him in the scene, with its rock 'n' roll and drugs and wondered why he had to be there, because he had it all. He had the money. He had the fame. He just didn't fit into this hard-edged Gainesville dope scene. And I believe that River also felt that he didn't fit in and he was doing the drugs because he wanted to fit in so desperately. Drugs made him part of the scene. It was peer pressure and he wanted to be cool."

Campanaro also noticed a darker influence: "River had a definite fascination with the dark side," said Campanaro. "Rock 'n' roll and drugs had a lot to do with it and I think a lot of it had to do with the way he had been brought up. He had been so sheltered. He had also experienced a lot growing up but he had also missed out on a lot of things."

Bobby Bukowski, soon to become a close friend and major support, remembers their first meeting:

"He had very long hair and he struck me—as he came out of an elevator—as an angel, some kind of supernatural being," Bukowski told Premiere magazine.

"An angel could be Gabriel, but an angel could be Lucifer too. He would as readily delve into the deep, dark recesses as he would fly up to the lofty, illuminated [places]."

## Chapter Twelve

# COASTING

IN SUMMER, 1989, RIVER Phoenix put Aleka's Attic on hold to fly to California for his next film, *I Love You to Death,* which he described as a "whacked-out comedy." The film, which was based on the true story of a woman who made five unsuccessful attempts to kill her cheating husband, was an attempt at comedy to lighten up his serious image. Complaining that journalists only wrote about "my boring side," River said: "They bring out this intense River, a goody-goody boy and not the River who's into a good kick. I've always had a fine sense of humor."

River was perfect for the part of New Age pizza boy Devo Nod, and was cast over the phone by director Lawrence Kasdan. The director of *The Big Chill, Body Heat* and *The Accidental Tourist* had gathered an impressive ensemble of actors, including Kevin Kline, Tracey Ullman, William Hurt, Joan Plowright and Keanu Reeves.

The black comedy centers on a Tacoma pizzeria owner Lothario, played by Kevin Kline, whose devoted wife Rosalie (Tracey Ullman), accidentally catches him making a romantic rendezvous at the public library. Encouraged by her mother, played by Joan Plowright, Rosalie enlists the support of her ardent admirer Devo in the murder.

"It's kind of 'how to kill your husband and save your marriage,'" said River. "I'm the middle man who helps arrange the extreme acts that happen in the movie."

River totally immersed himself in the part of Devo, with his Eastern philosophy and heavy mysticism. Veteran British actress Miriam Margolyes, who played Kline's mother, saw some dangers in River's intensity.

"He's a young man and he's serious and more thoughtful about his work," she said. "At the moment he has no way of distancing himself from a part."

River, with his New Age background and his strict vegan beliefs, was offended when it was suggested that he closely resembled the spacy runes-casting Devo:

"I don't confuse myself with the characters I play," he said. "Anyway, Devo is such a psychological mess-up. He's got a twisted idea of spiritual things and all that crystal stuff. He's so serious about life."

While on the set of *I Love You to Death* River cemented his friendship with Keanu Reeves, whom he had been introduced to a year earlier while Martha Plimpton and his brother Leaf had been making *Parenthood,* and soon the two became inseparable.

"Leaf and Martha were his [Reeves'] buddies before I was even a friend of his," said Phoenix. "Then I met up with him on *I Love You to Death.* And I liked the guy. He's like my older brother."

Like River, Reeves had had an unstable childhood and had always been on the move. The son of a Chinese-Hawaiian father and an English mother, Reeves was born in Beirut, Lebanon, and his parents separated when he was two. Raised by his mother and stepfather in Toronto, Keanu, which is Hawaiian for cool breezes, attended four high schools in five years before dropping out and leaving home to become an actor.

Phoenix also developed a close rapport with English comedienne Tracey Ullman and they'd "just mouth off and get clever with each other" and play word games during any free time on set. To prepare the actors, director Kasdan conducted lengthy improvisation sessions to help the characters relate to each other. Rehearsing in this way with actors of the stature of William Hurt,

Joan Plowright and Kevin Kline was a valuable acting lesson for Phoenix.

During filming, River stayed with Bill Richert in his huge Malibu house. "He spent the whole summer here," said Richert. "He'd show up late every night and sometimes I'd be asleep. He'd sit in the kitchen and play songs on his guitar he'd written and then he'd still be there playing the next morning when I woke up. River was always awake. If he wasn't acting he was playing music. If he wasn't playing music he was giving advice to someone. He found it very hard to turn himself off and he'd just go on until he was completely exhausted. Then he would slowly wind down like a clock, grab a nap and start all over again."

Almost every day Richert would come home to find long stream-of-consciousness messages on his recording machine from River, who had now begun a study of surrealistic poetry. On the final day of shooting *I Love You to Death*, River left an especially strange, cryptic message:

"Hello, Bill. If you're sleeping, please, by all means ignore this message. But in fact if you are awake, then you'd better not ignore me. . . . I had the most amazing day. It was just beautiful, the things I learned, through pain and through misunderstanding, and through being displaced, discombobulated.

"I came out on my last day of work as a triumphant failure. I stand here, need not I die nor need I drink, for I know that my soul will keep. And who's to say he or she or it is the one, for I only know from where it has begun."

Richert took River's spiritual forays seriously: "River lived in an area where truth lies. He lived surrounded by echoes of real things, the past, the future, life and death. He found it very difficult with studio deals, negotiations, photo shoots and paparazzi."

After completing *I Love You To Death* River resumed his "normal" life in Gainesville. Actually he was now leading a double life, delicately balancing the pressures of Hollywood with his new rock 'n' roll lifestyle in central Florida. Josh Greenbaum believes Gainesville centered River and to a degree kept his feet on the ground:

"His friendships here got him back to being River," Greenbaum said. "I don't know that anyone ever really understood the separation or connection between his two worlds."

But he also faced growing pressures in Gainesville by being accessible and trying to live a normal life.

"Fame is an amazing phenomenon," said Greenbaum. "First, you have your real true friends and then there's the people that just want to hang out with you because they think they can benefit." Greenbaum says Phoenix had to deal with people who pretended to be his friend and then bad-mouthed him behind his back.

"The thing that River most hated about fame was that people would say, Oh, you're rich. You've got a lot of money. Why can't you do this? They never realized that River bought hundreds of acres of rain forests in Chile to stop it from being developed into beach-front hotels. It wasn't like he was going out buying Cadillacs, Porsches and Ferraris."

Anthony Campanaro also noted a wave of resentment from local musicians against River as Aleka's Attic became the biggest draw in Gainesville.

"There's a lot of politics among the bands here," said Campanaro. "A lot of people said, Well, they're a draw because River Phoenix is in the band. They have no problems. They're not hurting. They don't have to work hard. But they did work hard. It doesn't matter if you have money or you don't have money, you still have to work to make your art as good as possible."

One of the more established Gainesville bands was an all-girl punk trio called Mutley Chix. Formed in August of 1984 by Dirk Drake's wife, Debra Fetzer-Drake, the band had progressed from loud three-chord covers of the Sex Pistols to widen their repertoire to include thoughtful modern rock songs. Like Aleka's Attic, Mutley Chix regularly played the Hardback and had just released a new cassette called *Burn Your Bra* on their own independent label.

"To me, punk rock is kind of like a culture," said Fetzer-Drake in 1990. "I wouldn't throw away a lifestyle just because I got a job or had a kid or something."

On Halloween, 1989, Fetzer-Drake added a new singer/saxophonist called Sue Solgot to the band. Nicknamed Suzy Q, the blonde twenty-five-year-old Detroit native left her adoptive parents to come to Gainesville to study fine-arts photography and earned a bachelor of arts degree. Solgot played saxophone briefly in junior high school but it was not until her student loan came through that she decided to buy a saxophone at a Gainesville pawnshop and brush up her technique. Now a member of Mutley Chix, Sue was studying at the Florida School of Massage by day and going punk at night, which made her something of an outlaw in rural Gainesville.

"When you're a Mutley Chix, Gainesville rolls out the red carpet for you," Solgot sarcastically told Tom Nordlie of the Gainesville *Sun* for a 1991 profile on the group called "The Girls in the Band." "People stop me on the street all the time and say, 'Aren't you in the Mutley Chix?' "

Moving as she was in local musical circles, it was only a matter of time before Solgot would meet River Phoenix, who was sporting a new marine crewcut for his next movie, *Dogfight*. When the actor saw her at a party he walked up to the singer and introduced himself as "Rio," then denied being River Phoenix after a friend of Solgot tried to unmask him.

"I'm not that guy," claimed Phoenix. "I'm nothing like him."

Eventually he admitted his true identity and asked Solgot out.

"He was very private and mysterious," Solgot told Esquire in March of 1994. "We never talked much about our pasts or who we were, though I was always curious."

River and Sue found they had a lot in common, with music and their concern with environmental issues, and soon they began dating and hanging out at each other's shows.

Soon River asked Sue to live with him and she readily agreed. He found a huge one-bedroom apartment in Gainesville's most prestigious area, the Duckpond. Their new home took up the entire first floor of a restored two-story house and was only a twenty-minute drive from the Phoenix family home in Micanopy.

"River didn't want anyone to know he was living here," said their landlady Melanie Barr. "He would hardly even look at me or talk to me. He didn't want me to know that he existed, which was stupid because he'd signed the lease and I knew who he was. I thought, Well, why are you trying to hide yourself from me?"

Each month River's mother would drive up to the house in a truck and send one of the kids in with the rent check, then drive off without saying a word. Now that River had a Gainesville base and did not have to go home he started staying out later with his band members, partying in the Hardback and the Market Street Bar.

"River was basically shy," says Melanie Barr. "Even though sometimes he could be a loudmouthed troublemaker in the bars. He'd get very drunk. My friends would see him and say, We saw your tenant outside so-and-so bar looking like he was going to puke or something.

"Because he was so famous he was very reclusive and quiet but not in the bars. Once he had a few drinks inside him he didn't seem to care. He would just be a typical twenty-year-old getting drunk, yelling rude things and acting stupid."

Unlike his friends, River Phoenix did not have to be up early for work every day and have the discipline and responsibilities of a nine-to-five routine. He had long periods between movies during which he could indulge his appetites.

"River had a little too much time on his hands and I don't think he knew how to handle it," says Anthony Campanaro. "I would look at him and say, 'If you can just survive these next three or four years you're going to be one hell of a star. He was going to be a great actor, if he could just hold on.'"

\*    \*    \*

A few days before Christmas of 1989 Keanu Reeves drove his 1974 Norton Commando motorcycle from Canada down through Charleston, North Carolina and into Florida to visit his friend River Phoenix. He was on a special mission, bearing a treatment that he had been given by film director Gus Van Sant for a new movie named after a B–52s song, *My Own Private Idaho.*

Van Sant, whose last movie, *Drugstore Cowboy,* cast Matt Dillon as a junkie thief who robbed drugstores for a living, had been trying to get his new script to Phoenix but was having no success bypassing his watchdog agent Iris Burton. In spite of Van Sant's pleas, Burton declined to show her bright young star the treatment about two young drug-taking homosexual hustlers, a disastrous property for his clean-cut image. She had erected a wall around River Phoenix, screening each script before sending it on to Heart Phoenix. Reeves' agent had also turned down the script, but Van Sant was determined to give young actors the opportunity to make their own decisions and telephoned the young star of the *Bill and Ted* adventures and arranged to send him the script.

"Some of the older people, like agents, just didn't get it," Van Sant told US magazine in November of 1991. "They just couldn't get past the first scene."

At the beginning of the treatment Mike Waters, who would be played by River Phoenix, is seen picking up an ugly, fat man and taking him to a hotel room for oral sex.

"As soon as they read that they're thinking of their client, picturing him giving head, and that prompted them *not* to get it. The idea of young guys having sex with older guys for money—it's like off the scale of life," Van Sant told the Advocate.

Reeves read the treatment, liked it and agreed to play the part of Scott Favor. Agreeing with Van Sant that River Phoenix was perfect for the other starring role, he offered to visit River and show him the treatment. When Reeves arrived at Micanopy and showed it to Phoenix, he was moved by the sad plight of the young hustler Mike Waters and committed to it, telling friends, "This will get me off the cover of Tigerbeat."

River recalled: "We said, 'Okay, I'll do it if you do it. I won't do it if you don't.' We shook hands. That was that."

On New Year's Day, 1990, River and a group of friends watched a rough cut of Van Sant's film *Drugstore Cowboy,* fascinated by the realistic on-screen portrayals of the actors shooting heroin, "spiking." Since moving to Gainesville, River had often visited Jacksonville Beach and had been beguiled by its drug culture. He was beginning to wonder about what it would be like to take heroin and began questioning people about it.

According to Esquire, in an April, 1994 piece, when the opportunity to try heroin presented itself he was ready. River Phoenix was ready and willing to experience everything. The only question: how far would he go?

## Chapter Thirteen

# THE DOGFATHER OF GAINESVILLE

RIVER PHOENIX AND Aleka's Attic flew to Charlotte, North Carolina, at the beginning of 1990 to record a song for an upcoming album called *Tame Yourself* to benefit his favorite charity, PETA. They joined R.E.M. vocalist Michael Stipe, later to be come a close friend of River, country singer k. d. lang and Natalie Merchant of 10,000 Maniacs, all of whom donated songs for the album to be released on the Island label.

River's moody mid-tempo tune, with its cryptic lyrics and strange animal imagery, would be the first and only Aleka's Attic recording ever to be released.

During the recording session at Reflection Studios Phoenix, surrounded by his fellow band members and wearing a red corduroy workshirt, baggy gray pants and canvas hiking boots, gave his environmental manifesto to the press:

"Priority number one on the whole list for us and for the whole world really is the environment," he said. "It's the life support system that keeps all of us, men and women in our civilized realm, alive. Animals can't really voice their opinion. We feel as though we can be one of the spokespeople on their behalf."

Asked by the Toronto *Star* to compare his movie and music careers, River said he preferred making music, since films were becoming a "production line" and too much like "work."

"Music is a whole oasis in my head," he said. "The creation process is so personal and fulfilling."

River also took another public stand at this time—against drugs. When his childhood friend and *Stand By Me* co-star Corey Feldman was arrested and charged with two counts of possession of drugs and intent to sell, Phoenix questioned the system:

"It's very sad," Phoenix told People magazine in April while in New York for the opening of *I Love You to Death*. "It makes you realize that drugs aren't just done by bad guys and sleazebags, it's a universal disease. Yes, possession is completely wrong, but the way it's dealt with is questionable because a lot of people are just products of the system. I mean, how many people want to see Corey Feldman go to jail for years?"

Although using drugs himself, River was shocked to see Feldman and other of his Hollywood actor friends becoming addicted to drugs. He was in denial of his escalating drug use, which would soon lead him to experiment with heroin. The growing chasm between Phoenix's increasingly erratic private life and his public persona as the clean-living vegetarian was never more pronounced than when Vogue magazine flew to Gainesville to shoot a photo spread with the actor, who in his disheveled appearance was now considered ultra-chic. Trying to live up to the public's expectations of him as the healthy environmentalist, River came down strongly against drugs and even aligned himself with Nancy Reagan.

"Nancy's said it all for me, anyway. *Just Say No!,*" he told journalist Vicki Woods, who was "charmed" by his performance, according to Vogue in May of 1990.

"I just stay away from [drugs]. I don't even like talking about it. It depresses me. The biggest thing that really gets me are the girls . . . because of being used, the way men use women. It really upsets me—the wonderful extra-virgin-oil young ladies who are so wholesome and so together and their heads are on tight and they've been straight, and they get caught, and you see them a year later and they're . . . and all they've got left is a recorded message in their heads.''

In the same way that River, the actor, at times fooled his parents and many of his friends, he managed to fool Woods. Introducing her as his ''aunt from England,'' he took her on a tour of Gainesville before posing with Suzy Q Solgot, who hid her blonde hair under a brunette wig as a joke, for fashion photographer Bruce Weber in chic clothes by Ralph Lauren, Paul Smith, Emporio Armani and Yohji Yamamoto.

In a feature piece entitled ''Tofu Men Don't Eat Meat,'' Woods described the Phoenix family's clean-living hippie lifestyle in which even the two pet dogs were vegans:

''Arlyn and John seemed to have followed the beat of the sixties drum harder than most,'' wrote Woods. ''And instead of turning into eighties yuppies they've hung on in there. They are now perfectly regular folks with twenty acres of property, a few cars, a few bank accounts, a cook, a gardener, a business manager and five handsome kids. They do vegetables instead of drugs now, they don't eat animal products, don't waste paper, wear leather, or over-consume any of the planet's resources.''

Taking Woods on a walking tour of Gainesville, River passionately laid out what was wrong with the environment and how man could improve the planet. At one point he even reprimanded Woods for leaving half a page blank in her notebook, telling her not to waste paper. From there he went into a somewhat rambling monologue about trees being a ''diminishing resource'' and the terrible waste of paper in American offices:

''I mean, if they can make a plutonium generator that will orbit Jupiter and stay there for *forty-three years,* surely they can make a receipt that will save paper. Drives me nuts! We have amazing superpower technology that will now never be needed to be devoted to . . . to arms, and instead of putting money into building safe sewers and protecting the groundwater, they . . . they . . . can't even make a damn *birth control device* that will limit the world's population.''

Then he spoke about his failure to recognize himself in interviews which portrayed him as a "teenage messiah" who wanted to save the world. "The whole collage rings false," he concluded.

After the interview he took Woods for lunch at the Coney Island restaurant, a vegan place in the center of town that had lately become his favorite hangout and meeting place. Owner Jim Kesl, a friendly man in his early forties with long, thinning brown hair tied in a pigtail, had become friends with the actor and his family, who had started to hold their birthday and anniversary celebrations in the restaurant.

"I think River liked Coney Island because he was left alone and just treated like a normal kid," said Kesl. "He had a lot of friends but it wasn't like he was a Hollywood glamor boy and people were trying to get his autograph."

The millionaire young actor never bothered to carry money around with him and he would always be borrowing cash for cigarettes or drinks. When he was feeling generous he loved to take a group of friends to Coney Island and invite them to choose anything off the vegetarian menu, which included dishes like Curried Lentils and Rice topped with Yogurt and Raisins, BBQ Tempeh, Carrot Dog and Tofu Burger. But when the check came he would always have empty pockets and Kesl would have to bail him out.

Kesl was more than happy to oblige. The Phoenixes, after all, had put his restaurant on the Gainesville map:

"It was underground hip before River started coming in," said Kesl. "Then I started seeing the sorority girls coming in and we started getting a bit of a reputation, which helped my restaurant a lot."

Although River mostly stayed in town with Sue Solgot he found himself supporting more and more members of the ever-growing Phoenix tribe. There were now more than a dozen people sheltering on the Phoenixes' Micanopy spread, living in two travel trailers, a motor home and in the actor's vacant apartment above his recording studio. The actor's self-sufficient friends resented these hangers-on and called them "Klingons." They justified their existence by helping out as gardeners, secretaries, security and shoppers. Many believed the rich actor, who felt paternal toward them, was being exploited, and some even compared the extended Phoenix family to a "Stalinistic cult."

John Phoenix, now seeing his longtime fears for his family proved right, became so unhappy with life in Micanopy that River bought him a spread in Costa Rica. From then on his father spent nearly all his time in the village of Montezuma, a seven-hour ferry-and-bus-ride from the capital San Jose, running a bed-and-breakfast operation. From time to time River and the other children would fly out with their friends to spend time with their father.

John still tried to direct River away from show business but now had little influence with his beloved son, who was much in demand and one of the hottest young actors in films.

"The pressure was there to keep going, make more," said John Phoenix. "Iris Burton said ten years ago that young actors were like pieces of meat and River was a filet mignon. It might sound harsh but she was only telling the truth. As he got famous the scripts poured in. Everyone wanted a piece of him. He was constantly under pressure to make more films, make more money."

Heart Phoenix now divided her time between managing her children's movie careers and attending environmental workshops. She was often accompanied by John Robbins, the one-time heir to the Baskin-Robbins ice cream fortune who had given up his inheritance to devote himself to helping the environment. By now Heart was one of the nation's most vocal environmental campaigners and a leading member of the Mother's Movement—a group to help protect Mother Earth.

"River's mother does nothing but travel all over the world to all the different conferences and retreats she is invited to," said Gainesville environmentalist Holly Jensen, who has known the Phoenix family for more than twenty years. "She devotes her life to increasing earth-consciousness."

Ultimately it was River who had to earn the money to pay for everything. He cheerfully bought a house for his grandparents,

Meyer and Margaret Dunetz in West Palm Beach, helping to support them in their retirement and would always assist hard-up members of the Bottom family when they were down on their luck.

"River always felt that responsibility," said Bill Richert. "He always told me, 'I've got a lot of people to take care of so I've got to make good choices. He took it unbelievably seriously."

Increasingly, River Phoenix became a benefactor who gave but never asked for anything in return. And it was not only money that he gave. When his friend Anthony Campanaro was going through a difficult divorce and was very depressed River helped him through it.

"I was going through a lot of personal turmoil and I was very down," remembers Campanaro. "I would pass River on the street and he'd call my name—'Anthony!' And I'd turn around because I wouldn't recognize the person's voice. And it would be Riv, and he'd just pick me up right away. He made me realize what I had in this world and made me believe in myself. I'd sometimes be so down but he could always bring me out of it by saying, 'I'm always here for you.'"

River, who had grown up in such abject poverty and knew about going hungry, became the champion of the underdog. His generosity knew no limits, whether it was a bum on the streets of New York or fellow members of a Gainesville band stranded penniless on the West Coast when their van's engine blew up. But over the years many people took advantage of his good-natured generosity.

"River was built to take people at face value," said Dirk Drake. "To find out what was good about them, pull it out and expand on it. And River set himself up to be disappointed and overburdened because he was so loving and caring."

In May River flew to Seattle to prepare for his next film *Dogfight*, in which he had been cast as Eddie Birdlace, a marine who falls in love with a girl he tries to humiliate in a dogfight. The peace-loving Phoenix, who never played with a toy gun when he was growing up, insisted on spending four weeks in a simulated boot-camp on Vachon Island outside Seattle.

"If there's anything about River that he's not, it's military," said *Dogfight*'s producer Peter Newman. "I think this was a real dicey thing for River to do."

Actor Anthony Clark, who became close friends with Phoenix on the set of *Dogfight*, watched him transform himself into a violent marine during the military training exercises.

"When we first got to Seattle we were all these meek and mild actors ready to work together and give each other back rubs," said Clark. "Then they put us through marine boot camp."

The camp instructors targeted River for extra rough treatment because of his unusual name and his special vegan diet. They delighted in trying to ridicule him publicly by asking how he was "going to be able to kick ass on that kind of hippie fruitcake diet." But while he was making *Dogfight* Phoenix was anything but a peace-loving hippie.

Remembered Clark: "On the first night we're out of boot camp we went to this party and it ended up that the police were called. All of us were on stage making rude gestures, and some of the guys were projectile vomiting off the stage. River was the head of that whole thing. I hate to talk bad about him, but he had a mean streak. He wanted to get into a fight. That night he was a marine."

Phoenix was proud that he had gone through bootcamp and would later boast about it to his friends. The film's director, Nancy Savoca, said undergoing bootcamp was essential to the actor understanding the military pride of the marines, a major theme in the movie.

"They came out of there an incredible unit," she said. "I mean, it was scary, the way they bonded."

In the film River gave one of his best performances, as the young marine who falls in love with an ugly duckling, played by Lilli Taylor, the night before he ships out to Vietnam. The dog-fight is a marine ritual in which four marines bet each other to see who can find the ugliest girl and bring her to a party. Phoenix picks up Rose, a plump plain-Jane waitress, as his entry. When she discovers what is going on she confronts Birdlace, who feels guilty and ends up staying the night and falling in love with her.

"I like the character of Birdlace because he's a simpleton," River said during filming. "An average boring guy with a boring life, like so many who joined the marines. Birdlace is your average goon-squad leader. He's an easy read. He just wants to go out and have a good time. And one day his conscience catches up with him."

Phoenix seemed to feel contempt for Birdlace, who he felt was the polar opposite of himself:

"He's very naïve and probably believes in the American dream. He doesn't know that it's about to shatter with Kennedy's death, the loss of trust in authority, the deceit."

On a rare day off in the middle of filming, River invited Anthony Clark to join his mother, Heart, and a friend on a short trip to the rain forest in the northwest corner of Washington state.

Remembered Clark: "His mom's going, 'Hug a tree, Tony,' and I'm like, 'I don't feel good about hugging a tree,' but you know something? I've never seen trees like this in my life—they're thirty stories tall and they're swaying in the wind and they're making music and you hear *rrrrrr*. And all of a sudden I realized how important these issues are to his family."

*Dogfight* would be the first time that River Phoenix consciously moved outside Hollywood stereotypes in his movies, taking increasingly bigger and bolder chances to play real people, not celluloid heroes.

"The media dictates how you're supposed to look," he told writer Dan Yakir. "And if you don't, you're out. That can destroy your life, especially when you're young and impressionable. Suicide can be sparked by how someone feels about himself. But who's to say what's beautiful and what's ugly?"

After shooting the movie River found it difficult to shake off the "bitter" Birdlace character, likening it to "an emotional harness." "When I walked away I was kind of tormented," he would say.

The film's cinematographer, Bobby Bukowski, who would become one of River's most intimate friends, said the actor stayed in character long after the cameras stopped rolling.

"After *Dogfight* I remember thinking he was being a real jarhead asshole," said Bukowski. "It took a month for him to become sweet again and then the whole street-urchin character in *Idaho* stayed with him and played into the whole drug thing."

*The young River Phoenix's peaches and cream looks made him the idol of millions of young girls who wanted to be his girlfriend. (Copyright © Fran Cerce/ Retna.)*

*In* Mosquito Coast, *13-year-old River adopted Harrison Ford as his second father and learned a lot of his movie techniques from the superstar. (Copyright © Nancy Ellison/SYGMA.)*

*River Phoenix hated the city and loved the freedom of the wide open spaces. (Copyright © Lance Staedler/SYGMA.)*

*An early pin-up shot of River on the set of* Mosquito Coast. *His thoughtful, sensitive looks helped turn him into a teen idol who received thousands of fanletters every week. (Copyright © Nancy Ellison/SYGMA.)*

*River with fellow animal rights*
*activist k.d. lang at a benefit for*
*PETA in New York.*
*(Copyright © Bill Davila/Retna.)*

*A publicity shot of the gang in River's breakthrough movie* Stand By Me. *From*
*left to right: Wil Wheaten, Jerry O'Connell, Corey Feldman and River Phoenix.*
*(Copyright © Stills/Retna)*

*River Phoenix, who received an Oscar nomination for his moving performance as Danny Pope in the 1988* Running On Empty, *in a dramatic confrontation with his father, played by Judd Hirsch. (Copyright © SYGMA.)*

*River and his mother Heart share a touching moment together during the filming of* My Own Private Idaho *in 1990. (Copyright © J. Huba/SYGMA.)*

*During his meteoric career, River Phoenix's thirteen films turned him into a genuine Hollywood legend. (Copyright © Walter McBride/Retna.)*

*Millions of his fans will always remember the innocence of River Phoenix. (Copyright © John Moran/The Gainesville Sun.)*

*Nature lover River Phoenix climbing trees in one of his favorite hideaways—The Paynes Prairie State Preserve in Gainesville. (Copyright © John Moran/The Gainesville Sun.)*

*A classic shot of River Phoenix the dreamer. (Copyright © John Moran/ The Gainesville Sun.)*

*River Phoenix had a lazy eye which he had to flutter and blink to center his iris. This often gave him an extra layer of depth on camera. (Copyright © John Moran/The Gainesville Sun.)*

*River's best friend and musical collaborator Josh Greenbaum with his father Kenny, who live with the Phoenix family and are in its inner-circle. (Courtesy of John Glatt.)*

*Farmer Roy Nance outside his tiny house in Metolious, Oregon where River was born on August 23, 1970. (Copyright © The Madras Pioneer.)*

*One of the original grunge rockers—the millionaire actor often looked like a homeless person. (Copyright © Steve Eichner/Retna.)*

*Rain Phoenix rocks out with her brother River during a performance by their band* Aleka's Attic. *(Copyright © Steve Eichner/Retna.)*

*River Phoenix played his last public show in Gainesville at a rally to support Bill Clinton's presidential campaign in October 1992. Also pictured is bass player Sasa Raphael. (Copyright © John Moran/The Gainesville Sun.)*

*River Phoenix always believed that his music would catch on with the public and help change the world. He was disappointed when Island Records failed to take up their option for him to make a record. (Copyright © John Moran/The Gainesville Sun.)*

During the filming of My Own Private Idaho *it was impossible to tell the difference between River Phoenix and his street urchin character, Mike Waters. (Copyright © Henry McGee/ Retna.)*

*River Phoenix never played the Hollywood game and raised many eyebrows when he arrived at a movie premiere in a Bob Marley T-shirt. (Copyright © Steve Granitz/Retna.)*

*Dan Aykroyd (left) was a positive influence on River when they starred together in* Sneakers *in 1991. Also pictured is David Strathairn. (Copyright © SYGMA.)*

*A few seconds into this passionate love scene with actress Grace Zabriskie, River's character from* My Own Private Idaho *Mike Waters fell unconscious from a narcoleptic attack. (Copyright © SYGMA)*

*River and his co-star Keanu Reeves spent weeks carefully researching their roles as male hustlers in Gus Van Sant's,* My Own Private Idaho. *(Copyright © SYGMA)*

*River Phoenix and Mike Parker became great friends while filming* My Own Private Idaho. *(Courtesy of Mike Parker.)*

*River in deep conversation with his friend Bob Pitchlynn during a break from filming* My Own Private Idaho. *After the polaroid shot was taken River drew a beard on Pitchlynn and scrawled "Hump Night" on the photo as a joke. (Courtesy of Bob Pitchlynn.)*

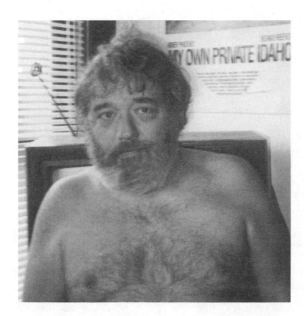

*Bob Pitchlynn was the real Falstaffian character that* My Own Private Idaho's *Bob Pigeon was drawn from. (Courtesy of John Glatt.)*

*German actor Udo Kier and Keanu Reeves share a beer during a break in* My
Own Private Idaho. *(Courtesy of Bob Pitchlynn.)*

*River's birth certificate showing his real surname of Bottom which was crossed
out when the family name was finally changed officially to Phoenix on April 2,
1979.*

*A tuxedoed River Phoenix and his girlfriend Martha Plimpton were "putting on the Ritz" for this gala event. (Copyright © Steve Granitz/Retna.)*

*River Phoenix did a photo session at the Chateau Marmont in Los Angeles where comedian John Belushi od'd on a speedball in 1982. (Copyright © Kim Kulish, Los Angeles Daily News, SYGMA.)*

*The cast of* My Own Private Idaho *partied hard during the making of the film in Portland, Ore. From left to right: River Phoenix, Keanu Reeves, Rodney Harvey, Udo Kier and Mike Parker. (Courtesy of Bob Pitchlynn.)*

*A mourning fan of River Phoenix lays a flower on the sidewalk outside the Viper Room on Sunset Boulevard the morning after the actor's tragic death. The Viper Room became a place of pilgrimage for distraught fans in the months after his death. (Copyright © Tina Gerson, Los Angeles Daily News, SYGMA.)*

*The Viper Room logo.*

*The sidewalk outside
the Viper Room where
River Phoenix died.
(Courtesy of John
Glatt.)*

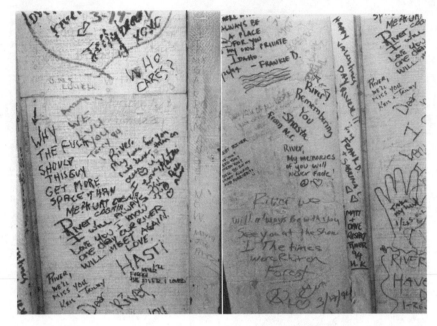

*Mourning fans scrawled their loving tributes to River Phoenix on the walls out-side the Viper Room. (Courtesy of John Glatt.)*

## Chapter Fourteen

# LIVING IN IDAHO

TWO WEEKS AFTER River Phoenix agreed to do *My Own Private Idaho* Gus Van Sant flew to Gainesville to meet his new star for the first time. The thirty-eight-year-old director instantly hit it off with Phoenix and they spent an hour talking before Van Sant asked to photograph him.

"We had been talking very intensely on the phone about *My Own Private Idaho,*" remembers the director to Mademoiselle magazine. "He was the kind of person who was very analytical and he wanted to know everything there was to know about the movie and what we were planning to do."

By the time Van Sant flew back to Portland, Phoenix, uneasily, told friends such as Dirk Drake that he thought the director had a crush on and was pursuing him. But River did like Van Sant's quiet intensity and the fact that he played guitar in a Portland rock band called Destroy All Blondes. He was also excited about doing *Idaho,* which he felt could establish him as a serious actor and finally bury the teenage heartthrob image he so detested. To help him prepare for his role, Van Sant had made videotapes of a former Portland street hustler called Mike Parker, who was the real-life model for his character Mike Waters, talking about his life and his experiences as a male prostitute.

Parker, then aged twenty-one, was originally to play the Mike Waters role in *Idaho,* and Interview magazine even ran a picture of him and Van Sant together to announce it in June, 1990. But then the success of *Drugstore Cowboy* gave Van Sant the clout to go after the two young stars he called "the best of their generation."

Gus Van Sant had been smitten with Mike Parker when he was first introduced to the cherubic-looking blue-eyed boy when he was just sixteen years old. At the time Parker had just come off the street after three years of hustling, and Van Sant was fascinated by his tales of prostitution.

"He's very voyeuristic when it comes to that kind of thing," explains Parker. "My time on the street was really a search for acceptance. My father left when I was very young and I was looking for acceptance. And I was going to get that any way that I could, even if it was a dirty old man that wanted my body. It wasn't a gay thing. It wasn't a straight thing. It was a search."

Van Sant, who came from one of Portland's most affluent and respectable families, courted Parker and adopted him as his young muse, giving him lead roles in his first award-winning short films, *My New Friend* in 1985 and *Switzerland* a year later. As their friendship grew, Parker moved into Van Sant's sprawling mansion high up on a hill in the Vista district of Portland. This way the director could observe his life closer.

"I was still streeting," explained Parker. "I wasn't a street person but I still hung out on the street. I knew what was going on. I guess Gus was attracted to that and wanted to know more."

In 1987 Van Sant produced his first full-length feature film, *Mala Noche* ('Bad Night'), about a Portland grocery clerk's infatuation with a street boy less than half his age, incorporating much of what he had learned from Parker. Made with just $20,000 from his own savings account, *Mala Noche* won the Los Angeles Film Critics prize for best Independent/Experimental film in 1987 and brought Van Sant the recognition and financing he needed to make his next film, *Drugstore Cowboy*.

In April of 1990 Parker, who had a small part in *Drugstore Cowboy*, flew to San Francisco to meet River Phoenix, who was in town to shoot some exterior scenes for *Dogfight*. By now River knew about Parker's hustling days from the heart-rending interview videos he had watched back in Gainesville with his tutor Dirk Drake. With his work on *Dogfight* almost finished, River was slowly easing out of the macho Eddie Birdlace to prepare for his most challenging role. To help him research his new role Phoenix befriended Matt Ebert, a production assistant on *Dogfight,* who had been a real-life street hustler and a former heroin addict.

"River started with heroin out of malaise," Ebert told Esquire in March of 1994. River brought Ebert with him to work as his assistant on *Private Idaho.*

"River had an involvement with a minor member of the [male] cast, so he could be ready for *Idaho,*" according to Mike Parker. "I think maybe he had feelings that way. Everybody has a level of curiosity. River struck me as real curious. Maybe not because he was gay but because he wanted to understand. I can see him doing something like that, getting into it, figuring the role out and coming to see it from every point of view. River wanted to become Mike Waters."

In June, five months before the cameras were set to roll, River flew to Portland to research the world of gay hustling. Staying with Van Sant, he began meeting some real-life characters from Portland's underground. During the summer Van Sant introduced River, Keanu Reeves and the rest of his actors to such people, not revealing that they were to form the basis for the characters in his film.

Bob Pitchlynn, known in Portland as a "sage of sorts" and a "raconteur extraordinary," was the prototype for the Falstaffian Bob Pigeon in *My Own Private Idaho.* Pitchlynn, a one-time rock 'n' roll promoter who had fallen on hard times and become a street person, now lived in an old house on Missouri Street in the midst of the Portland ghetto. His home had become a sanctuary for street kids, and Parker had once briefly lived with Pitchlynn when he was in trouble. Now in his late forties, Pitchlynn, suffering from emphysema, was being looked after by his friend Conrad "Bud" Montgomery, a street-smart man in his late twenties.

"Gus showed up one night at my house saying he had a birth-day present for me," said Pitchlynn. "He had River with him and I was mad because he had brought somebody over without asking me first. We were sitting on the porch talking for about an hour before I even realized that he was River Phoenix."

River Phoenix and Keanu Reeves became frequent visitors to Pitchlynn's, where they would play guitar and soak up the bohe-mian atmosphere. Pitchlynn and Montgomery did not realize how intently they were being observed until they attended the pre-miere of *My Own Private Idaho*.

"Gus had already talked to me about doing the movie which had something to do with me as a character," said Pitchlynn. "I just didn't realize how much so. We were tutoring River and Ke-anu and they were picking up characterizations from us. We never ever got paid for it."

On one occasion Phoenix brought Michael Balzac, better known as Flea, the bassist of the chart-topping rock band the Red Hot Chili Peppers, so he could study Bud Montgomery, who he was to play in *Idaho*.

"Flea kept coming in excitedly and saying, 'You can't believe what Bud just said,' " says Pitchlynn. "We were both pretty naive about what was going on."

Van Sant asked Mike Parker and another former friend of his, Scott Green, who was now working as his personal assistant, to guide the two young actors through Portland's hustling scene. Green, who came from a respectable family, was the model for Reeves' Scott Favor character.

Phoenix was low key at his early meetings with Parker, just get-ting to know him and making small talk about music to win his trust:

"When I interview someone I don't want to talk about them-selves," said Phoenix. "I find that doesn't give me anything. To talk about someone's 'self' makes their guard go up, so we just talked about things that we liked, that we had in common. There's no need to get right up in someone's face and say, 'What did you do on this day?' "

Mike Parker says that he never felt "interviewed" by Phoenix and found it easy to open up to him. On their first day together Parker and Phoenix sat on the grass in a public park, high on a hill with a sweeping view of the entire city.

"We talked the entire day," said Parker. "Even though he had never been in my particular situation I felt he understood me. He knew the pain. He told me about the times as a child when he'd played on street corners in Hollywood without knowing where he was going to sleep that night or where his next meal was coming from. In his own way he had also been there.

"I think River caught the drifting part of it. I felt that even though River had a deep sense of family he had no solid base or anything really to call home."

Later Phoenix would admit just how much he related to Mike Waters' search for his mother and a happy homelife after his own unsettled childhood:

"For me there's something so universal in his quest for home," said the actor. "It has the sentiment of so badly wanting that home, that Beaver Cleaver reality that so many kids don't have in this country.

"There were times, walking through suburbia, that I saw houses where I knew someone grew up, went off to college, and came back and visited their parents. That's kind of a neat idea and at times I thought that's what I wanted."

During the summer Phoenix and Reeves became frequent visitors to Portland's Old Town district and spent nights with the hustlers who cruised a strip outside the gay City Nightclub on Thirteenth and Burnside known as "Vaseline Alley," where boys as young as twelve sold their bodies to passing motorists on forty-dollar "dates."

"I took River and Keanu down to where boys prostitute themselves and we'd sit on the corner and just watch," remembers Green.

After a couple of nights Phoenix told Green that he wanted to explore further and see exactly how the "dates" were arranged.

Green said that "River didn't pull 'dates' but he did get into the johns' cars with me so he could see me make the deal. Sometimes River would even talk to them, saying what he would and what he wouldn't do. But after we agreed to the deal I'd say, 'I'm sorry. We can't do this.' And we'd jump out of the car leaving these guys wondering what the hell was going on."

Phoenix said he felt like a "guerrilla" hanging out with the hustlers, whom he befriended.

"It was very sensational for us," he told Interview magazine in November, 1991. "It was all in character. We were just hangin'. If anything, they thought this is another cat who's trying to take my spot on the street. It's a brotherhood on the street, man. You all watch for each other's backs because no one wants to see anyone get stabbed."

To enhance their research, Phoenix and Reeves studied John Rechy's 1963 novel, *City of Night,* which is about drag queens and male prostitutes, and Werner Herzog's film *Stroszek.* Keanu Reeves said all their research was done on their own time as part of their strong commitment to the film.

"It's our responsibility to go as deep as we can," said Reeves, who also wanted to be taken seriously as an actor after his teenage *Bill and Ted* "dude" roles, "and to explore all the directions that might be suggested in a script. Just so we have all our bases covered."

*My Own Private Idaho* revolves around Mike Waters' search for his mother, who had abandoned him as a child. Surviving on the streets by selling his body, Waters dreams of finding his mother and living with her in the safety of the little wooden house in Idaho where he was born. He is helped by his best friend, Scott Favor, the mayor's son, who is hustling for excitement and biding his time until he comes into an inheritance at the age of twenty-one. Favor joins Waters to travel to Idaho in search of his mother and then takes him to Rome. Although Waters' mother has disappeared, Favor falls in love with a beautiful Italian girl and returns to Portland after his father dies to become a pillar of the establishment. The film starts and finishes with Phoenix collapsing on a long straight road, which was filmed just fifteen miles from where he was born in Madras, Oregon.

Van Sant's script used Shakespeare's *Henry IV, Part One,* freely injecting Shakespearean dialogue into Favor's mouth. Van Sant also made Mike Waters a narcoleptic who often has attacks that send him in a dream-escape to the security of his earliest memories of his home and mother.

Describing *Idaho,* Phoenix said: "Shut your eyes and you're in a surrealistic state. Open them and you're in a documentary. Shut them again and you're off in dreamland."

Before production, Van Sant introduced Phoenix to his friend Jake, a narcoleptic whose condition made him fall asleep at inopportune moments.

"I spent a lot of time talking to him about why narcolepsy happens," said Phoenix, who never actually saw Jake have an attack. "I understood it completely from the medical and the scientific standpoint, though they don't know exactly what it is. He goes directly into the REM (rapid eye movement) state where your dreams are very lucid, very fast and where everything looks real. After I'd done a few of the fits, Gus said they were exactly the way Jake had them."

During the next few months Phoenix and Reeves flew in and out of Portland to research their roles. Parker patiently taught Phoenix "all the marketing tricks," showing him how to lure "dates" by adopting a look of wide-eyed innocence while giggling nervously like a little child:

"I showed River how to market himself on the street," says Parker. "You have to look real innocent and display. In my experience there are two kinds of hustlers. The ones that are rowdy and look like they haven't taken a bath in a week and the glamorous ones, who don't have a hair out of place. River took the underdog, grunge-type look, which is a definite pick-up on the street. You see a lot of guys are into that for the power thing. It's a power thing, getting somebody who's really innocent, who doesn't know and is totally naive. The customers like people who are not too smart so they can be easily talked into something.''

River spent hours questioning Parker about every part of his life so he knew the character so thoroughly he could step into it. He studied Parker's soft-spoken voice, his nervous darting eye movements and the way he would make a point by using his hands. Phoenix was extracting what he needed from Parker until he was fully transmuted into Mike Waters.

"I think he pulled out all the stops to get into his role for *Idaho,*" says Parker. "He found it so challenging that it took over his whole being. Maybe he just went a little too far."

Phoenix would later describe Mike Waters, saying: "His cut-open flesh is as close to a stone brick wall as anything. He's part of the street. He's a rat."

In his search for Mike Waters, Phoenix journeyed into his depths to confront his own troubled childhood and his still unresolved sexual identity. Using what he termed "self-brain-washing," he went farther than he had ever gone before in his dangerous quest into the dark side of himself, a journey from which he would never completely return.

"I had to block all the River input," he explained. "All the memories were owned by the character. I was a nerve-ending in service to the project."

Later in October, 1991, he compared his own instinctive acting method with the more conventional one used by Keanu Reeves:

"You can never quite explain or understand, even if someone wants to, the inside of their mind and what their secret recipe is," Phoenix told Steven Rea of the Philadelphia *Inquirer.* "But I think Keanu has more of a theater base [than I do]. I just have a more abstract place that I go to, that hasn't really been defined traditionally. . . . I think he probably uses things in his life. I don't know exactly, but I think that he has life references that he draws on, whereas that's my big no-no. I don't ever do that. I assimilate everything."

Keanu Reeves, who credits Phoenix with helping him fully understand his role in the film, said: "River's a heavy actor, man. I kind of like rode his wave sometimes. His character, Mike, is like totally estranged from everything. He's overwhelmed. He knows how to hustle, though. Mike is a strong hustler."

Bobby Bukowski saw many similarities between Phoenix and Waters, who was "kind of isolated, a nerd, a misfit."

The more deeply Phoenix got involved in *Idaho,* the more he wanted input into every aspect of production from the script to the soundtrack. At one point he decided his old friend William Richert, who had written and directed *A Night in the Life of Jimmy Reardon,* was perfect for the role of Bob Pigeon, the obese, middle-aged Falstaff character based on Bob Pitchlynn, and embarked on a no-holds-barred campaign to get him the role.

"River's the one who cast me in that movie," says Richert. "Hell, I didn't want to do it at first."

At that time Richert, who was in his mid-forties, was dating a beautiful twenty-two-year-old woman and thought playing a "fat, ugly and gross fifty-five-year-old pederast" would turn her off.

"One day River called and asked if he could come over to my place in Venice and show me the new *Idaho* script," says Richert. "I looked at the script and there is the same description of the part: 'On comes fat, gross Bob Pigeon.' I said, 'River, I'm not going to do this. It's not going to be a wildly successful picture anyway because a lot of people aren't going to understand it.' "

Phoenix then announced that Van Sant was on his way over to talk about the role, placing Richert in an embarrassing position since he had never even met the director. When Van Sant arrived Phoenix explained Richert didn't want the part but then asked if they could read the script outside on the terrace.

"River put a gun to my head," said Richert. "There was no way out and I was mad at River for tricking me. So I went outside and read Bob Pigeon for the first time. But even then I decided not to do it."

Another actor was then cast in the Pigeon role by Van Sant, but River Phoenix and Keanu Reeves persuaded Van Sant to fire him, saying he didn't have the right energy necessary for the part. They then waited until the day after Richert got married before begging him to take the role, saying the whole project would fall apart if he didn't. This time he agreed.

In September of 1990 River Phoenix briefly surfaced from being Mike Waters to accept the Humanitarian Awards from PETA for his fund-raising. He traveled to Washington, D.C. to collect the award and then played at the Bayou Club in Georgetown with Aleka's Attic as part of a fund-raiser for Save the Forests. It was the first time Josh Greenbaum had seen Phoenix since he had been to Portland and he was stunned by the change in his friend:

"River got progressively deeper and deeper into his characters," said Greenbaum. "He looked into people and he saw their pain. He thought this was an important story to show the general public that there are teenage guys selling their asses on the street for money or drugs. It was also one of his most challenging roles and completely different from anything he had personally experienced."

Conrad "Bud" Montgomery, who would be portrayed by Flea in the film, developed a close and lasting friendship with Phoenix, which gave him special insight into the actor:

"I was on the streets for five years, living under a bridge before Bob took me in and gave me a place to stay," Montgomery, whose song "Getting Into the Outside" is featured on the film's soundtrack, told the author. "You have to live by your wits or else you don't survive. There are a lot of kids out there who run away and drop out of school and just don't have their heads about them.

"I think River related to not having a really anchored home. A real stable home life. River didn't have those family values drilled into him when he was younger and therefore he didn't have that anchor for him to say, 'I can grab onto that and weather this.' If you don't have that anchor there's nothing you can tie down to and say, Okay, this is who I am. And if you don't have that mooring, that safety zone, you're lost."

## Chapter Fifteen

# THE LOST BOYS

IN NOVEMBER OF 1990 River Phoenix joined the rest of the cast and crew in Portland to begin work on *My Own Private Idaho*. He had been using Gus Van Sant's Vista home as his base for the previous two months as he metamorphosed into Mike Waters. Fresh-faced River Phoenix had all but disappeared and now in his place was a pasty, sad-eyed pimply lad dressed in thrift-store clothes and in need of a wash. It was impossible to know where River Phoenix ended and Mike Waters began.

"He seemed to be changing into this character," said Gus Van Sant. "He sort of assumes the character."

The actor was also subtly changing the Mike Waters character that Van Sant had written, making him his own creation.

"River made the character gay," said Van Sant. "The character wasn't really gay in the first place. Because [he was a hustler] he didn't really have a sexual identity."

When Van Sant sent the actor to hang out at the City Nightclub, where the young street hustlers relaxed after work, owner Lannie Swerdlow threw him out, not believing he was River Phoenix. "He looked like a bum off Old Town," said Swerdlow. "He was ragged and he looked horrible. He said, 'I'm River Phoenix.' I asked to see his I.D. He didn't have any so I said, 'Well, if you're River Phoenix you can certainly afford to pay the six-dollar cover charge.'

"He said he didn't have any money so I told him to stop putting me on and had the bouncers escort him out of the club."

It was only after someone working on the film, who happened to be at the club, recognized Phoenix and asked Swerdlow why he had thrown him out that the actor was allowed back in. Later, Phoenix filmed a scene at the City, where he has a narcoleptic attack on the dance floor; it was not included in the final cut.

Eric Alan Edwards, *Idaho*'s director of photography, says Phoenix wore his role "in a very raw way."

"He looked like a street kid. I've never seen anybody so intent on living his role."

But even though Phoenix outwardly seemed to feel comfortable in the Portland gay scene he was still very nervous about actually having to play homosexual nude scenes in front of the cameras:

"They were still very leery of what they had to do," said Wade Evans. Evans was an old friend of Van Sant who played a john that River picks up in the film. "They knew it was a career boost for both of them but I think they felt uncomfortable about getting naked and appearing in some of those nude scenes. I often told them, 'Christ, you guys are actors getting paid for this. Act!' "

A year later River would play down his nude scenes with Reeves and German actor Udo Kier: "Hey, it was just this mass of flesh. And Keanu and I have known each other for a long time."

On the first day of shooting River had to do a scene in which he gets into Evans' car for a "date."

"That was the first time I had met River," said Evans. "During one of our many takes, when we're driving around the block, River asked me, 'So how many guys do you pick up?' He just figured I was one of those guys. I said, 'No, I'm not. I'm helplessly heterosexual.' "

Bob Pitchlynn was surprised to walk into his front room and find River and Keanu debating whether Van Sant was bisexual or gay.

"They wanted to know if Gus had a girlfriend and whether he was staying with her," said Pitchlynn, who had a cameo role as a john at the beginning of the movie. "River says, 'No, I don't think he likes girls.' Then they asked me if Gus was gay and I sort of begged off and said, 'I don't think Gus is particularly sexual one way or the other.' I thought that was pretty naive for how worldly they were supposed to be."

As River got to know Van Sant better he started quizzing him about his sex life. Van Sant remembers River asking personal questions about his gay relationships: " 'What exactly do you do in bed? Which side do you sleep on? Do you ever tell him to shut up? If you're angry at him do you still buy him an expensive birthday present?'

"River dropped clues about his sexuality but I never really followed them up," said Van Sant.

But the director apparently suspected that River and the other actors had secret liaisons and questioned Bob Pitchlynn about it:

"Gus asked me if I had been in the sack with anybody or whatever," said Pitchlynn. "One night he was jokingly asking me about it, saying, 'Come on, come on. I know.' I said, 'I don't know who told you that, Gus, but it's not true.' "

During the filming River constantly looked to Van Sant for approval:

"River was always doing things like saying, 'I just love you,' and lunging to hug me,' " said Van Sant. "I'd freeze, maybe because my father used to grab my knee in a certain way. River didn't like that, so he'd hug me again, and I'd freeze again, and he'd yell at me."

During the making of *Idaho* River became taken with the difference between love and sex, which he felt was the dominant theme of the film. With this in mind he actually wrote the film's pivotal scene, in which Mike Waters declares his love for Scott Favor and kisses him, saying he can make love to a man without being paid for it.

"River wrote that entire scene after a conversation with me about being able to love people, maybe even a man, without getting money for it," says Mike Parker. "It was intense. River incorporated what he felt inside for real with what I felt and it just all came out in that kiss with Keanu to make one of the most brilliant scenes in the movie."

River said the campfire scene was totally scripted down to the last stutter and cough:

"I wrote them all," he told the Advocate. "In society there's this confusion between love and sex. People think they want love and that they'll get it through sex. Very rarely do the two merge cohesively. Mike [Waters] is very clear on the difference between love and sex because he has sex for a living. That's why his line was so important: 'I love you, and you don't have to pay me.' I'm so glad I wrote that line."

Van Sant said he gave Phoenix a free hand in writing the scene. "He didn't discuss it," says the director. "He added all that stuff where he was in love with Keanu. River transformed that scene into what it is. The way it was originally written, it was pretty much innocuous: Mike makes a pass at Scott very routinely because he's bored, he's in the desert . . . he wrote all that stuff. He created that scene."

River was so nervous when they shot the scene on a closed set that he almost ruined it by trying to break the ice and telling Reeves, "Just think, Keanu. Five hundred million of your fans will be watching this one day."

Reeves became embarrassed and self-conscious but managed to pull himself together to finish the kissing scene, to the horror of Van Sant, who thought his key scene had been jeopardized by River's outburst.

"He scolded the shit out of me," said River. "I almost cried."


Away from the set the cast and crew had split into different social groups. Phoenix was the enthusiastic ringleader for the inner circle that liked partying and playing music. The group included Reeves, Flea, Mike Parker, Scott Green, Rodney Harvey and another actor called Shaun Jordan. They were all living at Van Sant's ten-room Tudor-style house on a hill overlooking Portland.

"The atmosphere was totally medieval," remembers William Richert, who stayed in town. "Half the people were staying with Gus and sleeping on the floor because there was no furniture."

Nights they would often get drunk and stoned in the garage and jam late into the night next to Van Sant's collection of BMWs before falling asleep on the futons scattered throughout the house.

"River would just start playing these tribal rhythms on guitar and he'd go into a trance," says Parker, who joined in on a drum machine. "We'd play these amazing jams that would last for three hours without stopping. River loved it. He would just shut his eyes and just go on for hours like nothing else around him mattered at all."

Even after everyone else had put down their instruments to go to sleep, River would carry on alone, playing in his favorite alcove until his fingertips bled.

"It was great therapy," said Phoenix. "We had lots of fun in Portland when we were filming *Idaho*. After a day's work, to be able to jam and fall asleep playing your instrument is the best! Both Keanu and Flea brought their basses. I brought a beautiful hand-made guitar from northern Ireland called a Lowden at a great music store in Portland called Artichoke Music."

River's ad-hoc garage band consisted of Van Sant and Green on guitar, Flea and Reeves on bass and Parker on percussion. Wade Evans later replaced Flea when he flew back to Los Angeles early after wrapping up his part.

"It really clicked," said Evans, who is Van Sant's film editor and later worked on his videos for Flea's band, the Red Hot Chili Peppers. "Gus's garage, where we'd play, had such great sound quality. I set up the amps and we'd play for hours and hours. Any excuse to play and we'd jump on it."

The jams, which River described as "a sort of fusion-funk Latin-jazz thing," led to an on-going musical collaboration between the actor and Flea after the movie, and they became good friends. At one point during the filming Rain and Leaf Phoenix flew down to stay and joined in the jams. While in Portland, Rain began a relationship with Scott Green, which lasted for nearly a year.

"Rain's a real down-to-earth person," said Green. "She and River were so close."

Scott Green and Mike Parker, who had once had to survive on the streets of Portland's Old Town, showed Phoenix the squalor and decay in the tough, rundown area of homeless people and runaways. Spending so much time filming there, River was genuinely moved by the plight of the hungry down-and-outs hanging around the Burnside Bridge and did his best to help them.

"Once we were going to this health-food store to get the makings for a feast River was cooking," remembers Mike Parker. "He bought a hundred dollars extra worth of food and we took it to Old Town, where he passed it out to all the homeless people he could see. That's the way he was."

Scott Green said Phoenix was always very generous to the Portland street kids:

"I saw him give money to people a lot," remembers Green. "He wouldn't hand it out like some big roller, but on a few different occasions I saw him give twenty-dollar bills to kids on the corner."

"Maybe River thought drugs were part of the street mentality and that's how his character Mike Waters escaped his problems and helped him in his search for his mother, his home and his identity," says Mike Parker.

Matt Ebert, who was looking after River and Reeves on the set of *Idaho* and played a cameo role as one of the gay coverboys, says that heroin made River withdrawn and introspective:

"Heroin makes you reflective, you look inside—and then you face the consequences of looking into the chasm," he said.

A few weeks before going to Portland to start work on *Idaho*, Reeves told Denis Cooper of Interview magazine that he wanted to try hard drugs.

"I want to be on speed," he said. "I've never been on speed. I want to be a speed freak for a while."

William Richert says that although he never saw any hard drugs during the filming it would not surprise him if Phoenix and the other actors used them as an essential part of their characterizations:

"They'd been going down and hanging out with real addicts," said Richert. "Staying on the streets. Holding stuff. Looking at it. They may have sniffed it. You've got nineteen-year-old kids trying to play drug addicts in a contemporary, deeply involved and committed artistic feature, teetering on the edge of reality. John Doe and Mrs. Doe might find that a dangerous and iffy situation. Whereas to someone who's trying to do a work of art it's *de rigeur*. It's absolutely necessary."

Scott Green, who played a street kid in *Idaho* and a gay coverboy, says Phoenix had already tried the drug:

"River had tried heroin a couple of times out of curiosity," says Green. "He didn't inject it with a needle but he smoked it once during the film—he didn't get it from me. I don't think he liked it very much."

Pitchlynn says he couldn't handle Phoenix when he was on drugs:

"We grew apart because of the drugs. It got to the point where they'd just call at midnight or two in the morning and I'd just say, 'I'm in bed.' I didn't want to deal with it. They just wanted to party."

During the filming Sue Solgot flew out to Portland to visit River and he made everyone promise not to tell her he'd been taking drugs.

"River asked me not to tell his girlfriend what he was doing with drugs," remembers Pitchlynn. "I don't like that sort of situation. He had asked me to collect her from town but told me not to say anything."

Nick Richert, who had come to see his father, also spent some time on the set with Phoenix and saw a change in his old friend.

"*Private Idaho* was a turning point for River," said Nick. "I have to put some of the pieces together because he was very secretive. He was well aware of the rumors that started but he never talked about it. There's a good chance he would have taken [heroin] to get into character."

Although Phoenix was on drugs when he was in front of the cameras for many of his scenes in *My Own Private Idaho,* he was always in control and his work never suffered. At this time he was still able to juggle drug-taking with maintaining his professional approach to acting. As an intrinsic part of his acting method, Phoenix wrote piles of notes on what he called "parallel scenes for his characters."

"It's my own stream of consciousness," he would say.

Mike Parker watched Phoenix's work in front of the cameras and was amazed by his thoroughness:

"I'd never seen anybody who was so meticulous and clear-headed about their work," said Parker. "He would make these footnotes in a script so if he'd walk in a doorway in a certain way he'd write it down so he could go back to that scene a week later and be able to come in the same way again. River was very analytical. He was just very intense about his work."

Phoenix was also extremely generous to the other actors, especially Mike Parker and Scott Green, who had been given secondary roles in *Idaho* although they had little acting experience.

"I remember one time I had to deliver a line during a Shakespearean scene," said Parker, who played the part of a street kid called Digger. "And as soon as it was over River came over to me and told me he thought the imaging was really good. He's a great actor and I took it as being very real when he took the time to come over and tell me I did a great job. I mean, it was the first real acting role I had ever done."

Toward the end of filming in Portland, Phoenix, totally burned out and exhausted, would come around to Bob Pitchlynn's house late at night to get away from everyone and be alone with his guitar.

"River would just sit in the living room playing guitar by him-self," said Pitchlynn. "It's not the classic idea of the lonely rich boy but obviously he was a human being too. He was just as lonely and as confused and worn out as everybody else. He seemed very tired. Nobody can stay up, no matter what drugs they are taking, and not pay for it one way or another. It goes up, it comes down. Believe me, that's a cliche, but it's true."


In December Gus Van Sant led his cast and crew north to Seattle for two weeks' filming. After nearly three months in Portland, River Phoenix had become a wreck. When journalist Dario Scardapane visited the *Idaho* set on a cold wet afternoon on assign-ment for US magazine he saw the toll that the film had taken on Phoenix.

"Quite honestly, he looks like crap," Scardapane wrote in his feature called "The Lost Boys." "His hair's a mess, stubble flecks his face, his grungy pants don't fit, and more than anything else, he appears in dire need of a good night's rest, which the actor seems intent on getting, promptly collapsing on a bench in the ferry's cabin."

The actors were shooting a scene aboard a ferryboat, which never made it into the movie. Scardapane writes: "Today's shoot, which takes place on the ferry's foredeck, showcases one of River's ill-timed naps, and the actor is definitely getting in the mood for slipping into another coma. As the cameras roll, Keanu and Rod-ney are seen taking a break from the harsh rigors of cruising for cash on the street.

"Getting a little R&R, they proceed to pass a pot-pipe back and forth and simply admire the view spread out before them. Almost unnoticed, River lies immobile in a puddle near his co-stars' feet, a position he'll keep for most of the day. Frankly, there's not much difference in his performance when the camera is rolling and when it's not."

On the last day of shooting in Seattle, Scardapane joined Phoenix, Reeves and Van Sant for a morning cappuccino at their new local haunt, the Virginia Inn.

"River enters, eyes half-open, looking as if he has slept in his red, high-water pants," says Scardapane. "Slowly he makes his way to Van Sant's booth and immediately gets horizontal. While River dozes off, Keanu is outside just burning with energy, prepping for his hustler mode."

After the day's filming the production wrapped up in Seattle and Van Sant took his "lost boys" to Rome for the final week's shooting before Phoenix returned to Florida to try to resume his life.

## Chapter Sixteen

# FLOWING DOWN

As RIVER PHOENIX came out of *My Own Private Idaho* it became painfully obvious to his friends that something had gone wrong with the gifted actor. After living and breathing his Mike Waters character for six months, it had, it seemed, become a monkey on his back that he couldn't shake off.

He did spend Christmas with his family before flying off to New York to celebrate the new year with friends, but temperamental and moody, he was veering out of control, fueled by the combination of cocaine and alcohol.

On January 2 he walked into the Limelight club after a night's partying. Still dressed in his *Idaho* street-kid clothes, he sat by himself in a deserted corner of the converted church club resting his head in his hands. After a few drinks he suddenly came to life and started talking about how he was still doing "research" for his part as a male hustler. Then without warning he ripped off his shirt, wrapped it around his head and ran onto the dance floor barechested and started dancing. When the club's paparazzi followed him onto the dance floor and started taking photographs he shouted at them to leave him alone.

"Is River Phoenix bidding to take over from Sean Penn as showbiz bad boy?" asked Star magazine, adding that the actor was seen "partying up a storm" and "hurling a flood of abuse" at photographers.

Celebrity photographer James Edstrom told the tabloid, "He started changing his clothes in the middle of the room. He was screaming for me to get out."

A few weeks later at another New York club, Danceteria, River had to be restrained after a fan tried to take his photograph. He grabbed the fan's camera and threw it to the ground and then, according to the Globe, started kicking him before two bouncers intervened and made him pay for the damage.

Nick Richert says Phoenix's drinking and drug use intensified after *Idaho*, beginning a pattern in which he would go on binges and then give it all up. Excessive by nature, Phoenix did everything in his life with a kind of fearless passion that literally knew no bounds.

"River was a regular partier," said Richert. "That was his life. He would never want to go to sleep, ever. He would just have too much going on in his head. He was always running, doing things."

But even when he stayed up for days, driving his body to the limit, Phoenix still maintained his strict vegan regimen.

"River was always the health guy. Pure," says Josh Greenbaum. "He was always the one eating a sprout-and-cucumber sandwich when I was eating greasy tofu. He was a carrot juice nut. River was always going for the cleaner and healthier choices."

Asked about the paradox of Phoenix taking drugs and drinking while advocating clean-living vegetarianism, Greenbaum replies, "It's irony at its best. River would still accomplish his goal whether he decided to be Mr. Health USA or smoke cigarettes and get drunk."

Sky Sworski says Phoenix's veganism had nothing to do with his health: "It was about not killing," said Sworski. "That's a real important point."

After he returned to Gainesville, Phoenix reunited with Aleka's Attic to prepare for a ten-week tour up and down the East Coast to coincide with the release of the PETA compilation album *Tame*

*Yourself.* The band's contribution, "Across the Way," was now getting play on college radio stations, spurring Phoenix to take Aleka's Attic out on tour with another Gainesville band, Ndolphin.

Since Phoenix had left Gainesville to do *Idaho* six months earlier, Aleka's Attic had been put on hold. Josh Greenbaum and Josh McKay, who had uprooted their lives to move to Gainesville to play in the band, were starting to get restless, finding it difficult having their lives dictated by River's movie schedule. Each time Phoenix took off on a movie project the two-year Island development deal would be frozen, leaving the band members waiting in limbo for his return.

"Having a movie star as the front man for a band is a double-edged sword," Josh Greenbaum would say. "That was one of the main problems for the band for a long time. There was constant change and adjustment of lives. We'd just be building some momentum, we'd be together for four or five months, and then River would leave for six months to make a movie. Those breaks definitely affected the flow."

Phoenix kicked off the tour by performing at a Vets for Peace rally in Gainesville at the university bandshell, opening for the sixties band, Country Joe and the Fish. Still sporting his scruffy *Private Idaho* haircut and sideburns, River was cheered by the audience as he walked up to the podium to give a speech before Aleka's Attic played.

"He was ranting and raving," said Bill DeYoung of the Gainesville *Sun.* "He made no sense at all and I don't think he was on drugs or intoxicated."

To everybody's astonishment, Phoenix began telling Gainesville's war veterans how he was never going to go across the world and fight, spending ten minutes carrying on about peace and love.

"I remember watching him and thinking that he just didn't have a clue what he was talking about," said DeYoung. "By the time he finally finished everyone in the audience was asking each other why he even bothered to do it.''


Chaperoned by Kenny Greenbaum and Sky Sworski, Phoenix and his band proceeded to New York for the first of three benefit gigs at the environmentally correct New York club, Wetlands, to raise money for rainforest campaigns in New Guinea, Ecuador and the Solomon Islands. As the opening act for the New York band the Spin Doctors, Aleka's Attic had improved almost beyond recognition from their first tour.

River's agent Iris Burton was not at all happy that her most valuable client was playing for a rock 'n' roll band with no new movie projects in sight. When the media called for details of his new career she refused to be connected with it: ''We don't know anything about it because he's handling bookings himself.''

Once in New York, Phoenix seemed unusually relaxed to the point of joking with a New York *Post* reporter who asked him how he felt about groupies:

''Yeah, the girls expect you to cater to that weird celebrity phenomenon, but I just negate that by being who I am—in a gorgeous kind of hunk, dude way.''

Josh Greenbaum said River Phoenix's fame drew huge crowds to shows: ''We get a lot of fans coming to our shows who just want to see River,'' he said. ''But that's cool because a lot of them end up really getting into our music.''

The high point of Phoenix's stay was the launch party for the *Tame Yourself* album at New York's Hard Rock Cafe, where he was photographed with country singer and fellow animal activist k. d. lang.

''We're second-to-last on the album,'' Phoenix boasted at the launch. ''That's a great place to be.''

While in New York to promote the album and play more gigs at Wetlands, where Aleka's Attic was headlining for the first time,

Phoenix uncharacteristically granted an interview to Sassy magazine writer Christina, with unfortunate results.

"I'd been trying to get an interview with the elusive River Phoenix for years," Christina told her readers in her story, "I Saw River
Phoenix Brush His Teeth." "Recently the publicist for *Tame Yourself,* an album to benefit People for the Ethical Treatment of Animals, was able to make my dreams become a reality. Which is how
I came to be sitting with the cute little thing in his hotel room. Of
course his whole band was there too, so we didn't have much
privacy."

In fact, when Christina arrived for the interview Phoenix was
anything but cute, having just gotten out of bed and looking the
worse for wear. Doing his best to kill the myth of being a nice
cuddly heartthrob, he was uncooperative, leaving Christina to
speculate about the change in him:

"I was stunned at how different River's once-shiny, silky blond
hair looked," she wrote. "It was short, a dirty color and kind of
brittle. I don't know if the Riv was trying to dread or what, now
that he has left his teenage years behind him."

Christina, however, took it in stride when Phoenix, hardly ac-
knowledging her presence, called for his toothbrush and proceeded to brush in front of her. The actor, wearing a blue Aleka's
Attic T-shirt, heavy black shoes and the olive green combat jacket
he had worn in *Dogfight,* which now sported an anti-fur badge,
appeared more than "a little hostile." He only seemed to cheer
up after room service bought him a bottle of Moet & Chandon,
which he proceeded to drink by himself.

"I am whatever I am doing at the time," said Phoenix mysteriously when asked about his next movie projects. "I put everything
into it. And so . . . we can be a million different people in a
single day if we try hard enough and if we run around enough. As
far as priority, what I feel is priority—with anyone, your feelings
fluctuate, like the tides."

Christina found Rain Phoenix, now eighteen, much friendlier
when Rain walked into the room during the uncomfortable inter-

view wearing jeans and a multicolored midriff top that showed off her "very flat stomach."

"Rain was very serene and quiet," wrote Christina. "She is short with dark skin and hair. She seemed like a nice person."

Rain told Sassy readers that when she wasn't singing and playing tambourine with Aleka's Attic she was studying opera and voice at the University of Gainesville.

"It's totally different from singing rock," she said. "It's a heavier, amplified sound. I really enjoy it."

Checking out the rest of the band, Christina found Josh Greenbaum "not particularly cute" and Josh McKay only "marginally attractive." But she declared Tim Hankins as the "real visual treat" of the band with "lovely skin, red lips and shiny hair."

When she asked the band how they felt about being known as "River Phoenix's band," Greenbaum's response was, "It sucks."

By this time Phoenix was well into the bottle of champagne and had become much friendlier to Christina. Making an effort to explain his lyrics, he said, "As a piece of music, "Across the Way" is probably the most extreme we will ever get in its regalness and its orchestration," which prompted Christina to note: "As a writer, I understood River's reluctance to analyze his art; however, as a reporter I was annoyed."

At the end of the interview Phoenix was given the news that Sassy had just voted him as one of the "20 Men You Can't Beat with a Stick."

"Oh, really," he said. "Is Tom Cruise in there?"

When the Sassy article, with the front-page teaser headline RIVER PHOENIX AND HIS LITTLE HIPPIE BAND, came out Phoenix was not happy and said why.

"I *will* say that I really feel sorry for all the true hippies that had to deal with me in the press as their poster child," he told US magazine. "I'm certainly not a good example of what the pure American hippie is. I find it quite hilarious every time that I see something as lame as Sassy's article about 'River Phoenix and His Little Hippie Band.' All that sort of stuff to me is like, please, don't insult the hippie families of America by using us as their poster children. It's just ridiculous. It underrates true hippies. It's a way of life, not an appearance."

Throughout the tour, which included appearances in Miami, where they opened for Sonic Youth, Chicago's Cubby Bear Lounge, and Boston's Rathskeller, Hankins and McKay were fighting with Phoenix, whose behavior was becoming increasingly erratic.

"I used to hear a lot of stories about River being drunk and obnoxious in the clubs where they played," said Bill DeYoung of the Gainesville *Sun.* "Tim had a lot of personal problems with River. He told me that River was a serious drinker and also referred to him as a junkie. Tim's a few years younger than the other guys and he just couldn't take it. He told me he was shocked and just couldn't get along with River anymore."

After the tour Phoenix went into the studio with Aleka's Attic to record what they called the "Here's Where We're At" demos as part of their Island deal.

"But as soon as we finished it, River went off to do the press stuff for three months," said Josh Greenbaum. "And so Island was sitting there with the demos. That was the really big period of change."

Hankins was the first to leave the band in late spring, saying they were working toward something "that never came to fruition. River always took this posture of trying to dissolve this myth that had been created," said Hankins. "If you saw the way he dressed . . . if you didn't know him you'd think he was a homeless person."

For the next four months Phoenix mainly stayed on the West Coast, alternating between Los Angeles and Portland and leaving Sue Solgot behind in their Gainesville apartment. The couple were now more often apart than together and left many of their friends wondering.

"I found their relationship a little confusing because of some of the stories I'd hear about him," said Jim Kesl, who regularly entertained the couple at his Coney Island restaurant. "I used to wonder how much she knew about his other life. There was a private part of his life I didn't know much about."

Their landlady, Melanie Barr, says Phoenix wasn't in town enough for them to have a "normal boyfriend-girlfriend relationship. They were separated a lot. It seemed to me that they hardly saw each other."

But Solgot claimed that being apart was actually good for their relationship. "It sucks and it doesn't suck," said Solgot. "Because it gives us space."

After finishing *My Own Private Idaho* Phoenix had become a hero and icon for the gay movement, leaving much speculation about his true sexual orientation. He seemed to add fuel to the rumors when he started hanging out in gay bars on Hollywood's Santa Monica Boulevard, where he took Nick Richert and Suzy Q Solgot when she visited.

"I would go to gay bars with River and Suzanne," said Richert. "River was extremely tolerant and open to gay people. He was certainly heterosexual but I thought he might do anything. I would hang out in the Hollywood scene with him and meet his friends in the bars."

Phoenix always hated labeling people straight or gay and gave cryptic answers when asked about himself, always leaving the answer in doubt:

"I have a real problem with separation," he told US magazine. "I don't see things as this person is this or that person is that. People just aren't at ease with their sexuality."

Solgot, who was supported by Phoenix as she trained to be a masseuse, said he didn't differentiate between men and women when it came to affections. "If he loved somebody, male or female, he felt he should check it out," she told Esquire.

Scott Green says Phoenix loved Solgot and, as far as he knew, was always faithful to her when he was in Portland making *Idaho*: "I think River was very curious about men and I don't think it had anything to do with *Idaho,"* said Green. "It was his own personal feelings."

That summer Heart Phoenix and River visited Heart's old friend from the Children of God, Bithia Sherman, and her son Jonathan at their Simi Valley home. Bithia Sherman had renewed her friendship with the Phoenixes after leaving the cult a few years earlier and they now regularly corresponded with each other. It was the first time Jonathan had seen River Phoenix since they were children.

"River had a lot of pain inside," Jonathan Sherman told the author. "There was a lot of stuff that he hadn't dealt with from when he was a kid and I think it was surfacing."

Phoenix talked about his career and about how he wanted to devote more time to music, but Sherman apparently sensed an underlying sadness in his old friend:

"He seemed distant. He seemed very unhappy. I know from my own experience how hard it was to cope with your sexuality after what we went through in the Children of God. I was very promiscuous for a time in my high school and even in junior high. I actually declared a second virginity and I've been celibate for two years now. I don't want to have sex until I find the right person. It was hard coming back. I think a lot of that stuff from the Children of God still affected him but he kept it to himself."


In June Phoenix visited Portland to see Gus Van Sant and hang out playing music with Wade Evans, Scott Green and Mike Parker. He then joined Suzanne Solgot to fly to Los Angeles and meet up with Flea and the rest of the Red Hot Chili Peppers, who had just finished recording their album *Blood Sugar Sex Magik* and were on the verge of hitting the big time. Phoenix's friendship with the band deepened as they played music together and talked and the actor invited them all to Costa Rica to stay with his father.

John Phoenix was now living full-time on the Costa Rica estate his son had brought him. He had become less reclusive than he had been in Florida, often venturing out to his favorite bar in Monzezuma, where the local people affectionately called him Don Juan. While they were in Costa Rica Phoenix got to know the other members of the Red Hot Chili Peppers—John Frusciante, Anthony Kiedis and Chad Smith. The band had been wracked by drug problems since it started in 1983. The original guitarist Hillel Slovak died in June, 1988, prompting Flea and Kiedis to focus on their rock 'n' roll careers. John Frusciante, who replaced Slovak in the group, was originally a Chili Peppers fan who taught himself guitar and so impressed Flea that he arranged for Frusciante to audition for the band after Slovak's death. Phoenix and Frusciante became close and were near-inseparable when the actor was in Los Angeles.

While in Costa Rica Phoenix and the Chili Peppers played music and explored the island together, taking in the breathtakingly beautiful full eclipse of the sun. During his visit Phoenix talked into the night with his father about the nature of their addictions.

"By now River was an alcoholic," said Scott Green to the author, and "used to talk about his father and the genetics of addiction. During one of our conversations he said he thought he might have inherited his dependence from his father but he didn't think it was in any way his father's fault."

On the flight back to Los Angeles the on-board movie was *Awakenings,* the film starring Robin Williams as the doctor who wakes up his patient, played by Robert De Niro, from many years in a deep coma using the drug L-dopa. De Niro has to come to terms with the modern world but once he does the drug begins to lose its effect and he slowly recedes back into a coma. Phoenix identified so closely with the story that he cried all the way through.


Back in Los Angeles and sporting bleached-blond hair as part of an attempt to play Andy Warhol in a projected Gus Van Sant film,

Phoenix started publicity for *Dogfight* and *My Own Private Idaho,* which were coming out in September and October respectively.

In an interview by Joe Dolce of Details, Phoenix was relaxed and in good humor after a night hanging out at Flea's Los Angeles home. He had been interviewed by Dolce a few years earlier and remembered the journalist, greeting him with a hug.

Describing himself as "sort of an Arnold Schwarzenegger with a Nigel Tufnel twist," Phoenix answered a string of lighthearted questions. During the interview Dolce asked him if there was anything he had done at an early age that he had wished he had waited to do. Suddenly Phoenix became deadly serious as he revealed he had lost his virginity at four to other Children of God kids.

"I was completely celibate from ten to fourteen," he told Dolce, adding that he was scared that his early experience could make him "perverse when I'm older."

"I haven't really fucked a lot of different people, five or six. I feel like I should get around more, but I just fell into relationships that were fulfilling and easily monogamous. It's how it is . . . monogamy is monogamy until you screw someone else. And who's to say when you will screw someone else?" Phoenix responded to the question of whether he ever felt sexy: "Only when I have a vagina in my mouth and I'm listening to the biorhythms of my girlfriend's belly."

His fear and anxiety about handling his growing fame was obvious when Dolce asked what he thought of when he heard the word *heartthrob:*

"I think of a heart with clogged arteries," he snapped. "It's manufactured and I have nothing to do with it. I don't believe in that image. It's abused. It's media projection and it makes me want to eat cheeseburgers.

"Fame is what gets people to go watch your film. I'm glad to be in a film that I believe in and if it takes fame, then it's my job. But let's put it this way: I'd rather be a ghostwriter than have my name down. Credit doesn't matter to me. I hate being reminded of it. I want to be innocent of it. I don't want to be ruined by it.''

Asked if he ever fantasized about death, River thought for a moment and then said that he wanted his death to be full of drama.

''I don't want to die in a car accident,'' he told Dolce. ''When I die it'll be a glorious day. It'll probably be a waterfall.''

## Chapter Seventeen

# TRICK HORSE TREAT

IN AUGUST 1991 RIVER Phoenix flew back to Gainesville to celebrate his twenty-first birthday. He seemed to have everything going for him. He was rich and successful and was considered perhaps the most promising actor of his generation. He was also in turmoil. After a month in the Los Angeles twilight zone he was glad to come home to the womblike security of his family.

Speaking to Spin magazine about his on-going fascination with L.A., Phoenix said: "It's really designed, I think, to strip you and blend out. It's like feeling like the invisible man. You just stand there, and you start disintegrating, and you can't see yourself, and you feel like you're being absorbed into this big blob of glitter."

A few weeks earlier he had told the four remaining members of Aleka's Attic to prepare to go back into the studios to lay down tracks for the long-awaited Island album. They were in for a shock when their leader came back and bought a new Volvo to celebrate his signing a million-dollar deal to star in the big-budget movie *Sneakers* with Robert Redford and Dan Aykroyd. He explained to his disappointed colleagues that the Aleka's Attic recording session would have to be put on the back burner for the time being.

"We started talking about going to L.A.," says Josh McKay. "And instead of making the record the band would practice when he wasn't doing the film. I sort of crumbled under that concept."

McKay's confidence in River could not have been helped by his

188

telling the *Hollywood Reporter* that his music was little more than a "fun adventure."

"It's not to be taken all that seriously," said Phoenix. "It's a fun adventure . . . . If it turns out there's nothing to offer [in my music] I'm not going to do it."

Bill DeYoung says that Phoenix now started to pull away from Aleka's Attic and gravitate toward Hollywood, leaving his fellow band members to question his commitment.

"They started to wonder why they were here and what they were doing," says DeYoung.

Disillusioned with Phoenix, McKay then left Aleka's Attic and formed a band with Tim Hankins called Emperor Moth.

On August 23, River turned twenty-one and celebrated in the Market Street Pub with his close circle of friends:

"I remember the day before he turned twenty-one, River came into the bar and I had to card him," remembers Pub manager Steven Ward. "I said, 'Sorry, man, you're doing fine sitting down there but if you come up to the bar I'm taking the fine.' I'm not going to be able to tell the cop, 'Hey, look, it's River Phoenix!'

"So the next day he came in and proudly showed me his I.D., saying, 'I'm twenty-one. Card me.' I bought him a round of Guinness to celebrate."

Phoenix considered his twenty-first birthday an important milestone in his life:

"Turning twenty-one was the first time I felt my age," he told the Boston *Herald*. "It was a nice age to arrive at. I felt synchronized and deserving of the two-one blast-off title."

A couple of weeks later Phoenix provided a more politically correct version of the event for the media.

"I went into a bar, showed the guy my I.D. and said I wanted an herb tea," he told Kenneth Chanko of the New York *Daily News*. "I celebrated with a chamomile."

Phoenix's act was so convincing that People magazine featured him prominently as a clean-living member of "Hollywood's New Squares."

After his return from Hollywood many people noticed Phoenix's attitude to Gainesville had changed. He boasted to Rolling Stone magazine: "I'm kinda like Gainesville's godfather or dogfather, I should say—it's a backwards town."

In a Rolling Stone photo spread with his sister Rain, Phoenix was pictured at the family's Micanopy ranch applying "their casual approach to formal wear" in a $3,000 green silk velvet suit by Italian designer Gianni Versace with a Calvin Klein black cotton T-shirt.

Reporter Lisa Bernhard wrote a tongue-in-cheek account of Phoenix's day-to-day life, wryly observing that the town's most famous resident "shuffles through the streets of Gainesville like the town hound."

"Nobody stares or seems to care that this is one of the actors who is restructuring Hollywood's caste system," wrote Bernhard. "They just turn their heads and smile, as if to say 'Nice doggie.' "

When Bernhard asked about his image as a hip young environmentalist, Phoenix seemed to take offense: "I don't care if people want to call you little goody-goody nature boy. They can shove it up their ass. The world's falling in on them and they're just going to be blind ducklings."

Bill DeYoung said Phoenix's comments to Rolling Stone did not go unnoticed and created bad feeling:

"I think everybody was irritated because he sounded so arrogant," remembers DeYoung. "I mean, River had a real arrogant side—the dogfather of Gainesville!"

In Gainesville, River led a protected life, with Sky Sworski acting as his personal assistant and watchdog to screen out unwanted media attention and protect his privacy. Interview requests were carefully vetted by his mother Heart and even when journalists were allowed to meet Phoenix in Gainesville precautions were taken so that the interview could be cut short if the writer was later deemed to be a "jerk," according to Michael Angeli in Movieline.

Phoenix's life in Gainesville now consisted of getting up at lunchtime, playing music with his friends, followed by late night bar crawls through his favorite haunts like the Market Street Pub, Club Demolition, the Hardback and the newly opened alternative music club, the Covered Dish.

Steven Ward of the Market Street Pub said Phoenix began drinking more heavily after he was twenty-one:

"When he was younger he knew not to push it," says Ward. "He'd come in and he'd have two twenty-ounce pints of Guinness. That's a hefty sum for a young lad. He started to drink much more as he got older and he would also come in later and later."

Usually Phoenix liked to stop in with Josh Greenbaum at the Market Street Pub at around one A.M. to listen to jazz and meet up with his musician friends after their gigs.

"River was always pumped up and running around," said Ward. "He'd be jumping around with his friends, saying, 'Hey. Let's go and do this.' He liked to drink here and then go to the Hardback to catch bands because it was really dark there and he could hide in the back. You could tell that he was too wide awake at one o'clock in the morning for it to be a natural high," said Ward.

Ward suspected that Phoenix was smoking the strong locally grown sensemillia and probably taking ephedrine, an over-the-counter stimulant popular with Gainesville students for all-night study sessions. By now there were strong rumors about River using drugs that were flying around town and making the actor extremely sensitive:

"I've copped some weird earplay about me and acid," he told Michael Angeli in Movieline in September of 1991. "I just thought it was a joke—I thought they weren't being serious. I thought it was this reverse psychology thing to get information out of some-one—'I heard you took acid.' I would just laugh. It would frighten the hell out of me to be a creature walking around in the nineties taking acid."

In September Phoenix flew to New York to attend the premiere of *Dogfight* escorted by Martha Plimpton instead of Suzanne Solgot, who had stayed behind in Gainesville, according to the New York *Post.* Solgot was very concerned about Phoenix's drug use and had been trying to get him to straighten up. But when she would point out the conflict between his healthy public persona and his drinking and drugging, Phoenix would lose his temper. He thought he was invincible and often referred to his body as a horse. But, as Esquire reported, in his more lucid moments he would ask Solgot: "What would those twelve-year-old girls with a picture of me above their beds think if they knew?"

Suzanne Solgot says that Los Angeles was the source of Phoenix's real drug problems, befriended as he was by some drug-pushers and hangers-on who plied him with their wares so they could be near him.

Said Solgot: "I think after a while being in L.A. and being vulnerable and confused, he would be tempted [by drugs] and say, 'Why not?' And there was this side of him that was stubborn and [thought] whatever he did he would be okay."

Solgot saw Phoenix change dramatically during their relationship:

"When we first met he seemed really sweet and gentle. There was a lot of pressure on him. His childhood had been so different from other people's that he had to catch up. He was always very responsible and serious as a child and then when he got older he started having more fun, partying more. It's really complex, but he became more hassled, more worldly."

Dirk Drake, who was now more of a friend and advisor to River than a tutor, saw first-hand the problems Solgot had with his behavior: "Suzy Q worked really hard early on in their relationship and intervened in her own ways," said Drake.

Phoenix, who often intervened to help his acting friends with their drug problems, appreciated Solgot's patient understanding: "She's really stuck with me and helped me grow," he told *Today* in October, 1991.

Ironically, just as he was at long last making the successful transition from teen star to mature actor, he found himself falling apart. It was as if street urchin Mike Waters were standing in the spotlight, stoned and unable to cope with the public attention and acclaim. River might have had the delicate skills of a magician in front of the camera, but he was like an immature child when it came to fulfilling the other side of his movie responsibilities.

At the Toronto Film Festival he was visibly nervous before he was due to face the world's press with his co-star and friend Flea.

"What should we do?" Phoenix asked Gus Van Sant, who would soon regret his hasty answer of "Whatever you want."

Walking to the stage in dark glasses, Phoenix seemed frozen like a deer in a car's headlights as the press conference began. His most complete sentence to the assembled reporters and photographers was: "Any comments I would have are built into the work," which he said so quietly it was almost inaudible.

Movie publicist Liza Herz said no one could understand Phoenix's speech: "He was incoherent," Hertz later told People magazine. "He looked unwashed. I thought immediately, He's really coked out."

The next day Phoenix was more articulate when he was interviewed by *Women's Wear Daily* and asked how he felt about *Idaho* being categorized as a gay film.

"I guess gays need a film 'cause they're a minority, because they need something like this as a social motivator," he said. "But the movie could just as easily be called an environmental film because of all the beautiful nature scenes of places that won't be around in the future."

Asked about his long-term plans, Phoenix gave the eerie answer: "If I'm living, I hope it's something I don't know anything about now."

At the New York Festival River Phoenix, Keanu Reeves and the rest of the cast of *My Own Private Idaho* were on stage at Lincoln Center taking questions from the audience after the film's premiere. None of the cast looked sober, giving the impression they would prefer to be back at the cast party at the China Club than having to discuss the film. At one point, Newsweek would report, Keanu Reeves leaned back in his chair, loudly clearing his throat and spitting on the stage."

In October River Phoenix was voted Best Actor for his role as Mike Waters at the Venice Film Festival, leading to speculation that he might receive a second Academy Award nomination.

"Venice is the most progressive festival," said Phoenix. "I don't want any more awards. Anything else would be a token."

*My Own Private Idaho* was released nationally on October 18, 1992, and River Phoenix was singled out for special praise by the critics. His performance was called "riveting" by the Philadelphia *Inquirer,* and Film Comment critic Donald Lyons said Phoenix was exploring deeper the acting territory that had first been opened up by James Dean nearly forty years earlier:

"It's not that he dares to play a hustler—lots of actors would be up for such a stretch," wrote Lyons. "But that he drives so deep into, specifically, Mike . . .

"If James Dean did anything really new in *East of Eden,* he used a looseness in limb, a fidgety floppiness, to signal sensitivity. Sliding on to various horizontals, balling himself into armadillo crouches, shivering hunched on street corners, Phoenix takes Dean's arithmetic into a dimension of calculus."

Phoenix, who had never fully grasped calculus, prompting his tutor Dirk Drake to dub him "our lad of perpetual distraction," was delighted with the review, which gave him an artistic last laugh.

"I like the idea of taking someone's good arithmetic and turning it into calculus," he told Steven Rea of the Philadelphia *Inquirer* while sitting in his hotel room, plucking Captain Beefheart blues riffs on his Yamaha guitar. "I like that idea but I've never seen one of James Dean's movies . . . if anything, Brad Pitt looks just like the guy.

"I should see *East of Eden.* I should see some of his films. I should. But in a way I don't want to spoil it, you know? I don't want to put too much information into my head. I like the idea that the only Brando film I've seen is *Streetcar Named Desire* . . . . One day I'll see some of these films but I have to do a few more movies before I start getting involved in past things, because it probably can influence you quite heavily."

Phoenix also revealed that his lack of movie knowledge extended to new films too: "I just don't want to get jaded with the industry," he told Rea. "I want to keep it more of a personal experience. I don't know how healthy it is to have too much information."

In Los Angeles, Mike Parker and River Phoenix took rooms at the Chateau Marmont, where John Belushi had died of a drug overdose a decade earlier, to do a string of publicity interviews for *Idaho*. Parker remembers having to wake Phoenix up one morning after he had overslept and thrown his tight interview schedule into disarray.

"River walked into the room, set up for the television interview with lights and everything, after just waking up," said Parker. "His hair was all matted and he looked a mess. The interviewer said, 'Oh, how are you today, Mr. Phoenix?' To which River replies, 'Not too bad except for the crotch rot.' He then started scratching himself. He had the whole TV crew laughing."


In Hollywood Phoenix's star was rising and he could now command $3 million a movie. He was offered the pick of the big-budget blockbusters, including a co-starring role with Sharon Stone in *Sliver*.

"I get offered a lot of stuff," said Phoenix. "And sure, you pause when they say on the phone, 'You won't do this for two, well, how about three?' But after the movie comes out I think, 'Man, I'm glad I didn't do that.' It's just not worth it. It's all in the script and whether I believe in it."

One script Phoenix loved was the aptly named *A River Runs Through It* based on the autobiography of Norman MacLean. The project was being directed by Robert Redford and Phoenix eagerly auditioned for the part of the young fly-fisherman growing up in beautiful Montana at the turn of the century.

"It's a great script," said Phoenix. "Just the best script that I've read that's come out of Hollywood in a long time. I auditioned—me and about a thousand other guys. It was a nice audition and I hadn't auditioned in a while. I thought I'd be nervous."

Phoenix had a long talk with Redford about the role and was stimulated by the veteran actor's passionate enthusiasm for his project.

"I believe so strongly in it that I want the best guy for it," River said. "If I get it, great. If I don't, I wasn't right for it."

Eventually Brad Pitt got the part but Phoenix would soon meet up with Robert Redford in the big-budget movie *Sneakers*, which he took mainly to please his agent Iris Burton, who, understandably, was still trying to persuade him to play the Hollywood game, where leading men can command $7 million dollars or more.


In late October, 1991 Phoenix moved to Los Angeles to start preparing for *Sneakers* and braced himself for life in the fast lane. During his five-month stay in Hollywood he wanted to go into the studio and complete the demo tracks for Island, so he brought along Josh Greenbaum and his sister Rain.

Flea, who was out of town, said they could all stay in his Malibu house, but when they arrived they found two of the rock star's friends, a part-time actor called Dickie Rude and his English girlfriend Abby Gorton, were already living there. They had nowhere to go so Phoenix good-naturedly suggested they all live together.

"We became really good friends," said Abby Gorton, a soft-spoken former model from Gloucester, England. "I'm the kind of person who likes to make everybody comfortable so I'd take care of him and do his laundry and everything."

Rude and Gorton not being vegetarians, Phoenix had to come to terms with living with meat eaters for the first time in his life.

"We used to torture him with meat," said Gorton, who was eventually converted to vegetarianism in Costa Rica by Phoenix. "We'd cook meat and drive him crazy.

Most days Phoenix, Greenbaum and Rain would rehearse in the house, and in November, billed as Tyrannosaurus, they made their West Coast debut at Hollywood's Gaslight. Throughout the set, Phoenix insisted on hiding himself under a stocking mask, and the audience, which included Keanu Reeves, were less than enthusiastic and booed him off stage.

Living in Flea's house gave Phoenix easy access to drugs and he soon found himself being surrounded by the hard-core Generation X Hollywood drug crowd.

"Los Angeles is a bad influence on anyone," says Josh Greenbaum. "It was on me. It sucks. There's a lot of phony people and a lot of bullshit all the way around. I think people in L.A. are very on edge. Very paranoid. You can't trust anyone."

Abby Gorton says that Phoenix took drugs to get away from the crushing pressures of his soaring movie career.

"He just wanted to relax," she said. "He would sometimes go to extremes to escape from all that pressure."

Phoenix would at times open up to the attractive English girl, telling her how hard it was to live up to his family and the world's expectations of him.

"River's had pressure all his life," said Gorton. "He's been supporting his family since a very young age. He wanted to give everybody their dream. He bought his grandparents a beautiful house in Florida and he bought the land that his father had always dreamed about in the middle of nowhere in the jungle. River wanted to make everyone's dream come true. He could do that, but the pressure was always on him to work and to make the money to keep the dream going.

"There was also always the pressure on him to be this pure-living vegan who could be everyone's role model. It was hard for him. It was unrealistic to expect someone to live up to that. He definitely felt that pressure."

To escape, Phoenix started withdrawing into heroin—and the further he went the more obvious it became that he was in danger of becoming hooked.

"You'd have to be really dumb or naive not to know he was high when he was," says Bobby Bukowski, who spent a lot of time with Phoenix in Los Angeles. "He was clearly so high he was like an alien."

Abby Gorton said Phoenix had a childlike curiosity about drugs: "River had that side of him where he'd like to defy things just to be a kid," said Gorton. "It was against the law and it was naughty but he was going to do it anyway.

"River was a kid in many ways because he'd never had a childhood. He'd lost a lot of his childhood because he was working and had to be this professional adult actor. He had all these responsibilities at a very young age. All these people telling him how he should be."

And Phoenix developed a strong bond with Gorton, who never censured him and instead encouraged him.

"He felt he could be himself with me," said Abby. "And I wouldn't put restrictions on him like his girlfriend or his family. I didn't expect him to be anything."

When *Jimmy Reardon* publicist Jim Dobson saw Phoenix on the set of *Sneakers* for the first time in five years he could not believe it was the same person.

"He was one hundred percent different," said Dobson. "He'd gone from a cute well-groomed kid to someone who wouldn't bathe, and his face was very gray. We all assumed he was on drugs."

Phoenix was also starting to get a drug reputation inside Hollywood.

"You started to hear in the media, 'Well, he was experimenting with drugs,' " said Peter Weir, who directed Phoenix in *The Mosquito Coast*. "Then I began to think that maybe River so carefully identified with his parts that he'd thrown himself into that [for *My Own Private Idaho*]."

In December Dirk Drake arrived to visit his former pupil soon after one of Phoenix's drug friends, wielding a butcher's knife, had chased the actor through the house in a rage after a disagreement about drugs.

"I told him I was furious about the glamor those friends attached to skag," said Drake. Phoenix's reply of "Don't worry, I have the fear of God," prompted an angry Drake to tell him to become a Baptist preacher. Phoenix told Drake that he had misunderstood and that he wanted to live "to see what the Higher Power's purpose is for me."

Drake says that Phoenix's erratic behavior was really starting to scare his friends: "He was taking life with so much passion it was frightening. There were interventions with people for his drug abuse, his alcohol. A lot of people were candid and as forward as they could be about their concerns for him. River had a strong passion and love of sensation whether it was watching a full moon or tossing some pints."

Josh Greenbaum says he also tried to warn Phoenix about drugs, with little effect: "He didn't like it," says Greenbaum. "He made that pretty clear to me. He just wanted to be able to do his own thing. Of course, as a friend I always told him how I felt about what was going on, regardless."

The one person Phoenix would listen to was comedian Dan Aykroyd, who realized the young actor had a problem and took him in hand. After seeing his partner John Belushi overdose on a lethal speedball combination of heroin and cocaine, Aykroyd warned Phoenix about the dangers and Phoenix agreed to lay off heroin.

"I think Dan Aykroyd was a very good influence on his life at that point," said Dobson. "They were good pals during the filming so I think having Dan with him helped him for a short time."

Phoenix found an instant rapport with Aykroyd and they kept the rest of the cast entertained with their antics.

"We called each other Mr. Woach and Mrs. Woach," remembers Aykroyd. "The catering truck we used to call the Roach Coach. And that somehow evolved into the Woach."

One of Phoenix's favorite tricks was to creep up behind

Aykroyd and blow on his bald spot or playfully pinch his "love handles" around his waist.

"Just complete, absolute, total irreverence," said Aykroyd. "And he could get away with it."

In *Sneakers* Phoenix played a nineteen-year-old computer nerd who joins Robert Redford's crack team of computer hackers who are recruited by a secret government agency to steal a "black box" that can be used to access any government system. The plot twists and winds through a maze of doublecrosses so that in the end the "sneakers" have no idea whom they are working for.

"I play this cyberpunk nerd," said Phoenix, who disliked the movie and told his friends not to see it. "I trashed myself in this. I will never appear in a teen magazine again. I've really degraded myself. He's very hyper, always twitching, the kind of guy you avoid playing if you want to walk with grace and dignity at the premiere."

Directed by Phil Alden Robinson, who was coming off the hit movie *Field of Dreams,* the film also reunited Phoenix with his former father-figure Sidney Poitier. Phoenix was key to the project, Universal Studios feeling they needed a bankable young star to attract young movie fans.

Josh Greenbaum spent many hours on the *Sneakers* set with Phoenix, jamming with him during the interminable downtime between scenes. Many of Phoenix's scenes had to be reshot because the director could not get the right takes, since the actor had difficulty concentrating.

"It doesn't feel like a movie for some reason," said Phoenix to Premiere magazine. "The work we do is very technical, and you have to keep the concentration for three, four months. After [*My Own Private Idaho*] I just did not feel like barreling through someone's psychosis, you know? I needed to do something that didn't involve so much guts."

Having his friends with him on set made *Sneakers* easier for Phoenix and tended to loosen him up. One day he almost got arrested for throwing a Frisbee with some friends outside the stage at Universal by studio security men who did not recognize him.

"The Universal police came over and told him to stop," said director Robinson. "And he said, 'I flipped them off.' Somebody had to talk to the cops and say, 'Please don't arrest him. He's in our movie.'"

Although Phoenix was heavily involved in drugs during much of the making of *Sneakers,* it never affected his work, and Robinson was delighted with his performance.

"He was in the scenes on the first day we shot, and I thought it was okay," said the director. "But once I saw him on film in the dailies, he was wonderful. He makes very quirky choices that really come alive on film."

After a vegetarian Thanksgiving spent at a fund-raising party for PETA hosted by the camp TV celebrity Elvira, Phoenix finally went into the recording studios with Josh Greenbaum, Flea and his sister Rain to lay down two tracks to complete the Island deal.

"It was overdue," said Josh Greenbaum. "This was it. Those were pretty much the crux of the deal. We had already gone over the two-year thing and we had got to the point where we had to make a decision."

Island's Kim Buie arranged for record producer T-Bone Burnette to produce the sessions and he soon became a surrogate musical father to Phoenix.

"I can say that he is without doubt my favorite person in the entire world," said Phoenix. "T-Bone Burnette is a confidant, a brother-in-arms. He has a lot of the same convictions and artistic commitments as me."

One of the songs they recorded was an ode of sorts to heroin called "Trick Horse Treat," which had been written by Phoenix and Flea on the set of *My Own Private Idaho.* Soon afterward, in a blow to Phoenix and Josh Greenbaum, Chris Blackwell heard the completed Aleka's Attic demos and decided not to pursue the option.

"It turned out that my voice wasn't star-quality," explained

Phoenix somewhat sarcastically. "I'm so glad that it didn't happen because I don't want to make music for the masses. I just want to make it for my friends and the people I play with."

When MTV asked River Phoenix for an interview for the 1991 MTV video awards he refused to have anything to do with the highly influential TV station.

"Fuck those awards!" he said to Paper magazine. "It's not that I don't like MTV, there's just nothing else. MTV is fine. I just don't want to be their poster child. I've done that in the past and I've never liked seeing myself spliced up, used and cut. If Aleka's Attic makes a video I'll direct and shoot it myself, and it wouldn't be a fake live performance or mouthing the words."

At Christmas the production of *Sneakers* closed down for two weeks so that Robert Redford could go on his annual skiing vacation. After pressure from Dirk Drake and Bobby Bukowski, River Phoenix moved out of Flea's house and stayed with his old friend Bill Richert high up in the mountains outside Los Angeles.

Now between film projects, Richert had developed a healthy alternative to coffee made from soya beans, and had opened a shop in Venice Beach on Main Street. Phoenix loved the idea and offered to put up $50,000 to become an investor in Richert's Incognito Coffee Company. When Richert ran out of money and was late with the rent on the store he asked the actor for some money to bail out the company.

"River came over to my house with the second check for twenty-five thousand dollars," said Richert. "He was hanging out, talking and playing me his songs and we were just having a good time. But after he left I couldn't find the check.

"I was embarrassed. I've lost a lot of checks in my time and now I'd gone and lost River's."

Eventually Richert decided that Phoenix must have changed his mind and taken the check home with him.

Richert remembered: "I called him up and left a message on

his machine: 'River, it's not polite to play with twenty-five-grand checks with businesses.' A little while later he called back and said, 'Oh, I'm sorry, I put the check in the freezer.' I said, 'Why did you put the check in the freezer?' River said, 'Well, when people give you money, Bill, you have to pay attention to it.' River was giving me lessons all the time."

When Incognito Coffee suddenly took off and Richert began distributing to the main health-food chains on the West Coast, River Phoenix started advising his old friend, who was getting out of his depth.

"My business sense was askew," says Richert. "I'm paying for my overhead out of my writing fees and it was a forty-thousand-dollar cash outlay one month. River kept telling me to get rid of the store and fire some of the employees. He'd tell me, 'It's your business and I'm an investor, but if I were you I'd hire someone to run the place and get back into movies.' "

Phoenix had now decided to put his words into action and use his money to buy rain forests and ensure their survival. In early 1992 he bought eight hundred acres of forest near his father on the border between Costa Rica and Panama and planned to buy a lot more.

"I have my reasons why I want to be filthy rich," said Phoenix. "It's so I can buy the last first growth and turn it into a permanent national park."

Abby Gorton said Phoenix was passionately committed to stopping the destruction of the rain forests years before other stars like Sting and Peter Gabriel adopted it as a cause. "He wanted to buy up all the rain forests that are being destroyed and stop the destruction," said Gorton. "River had this amazing plan to sell off the rain forests he'd bought in ten-acre lots as gifts. The lots could never be sold or built on and all you could do was hand them down to your children and say, 'Here's a piece of rain forest, please look after it because you're saving the world.' He planned to start a charity and use the money generated from selling the lots to save more and more rain forests. That was River's way of saving the world."

Bill Richert saw Phoenix as a Robin Hood figure who took money from the rich movie companies and gave it to the poor.

"And he didn't even have to steal," says Richert.

After *Sneakers,* Phoenix decided to get more involved in the business side of making movies so he could be "filthy rich" and finance a string of private projects including building a school in his father's village of Montezuma in Costa Rica.

He told a friend: "I want to make a million on my next picture, two million on the one after that and three million on the one after that."

But however much money he might be making, he never let it come between him and his friends. He was still as considerate and thoughtful as ever, and on Valentine's Day, 1992, he telephoned Conrad "Bud" Montgomery in Portland from the set of *Sneakers* to wish him a happy thirtieth birthday.

"We were surprised and flattered that he remembered," said Bob Pitchlynn. "It showed that he cared about us. We never heard from Keanu after *My Own Private Idaho* but River would come into town and we'd have dinner together with Gus every once in a while."

That phone call would be the last time that Pitchlynn and Montgomery would ever speak to River Phoenix.

## Chapter Eighteen

# SILENT TONGUE

AFTER FINISHING *SNEAKERS* in March River Phoenix plunged into his next film, *Silent Tongue.* Although rumors of Phoenix's drug problem were about in Hollywood, his star was on the rise and agent Iris Burton was still receiving tempting project offers from some of the town's top producers and directors.

For *Silent Tongue,* Phoenix would be in the acting company of such as Alan Bates and Richard Harris. The film's writer and director was Sam Shepard, a Pulitzer Prize-winner who enjoyed a reputation as one of America's great playwrights. But when Phoenix arrived on the set near Roswell, New Mexico, all he knew about Shepard was that he was married to film star Jessica Lange. It was left to his young co-star Dermot Mulroney to take him in hand and prepare him for working with Shepard.

"He was undereducated and overintelligent," said Mulroney, who became firm friends with Phoenix on the set of *Silent Tongue.* "I had to explain to him what a Pulitzer Prize was and what Sam won it for and why: 'Here's another play, River, I know you're not going to read the whole play, but please read these three pages before you have to jump up and do something else.' "

Phoenix was very excited to be working with actors of the caliber of Harris and Bates, and although his role required him to be on the set for only three weeks he insisted on staying for the whole seven-week shoot.

"It was his first experience working with theater people and he was excited about it," said producer Carolyn Pfeiffer, who hired a vegetarian caterer to cook special meals for Phoenix while he was on the set.

In the film, a western with mystical overtones, Phoenix plays Talbot Roe, a grief-stricken young man who guards the corpse of his half-breed wife Awbonnie, played by Sheila Tousey, in a burial tree after she dies in childbirth. Veering toward insanity, Roe refuses to bury her and is suicidal, at one point taking a shotgun barrel to his head. Talbot's father, Prescott Roe, played by Richard Harris, had originally traded Awbonnie for horses from Eamon MacCree, played by Alan Bates, who runs the Kickapoo Indian Medicine Show. To try to save his son, Prescott now decides to buy MacCree's second daughter, Velada, to take her sister's place and restore Talbot to sanity. Throughout the film Awbonnie's tortured ghost materializes from her body, demanding that Talbot free her to enter the spirit world by burning her body. In rehearsals, Shepard actually tied Phoenix and Tousey together with twine to reinforce the spiritual bond he wanted the actors to feel with each other.

River Phoenix was so convincing in his portrayal of madness, his wild eyes twitching and his hair looking as if volts of electricity had been passed through it, that director Shepard could not always tell whether he was acting or not.

Mulroney said: "Sam would always have that crooked smile, watching, trying to figure out how much of this was River preparing to play an uncultured mad dog and how much of it was really River. Sam was, in my opinion, completely and utterly perplexed by River. He was truly taken with him but couldn't figure him out."

On the set many wondered if Phoenix was stoned during the filming. One critic later remarked that the actor looked as if he was "zoned out on drugs."

During filming Phoenix soon gravitated toward the craggy-faced Irish actor Richard Harris, who had had his own problems with the bottle. Following the now established pattern for all his movies, Phoenix chose Harris as his paternal influence.

"He looked upon me as a kind of a father-figure," said Harris to Premiere magazine. "He'd knock at my door and ask if he could come in and sleep . . . . He'd sleep on the couch. I could hear him rehearsing his lines—at four in the morning. I said, 'Fuckin' go to sleep.' He'd be in the bathroom, taking a crap, doing his lines."

Each morning Phoenix insisted on personally driving Harris to the set, and once there he went out of his way to look after him.

"He bonded very, very strongly with Richard Harris," said Pfeiffer. "He always wanted to make sure that Richard was fine, that Richard wasn't lonely. He was like a mother hen, River."

Phoenix also became very close to Alan Bates and his family. After Bates' son Tristan died of a rare allergic condition in 1990 followed by the death of his wife Victoria two years later, River spent hours on the phone with his surviving son Benedick, comforting him. He also took care of him when he visited the *Silent Tongue* set to see his father.

"I think River was like my late son," Bates told Premiere magazine. "He was years ahead of his time, actually. He was ahead of his age. I think people like that are very vulnerable to . . . well, to other people. They are prey for the not-so-good."

Although he had third-star billing, Phoenix always acted humbly, going out of his way to help everyone on the set, no matter how low down the totem pole they were.

Carolyn Pfeiffer remembered: "We didn't have enough trailers to give to everyone, so we gave them to the first four above-the-line people. When River started working with Sheila [Tousey], he realized that she was in a honey wagon and he was in a trailer, and she not only had long makeup hours but a lot of preparation doing vocal exercises.

"So he came up to me and said, 'I'd like to give Sheila my trailer and I'll go into the honey wagon.' I'd never had an actor say, 'May I give up my comfortable space for a smaller one because one of my fellow performers needs it more than I do?' "

After finishing *Silent Tongue*, Phoenix flew to San Francisco to attend a surprise party for girlfriend Suzanne Solgot, who was visiting friends in Berkeley. As a joke he put a large paper bag over his head and arrived at the party with Bill and Nick Richert, who introduced him as their "mystery friend."

"Everybody was asking him questions and trying to guess who he was," said Nick. Finally after three and a half hours and long after the other party guests had given up trying to unmask him, Phoenix dramatically pulled the bag off to reveal himself to a burst of applause.

Phoenix's practical jokes were never spiteful or hurtful but they often confused his friends, who never knew whether or not he was telling the truth: "River," said Nick Richert, "would just bullshit and say anything and you'd believe it. He was a mind-fucker. I always had to try to stay aloof from him because I didn't want to get drawn in and seem gullible."

Growing up in a vacuum, Phoenix had not picked up humor naturally and consequently, however much he tried, his jokes were always slightly off the mark.

Gus Van Sant said: "He told me that he didn't have a sense of humor until he was nine and that he never really got its logic, the surprise of the unexpected. You know: An elephant and a hippo go into a bar, something is introduced, punch line. And he'd be like, 'Yeah, so what happened then?' "

Phoenix and his brother Leaf loved to entertain friends with their imitations of the cartoon characters Scooby Doo and Shaggy.

"River was one of the funniest people that I ever met," says Josh Greenbaum. "He would make up his own characters and come up with these original funny imitations. He wasn't like a Rich Little, he was wilder, like a Bobcat Goldthwait or George Carlin. He loved getting attention and making people laugh."

*   *   *

By the summer of 1992 Phoenix's relationship with Solgot had deteriorated further as his escalating drug use came between them.

"He didn't want me nagging him," explained Solgot. "Pointing out the contradictions between his public stands and what he was doing to his body."

Solgot says he would lie about his drug-taking when concerned friends would challenge him on it, telling them it was just "stupid rumors" being spread around by "those assholes."

"He fooled a lot of people and he fooled himself," said Solgot. "He was a great actor."

Through the last year of their relationship Solgot constantly tried to get Phoenix to clean up and get his life together but he was in denial, refusing to admit he had a problem. He alternated between going on drink-and-drug binges and could then be clean for days before falling off the wagon again. In the middle of the night, when he felt lonely and depressed, Phoenix would often call Martha Plimpton in New York to pour his heart out.

"He'd often be high when he called," remembered Plimpton in Esquire in March, 1994. "And I'd listen for twenty minutes to his jumbled, made-up words, his own logic, and not know what he was talking about. His language had become at times totally incoherent. He'd say, 'You're just not listening carefully enough.' "

Although he was now battling alcoholism and cocaine addiction, Phoenix was always there with help and support for others when *they* were having substance problems. Once, after hearing that a young actor friend of his had held up production of his new movie for three days after his arm abscessed from too much heroin, Phoenix staged an intervention. And when Phoenix started regularly calling Bob Timmins, a drug counselor, it was never to ask for help for himself.

"He called me twice in the last couple of years to ask me to intervene with friends," said Timmins. "And he made it passionately clear that he was committed with his time and money to making sure these people didn't die. In one case he drove [a famous rock star] to a clinic in Arizona.''

With no solid projects on the horizon, Phoenix spent most of the summer on the West Coast weighing movie offers. British director John Boorman, who had been impressed with Phoenix in *My Own Private Idaho,* approached him about starring in a film called *Safe Passage.* Phoenix and Boorman became friends, and the young actor took him to meet Bill Richert several times in an attempt to get his old friend involved in the project.

Phoenix was also interested in an approach by German director Volker Schlondorff, who made *The Tin Drum* in 1979. Schlondorff wanted Phoenix to star as the tortured young French poet Arthur Rimbaud in an adaptation of Henry Miller's *Time of the Assassins.* As soon as Phoenix started reading Miller's book he was stunned, as the book about the tragic nineteenth-century artist could easily have been his own life story.

"That book was River,'' said his friend Nick Richert. "He totally related to it and became obsessed. Who can know what effect it had on him?''

From then on Phoenix would carry the book around with him, often reading key parts he had marked to his friends. Seeing himself as an artist, River was captivated by the 1946 book about Rimbaud, who saw the civilized world as a jungle and did "not know how to protect himself in it.'' Like Rimbaud, River Phoenix felt like one of "the free spirits, who are the tormented ones— born out of time and out of rhythm.''

Born on October 20, 1854, Rimbaud was himself a child prodigy, who lived his life determined to experience everything. "He drives himself inhumanely. The goal is always beyond,'' wrote Henry Miller. Like Phoenix, more than a century later, Rimbaud wanted to "see all, feel all, exhaust everything, explore everything, say everything.''

In his description of the true artist, Miller talked directly to River Phoenix when he wrote: "They live like scarecrows, amidst the abundant riches of our cultural world."

For the first time Phoenix could artistically justify his preoccupation with the dark side with these words: "The road to heaven leads through hell, does it not? To earn salvation one has to become inoculated with sin. One has to savor them all, the capital as well as the trivial sins. One has to earn death with all one's appetites, refuse no poison, reject no experience however degrading or sordid."

Dirk Drake, with whom Phoenix would discuss Rimbaud, said: "Rimbaud is a unique parallel to River. It was real dark, real sad and real interesting."

Rimbaud burned himself out when he was just nineteen after three searing years when he "exhausted whole cycles of art." He then became a recluse wandering around Europe and was unable to create any new art before his death in 1881. After reading and rereading *Time of the Assassins,* River Phoenix launched into hyperdrive with his music as if sensing *he* did not have much time left.

"One of the things in the book that I think River recognized was how some poets and artists live with so much energy that they die at an early age," says Nick Richert. "It was as if they had just so much to say and that once they had spent it, they died."

Phoenix identified with Miller's description of Rimbaud being one of the "great spirits of the modern age" who were all "annihilated by Jovian bolts." With his drug-taking he was like "an inventor who, having discovered electricity, knew nothing about insulation. They were attuned to a new power which was breaking through, but their experiments led to disaster."

Chapter Nineteen

# THE THING CALLED LOVE

WHEN RIVER PHOENIX arrived on set to start work on his new movie, *The Thing Called Love*, it was the beginning of the end. The effects of his drug use were now unmistakable. His once rosy cheeks had a chalky pallor and his dirty brown hair fell limply over his eyes, which seemed permanently weighed down with black bags.

Phoenix—who was being paid $1.5 million for the film—brought a chilling new intensity to his role of up-and-coming country singer James Wright. For the first time heavy drug use was making him lose his creative objectivity, and throughout the nine-week shoot outside Los Angeles he fought Paramount Pictures executives for a say in every aspect of production.

The film's director, Peter Bogdanovich, who had made the 1971 hit *The Last Picture Show*, said of his new young star:

"When I met him, he was already in the role. But I didn't realize that because I'd never met him. So I thought, 'My God, he's really kind of like this part—moody, a little scary sometimes."

Anthony Clark, who had become close friends with Phoenix on *Dogfight* and now had a small role in *The Thing Called Love*, said the young star wanted a say in every aspect of the movie.

"It's one thing to be the star and carry a motion picture," said Clark. "But he wanted to write the music, perform the music and be in on the decision-making."

Although *The Thing Called Love* was a modern love story set in

212

Nashville, Phoenix turned the movie into a vehicle to show his contempt for his stardom. Changing his character into a moody temperamental singer, he insisted on playing it with a sneering scowl on his face.

Alan Moyle, who had directed the hit movie *Pump Up the Volume* several years earlier, was brought in at the last minute to rework the script.

"The producers were worried because River chose a darker, more introspective way to play the part than was written," explained Moyle. "At one point I said, 'River, who the hell are you playing here? I don't get it.' "

Phoenix then admitted he had modeled James Wright on the less flattering side of rock icon Bob Dylan, as seen in D. A. Pennebaker's documentary *Don't Look Back* about his unhappy 1965 English tour during which he was booed off stage at London's Royal Albert Hall for going electric.

"In that movie Bob Dylan displayed probably the most sour reaction to stardom possible," explained Moyle. "I don't think he smiled once in the whole movie and there are shots of Joan Baez gazing lovingly at him while he's just scorning her and all his friends. Okay, cool at the time but not someone you'd want to play a love scene opposite."

As production got under way Phoenix insisted on staying up all night with Moyle working on endless script rewrites for scenes to be shot the next day.

"It was like working without a net," said Bogdanovich in *US* magazine. "Everything on the picture was changing right up until the end."

Phoenix was also at odds with Paramount Pictures executives when they tried to rein him in and bring the picture under control.

"I took this project because Peter and I had an agreement as to how we were going to do it," said Phoenix in an interview with James Grant of *Detour* in July of 1993. "It has everything to do with me having the best understanding of the character and the movie. Me and the few people working on it from the creative end are the only ones that really understand what's going on."

Alan Moyle says Phoenix refused to compromise after his "agreement" with Bogdanovich.

"River was determined to keep his character from being bubblegum and easily figured out," said Moyle. "Unfortunately, one of my jobs as a ghostwriter was to make him accessible."

Bogdanovich had the actors improvise their scenes in rehearsal before incorporating the results into the script. Moyle would then run up against Phoenix's anger when he tried to edit the scenes down.

"It was a painful process," says Moyle. "Someone had to tell River that although the improvs were good, some of them didn't make sense. So he and I battled."

Phoenix then embarked on a game of subtle oneupsmanship with Moyle, who finally won the actor's respect and friendship by standing up to him.

"Let's say I wanted him to do a scene a certain way, River would automatically try to find another way to do it," said Moyle. "It was partly a game, partly his creative way of making it his own and partly his way of saying, I'm smarter than you. He was a kid basically and his aggressive side would come out in various ways."

The main reason Phoenix had taken the movie was to have the opportunity to play a musician and be able to perform music on film. But when he presented the songs he had written, Paramount executives balked and allowed him to have only one song in the finished film. It was called "Lone Star State of Mine," which he described as "an ode to solitude and preservation of one's independence."

"They just don't want to pay for songwriting," complained Phoenix. "Because they see it as just another political move on my part."

Phoenix's love interest in *The Thing Called Love* was a beautiful young actress called Samantha Mathis, who played aspiring country singer Miranda Presley, who arrives in Nashville with dreams of stardom. She falls in love with James Wright but is also pursued by another singer called Kyle, played by Dermot Mulroney, who completes this country love-triangle.

"Samantha agreed to do the movie because River was in it," said Bogdanovich. "She'd met him a couple of times but she didn't know him. He was crazy about her right away. He was anxious to have a lot of kissing scenes. He was saying, 'In the lovemaking scene, can we really do it? Can you just put us in there and close the door and let us go? He was only half-kidding.''

To the amusement of the other actors and crew, a visibly shy and nervous Phoenix started to woo Mathis with a boyish clumsiness.

"He'd say nasty sexual things to her," said Alan Moyle, who had been close friends with Mathis since they'd worked together in *Pump Up the Volume*. "As he was falling in love with her, he'd be goofing on her at the same time. River would do these imitations of coming on to her in a mock romantic way. You had to laugh because he was saying, I'm not really serious because if I was I wouldn't destroy all my credibility by talking like this. Unfortunately he couldn't pull it off."

Meanwhile the intense love scenes they were playing added spice to the true-life romantic drama. Finally, Phoenix made his move while they were doing a photo shoot together and they soon became inseparable.

"Samantha was a leveling influence on River," says Moyle. "She could be nothing but a good influence on anybody."

Throughout filming there were rumors that Phoenix was often high when he went in front of the cameras. When the dailies were viewed Phoenix seemed to have a glazed look in his eyes, as if under the influence of something. One day Bogdanovich challenged River about drugs when he arrived on set unfit to drive a truck for a key scene.

"He was very moody, kind of removed," Bogdanovich later told Premiere magazine. "Sam was upset. I took him aside and I said, 'Are you on something?' He said no. I said, 'Well you're acting kind of strange and Sam's upset.' He said, 'Oh Jesus, I'm just—this is a difficult character. I'm into this part and I'm just trying to deal with where's he's at this point. Jeez, I'm sorry. I don't mean to upset Sam.' I said, 'I don't want any getting into drugs. We don't need that.' And he said, 'No, no, man.' He said, 'I took a decongestant and half a beer and maybe that was a mistake. But I'm fine, I'm okay now, I'm okay. I'm cool.'

Bogdanovich was not convinced and a couple of weeks later again confronted his star about drugs.

"I wanted to see what he'd say," said Bogdanovich. "There were some rumors that he was on drugs on our picture, which angered me. We were all worried about the crowd he was with. L.A. bothered him. Something about it triggered all the more difficult parts of his life."

After his heart-to-heart with Phoenix, the director apparently decided there was no way he was taking drugs:

"It was impossible. I know how the rumor got started. We were kind of rewriting the script as we went along, and it was difficult to know how far to take the weirdness of the character. So we might do twelve takes or more of a given scene, and each one would be different.

"Unlike most actors, River never gave it to you the same way twice. I'd say to him, 'Why don't you do it in the way you just did it?' He'd say, 'You already have that. What's the point? Let me do it differently. Then I'd say, 'I think that's a bit too weird, River. Let's ease up on it.' He'd say okay, and he'd play it more normal. He had complete control over it. If he was on drugs he wouldn't have been able to control it. But some of the people at the studio, seeing some of the footage, said, 'Oh, he must be on drugs.' "

Alan Moyle claims that it was a tribute to River's acting that he fooled so many people into believing he was on drugs when he was merely playing a role.

"River made a choice to play a guy who was psychically fucked up, so on the rushes it would look like he's on junk because he was nodding," said Moyle. "It's clear to me that he's chosen that cool ultra-hip character and only idiots would think that was really him.''

But when English journalist Tom Daniels arrived on the set to profile Phoenix for the London-based *Mail on Sunday,* he found him incoherent.

"The most shocking thing on meeting him was his incoherence," said Daniels. "His conversation would become too abstract to follow, the connections cloudy. His mind would suddenly jump with no warning."

"I am being jerked around in the way you're always being jerked around," Phoenix told Daniels. "They want you to do what they want you to do." Then by way of a non-sequitur segue: "I have twenty personalities on top of the ten I already have. So I now have thirty people in my head."

Complaining he was having to go through "blood, sweat and tears" to deliver his performance, Phoenix said he was forced to play a simple scene involving a dog three different ways. His explanation was not simple.

"Having to do something like that changes your reactions," said Phoenix. "Somebody talks about a dog, either I had a dog that was hit or the other variation is I never had a dog and I always wanted a dog or I still had a dog that my dad left me when he died. Three different things to play."

Sounding tired and depressed, Phoenix told Daniels about his daily life on the set: "I sleep and I work and that's it. I don't do anything fun for myself. I have to immerse myself or else I feel false."

The crushing financial responsibilities he felt to support his family and friends also seemed to weigh heavily on the twenty-two-year-old when he spoke of his need for a hit movie.

"I need to get on up there with the big box-office types," said Phoenix. "You must have the conventional success to have the unconventional success. If I can do two unconventional films and one corporate monster film like this a year, three total, then I'll be happy."

Once content to complain quietly to his friends about his dislike of the studio system, Phoenix now publicly criticized Paramount for its handling of *The Thing Called Love:*

"The studio just releases all the obvious takes which will pacify the executives. Sometimes I do a take to pacify executives and it winds up in the movie, and I'm kicking myself. I try to be dark and humorous. The studio doesn't understand it. The reaction is fear. 'Oh my God! Look at this!' "

Conceding, that *The Thing Called Love* would either be "brilliant or just awful," River refused to take responsibility for the film if it was a box-office failure.

"I've worked my butt off for this," he said. "If this film doesn't work it's someone else's fault. I would like to make films where it's all my fault. But that's not my place. I'm just doing my job and it's someone else's fault then.

"I've learned, though, an awful lot on this shoot for *The Thing Called Love*—this is my college."

Then, like a battle-weary old soldier, he shifted into yet another gear to launch a revealing treatise on his own life and insecurities.

"Everything is ironic to me," he began. "There are moments I find hysterical, but I'm probably the only one who would find that, except for a few people.

"I don't think I'm a very good actor. Everything is kind of tentative and at a certain point you click in and you just feel the Holy Ghost move you. It's a great feeling. It's not like I reason and say, 'Oh, I want to do this.' It's just an inherent challenge that grips you and says, 'Do it.' Your subconscious says go with it, make it something. I think I can root out characters pretty well. I can be possessed pretty well. And I've got the psychiatrist's bills to prove it."

When the production moved to Nashville, Phoenix was in such bad shape that one night's filming had to be scrapped as unusable. But the studio was still wary of further unsettling their million-dollar star and refused to face up to his drug problem. His friend and co-star Anthony Clark watched Phoenix's decline on the set.

Clark said: "I knew maybe there were problems with . . . I didn't really know what . . . I was scared to even ask, because a few times I did talk to him about his intense situation with alcohol. I brought it up, but he was such a great actor that he would just totally calm my nerves. I mean, he would make you feel crazy for even asking him, 'Is everything all right?' And I wish to God that I could have stepped in and intervened, but he just seemed so incredibly together."

Phoenix had a disarming way of making friends feel guilty for daring to question him about his behavior.

"Sometimes you deny yourself the sleep you need because you're going to be working the next day," he would reply. "You stay up and you work very hard on the script or you write a song, which everyone is urging you to do."

Eventually River did agree to attend a couple of meetings of the West Hollywood group of Alcoholics Anonymous, which met in a mock log cabin. A member of AA told US magazine that during the meeting he spoke to Phoenix, who was still in denial.

"I'm here because my manager and my publicist and my agent want me to be here," Phoenix told him. "I drink and I do drugs, but I don't have a problem."

Around that time Alan Moyle was planning a remake of the 1966 British cult movie *Morgan—A Suitable Case for Treatment* [called *Morgan* in the U.S.), which starred David Warner and Vanessa Redgrave. As he got to know Phoenix better, Moyle decided that the unpredictable actor would be ideal to play Morgan, the husband who becomes unhinged after his divorce and goes off on a series of manic adventures dressed in a gorilla suit.

"I thought River would be perfect because you need someone who is truly slightly out," said Moyle. "So I told him about it and he pretended not to be interested at all. But that was River. If he knew you were pushing or you were overtly on a mission he would deliberately not be interested. Then after you had dropped the idea he'd start asking you about it and become interested."

Two days later Moyle was with Phoenix in his trailer when the actor suddenly became Morgan, going berserk and smashing everything in sight.

"I was frightened," said Moyle. "River's face was contorted like a demented gorilla. I was amazed and shocked by his transformation. He was hooting and pogoing and swinging wildly and dangerously and trashing everything in sight. I stood there dumbfounded for about thirty seconds and then, bang. He pops out of it. He goofed on me and blew my mind."

Moyle spent the rest of the shoot pleading with Phoenix to reprise his Morgan performance for Samantha Mathis and the other actors but he refused.

"Of course he wasn't going to do it on command," said Moyle. "He gave me that valentine and it was gone. It was a magical moment. Now I don't think I could make *Morgan* with any other actor after I saw River chimp around the trailer, squeeching and pounding his chest and being Morgan. I can't do it with anyone else."

During the filming in Los Angeles, Phoenix and Mathis spent most evenings at Alan Moyle's house eating vegetarian meals prepared by the actor. One night they threw a party for some of the cast and crew and Phoenix took Moyle to the supermarket.

"River wouldn't let me buy anything that had a preservative in it," remembers Moyle. "He'd look at the labels on the pickle jars and he'd check the ingredients. He just refused to compromise."

But even if everyone else tried to ignore the telling signs that River Phoenix was floundering, he could never fool the movie camera. When Chicago *Sun-Times* movie critic Roger Ebert saw Phoenix's shambling performance the following year he called it "a painful experience for anyone who remembers him in good health."

"[River's] performance should have been seen by someone as a cry for help," wrote Ebert. "He looks ill—thin, sallow, listless. His eyes are directed mostly at the ground. He cannot meet the camera or the eyes of the other actors. It is sometimes difficult to understand his dialogue. Even worse, there is no energy in the dialogue, no conviction that he cares about what he is saying."

## Chapter Twenty

# GOIN' DOWN

BACK IN GAINESVILLE, River Phoenix threw himself into a rush of activity. Regrouping Aleka's Attic with Josh Greenbaum, Rain Phoenix and, on bass, Sasa Raphael, a friend of his brother Leaf, he took over Pro Media Recording Studio in Gainesville, spending thousands of dollars a week on studio time. Now that Island Records had passed on Aleka's Attic, Phoenix decided to use his own money to put out a CD. He seemed a man possessed as he pushed his fellow band members through eighteen-hour days to capture the new music that was now coming to him in frantic bursts of creative energy.

"He was amazingly driven for a guy his age," said Pro Media owner Dave Smadbeck, who worked on the sessions. "I mean River just wouldn't stop. He'd get exhausted to the point of nodding out and he'd say, 'Let's do some more.' You would physically have to throw him out of the studio. He had an unusual passion."

Sessions would start at noon and often go on until six the next morning. After a couple of hours sleep Phoenix would be back in the studio again for another marathon session. Every day River's mother Heart would arrive at the sessions with vegetarian food and health drinks and the rest of the Phoenix family would come in and out.

"River was in charge of everything," says recording engineer Mark Pinske. "Whatever River wanted we did. He was a workhorse. He'd want to go, go, go, and sometimes we'd get past the point of no return. I'd say, 'River, we just need to go home and sleep.' "

Working in bursts of feverish energy, Phoenix would write song after song, each time announcing, "It's brilliant, brilliant." Then he'd refuse to take advice on how it could be improved, saying he didn't want to corrupt his original inspiration. Much of the work was left unfinished; Phoenix would lose interest and want to move on to the next song in his head. Dave Smadbeck saw Phoenix losing his perspective and tried to give him advice to get him back on track:

"At one point I told River, 'Hey, man, you've got to start focusing on this a little more strongly.' He was being so creative that it was just one raw piece after another. He just had to get it out at any cost."

Phoenix would keep driving his band members and the studio staff as he endlessly experimented on unusual effects to capture the sounds in his head.

"River would come up with all kinds of strange ideas," said Mark Pinske, who received three Grammy nominations for his work as the late Frank Zappa's chief recording engineer in the 1980s. "We'd set up long tubes and then miked them off the cymbals which he'd sing through to make his voice sound weird. River wanted to capture something that was different from anything that had ever been done before."

One day he told Pinske he wanted to incorporate the sound of the windshield wipers from Kenny Greenbaum's van into a song he had written. Pinske recorded the sound of the squeaking wipers in stereo in the parking lot using a portable recorder and then mastered it into the song.

"It was great," said Pinske. "At the beginning of the song you hear the windshield wipers going from side to side and you feel like you are in Kenny's van. River did great stuff like that right off the cuff."

Although Pinske never saw any drug use in the studio, there was heavy drinking. Several times he incurred Phoenix's anger when he halted sessions because the musicians were too drunk and started wasting valuable studio time.

"River would get mad at me," said Pinske. "The next day when he came in he couldn't even remember what had happened. I used to tell them, 'If you're going to party, don't mix it with work.' "

In October, 1992, Democratic Presidential candidate Bill Clinton came to a pre-election rally in Gainesville and River Phoenix decided to show his support by playing a free concert before Clinton's appearance. Billing themselves as the Blacksmith Configuration, it would be the only time that Phoenix allowed his name to be used in promoting a show.

"We need a new administration," said Phoenix at the time. "I like Clinton. I've met Clinton and Al Gore and they are both very capable."

More than ten thousand people turned out to see River Phoenix, who was due to play before candidate Clinton's ten A.M. appearance. Never an early riser, Phoenix stayed up all night practicing with the rest of his band to play what would be his last public performance in Gainesville.

"It was rawer and I think more nitty-gritty than ever," said Josh Greenbaum. "We became the tight garage band that we'd started as. We'd come full circle."


That winter Phoenix's Los Angeles friends Abby Gorton and Dickie Rude got married in Las Vegas, and as a wedding present, River took them to Costa Rica to stay with his father in his beautiful hacienda high above the Pacific Ocean. Attempting yet another reconciliation, father and son spent time together, writing songs together and telling the Rudes about the family history. John revealed that he was planning to write it down in a book to be called *By Way of Fontana,* but when Dickie Rude volunteered to co-author it he was politely but firmly turned down.

Although he was still drinking, the elder Phoenix seemed far more content and his dreams finally seemed to be coming true. Now running an organic farm alongside his bed-and-breakfast operation, he planned to open a vegetarian restaurant and employed local villagers, giving them land to live on and paying them good wages.

"John is known as Don Juan in the town," said Abby Rude. "He's very respected there because he treats people so well."

John and Heart were now married in name only.

"John lives in Costa Rica while Heart stays in Gainesville," said Abby Rude. "John prefers to be in Costa Rica away from everything while Heart's driving force is to inform people about the environment and bring peace and love into their lives."

The Rudes did their best to adapt to the Phoenixes' lifestyle by becoming vegetarians and joining in the long passionate family discussions about philosophy and the stagnating world condition.

"John's an incredible man," said Abby. "He is very strong and knows exactly what he wants. He just wants to live life in his own way and not have to put up with any of this civilization bullshit. Spending time with him in Costa Rica changed my life completely because for the first time I realized how little we need to survive."


Phoenix's three-and-a-half year relationship with Suzanne Solgot was now breaking up as he was spending more and more time with Samantha Mathis. He spent Christmas in Los Angeles with Suzanne, Sky Sworski and Josh Greenbaum. While he was there he embarked on a drug binge, buying heroin and cocaine from his group of Los Angeles drug friends. He saw much of Abby Rude, who was now managing a West Hollywood restaurant, and her husband Dickie, and with no professional commitments his other friends began to worry he was losing control completely.

Stories of Phoenix's drug excesses were part of the all-important Hollywood grapevine and he was getting a reputation as "largely unreliable." Late one night a former child actor, Paul

Petersen, who had started a foundation called A Minor Consideration to help young stars who become addicted to drugs, got a call from a friend about River Phoenix.

"He was absolutely shocked," said Petersen, one of the original Mouseketeers and a regular on the "Donna Reed Show." "He called me at one-thirty A.M. from a night club on Sunset Strip because he'd seen River and a bunch of others getting high on heroin in the men's room. He said he'd walked in and seen them shooting up."

Petersen managed to find out where Phoenix was staying and went 'round to challenge him.

"I knocked on the door and River answered," remembers Petersen. "I said, 'I don't know if you know me from the 'Donna Reed Show' but we have a group of former kid stars called A Minor Consideration. I hear that you have some real serious problems with drugs in your life and we can help.' And he looked me right in the eye and said, 'Oh, I think you've got the wrong person. It sure wasn't me. I don't even eat meat.' Then he closed the door in my face."

That Christmas Red Hot Chili Peppers bassist Flea was so alarmed at Phoenix's behavior that he urged the actor to get help. One morning, Phoenix staggered around to Bobby Bukowski's home, stoned on a speedball cocktail of heroin and cocaine, and collapsed into unconsciousness. When he eventually awoke and tried to cleanse his system with one of his patented "garlic-and-raw-veggies-and-serial-glasses-of-water" meals, Bukowski staged an emotional intervention: "I'd rather you just point a gun at your head and pull the trigger. I want to see you become an old man, so we can be old friends together."

Phoenix broke down in tears, swearing never to touch any drugs again.

"That's the end of the drugs," he promised Bukowski. "I don't want to go down to the place that's so dark it'll annihilate me."

Bukowski says that he then began to understand that Phoenix's preoccupation with hard drugs represented an adolescent rite of passage which he'd missed out on because of his ever-demanding acting career.

"He was a little boy and then he was a man," said Bukowski, echoing many others.

Phoenix was now in the grip of a serious depression, intensified by the drugs he was taking, and was finding it hard to break out of his moody spells. The only time he was now truly happy was when he was playing another character in a movie and could become someone other than River Phoenix.

"That's the only time I have security," said Phoenix. "Myself is a bum! Myself is nothing! I'm a peon. I'm an idiot. I'm totally removed. I'm in the closet. I'm out of sight. You can't touch me."


After ringing in the New Year over a champagne celebration with Abby and Dickie Rude, Josh Greenbaum and Suzanne Solgot, Phoenix went back to Gainesville to try once more to pick up the pieces. Now that he was involved with Samantha Mathis, Suzanne Solgot moved out of their Gainesville apartment to work as a masseuse in San Francisco. There was no bitterness in their split and the two swore to remain lifelong soulmates. Phoenix's friend Bill Richert witnessed their long breakup and his infatuation with Mathis.

"River and Samantha were close in a different way than he and Sue were," said Richert. "River used to call Sue his wife. She bought his clothes for him. She looked after him and I loved the way they were together. He and Samantha were more romantically involved but I don't think their relationship would have lasted."

In January, 1993, Heart Phoenix finally challenged her son about using drugs after noticing he'd lately become distant and withdrawn. She had also become alarmed after seeing a series of photographs taken on the set of *The Thing Called Love*. They showed an ashen-faced River, his long greasy hair slicked back rocker-style. At last she faced up to the fact that "a substance might be involved."

River was embarrassed and upset after spending so many years trying to hide his drug use from his parents and categorically denying having anything to do with hard drugs. Nevertheless Heart was suspicious and called John Phoenix for help. They agreed that River should get away from bad influences and urged him to take a long vacation in Costa Rica, where his father could keep a close eye on him.

Sky Sworski, known in the family circle as an "eco cop," claims he never even suspected River was on drugs.

"He was pretty secretive about it," said Sworski. "The people in his world were very loving and nurturing and would never have let him get involved with anybody who did things like that. He kept it from me. Because there would have been trouble."

After Bukowski's dramatic intervention, Phoenix made a serious attempt at cleaning up his act and would often call his friend for support when he felt the need for drugs. His friend and former tutor Dirk Drake, whom River had recently helped through a difficult divorce, also tried to help him stay off hard drugs.

"I would say River's real problem was the pressure of more people needing him," said Drake, who has agonized long and hard about the cause of River's troubles. "I think there was more to it than drugs. River was becoming more distracted. He was distracted by his distractions. The pressures were too much. There's a weird dichotomy here, because as the pressures and involvements were snowballing, it seemed like he was taking it well with his usual positive zeal. But if anyone with a heart and mind had paid attention, they would have seen it was all too much for him and he had nowhere to go. We were all guilty. We were all prolonging a lie."

Since his childhood in the Children of God, River Phoenix believed he had been born to carry out a divine mission to help save the world. Later his parents had refined the mission to utilize show-business success as the medium for the family's message. But trying to create good will for mankind in the climate of bottom-line Hollywood big business was doomed to failure, as John Phoenix had recognized years before.

"He could have been a lot less idealistic and a lot more focused," said Drake. "Drugs glossed over and glamorized the pressures and made it seem as if he was looking through rose-colored glasses."


During the next few months Phoenix rethought his life and decided to distance himself from his family so he could start living his own life and be more independent.

"He wanted to break away from the family," said Abby Rude. "He had always pretty much been with his parents and now he wanted to be on his own and have his own apartment."

Life in Gainesville was also becoming harder and harder for Phoenix to deal with as his fame increased, making him a target for a strange combination of resentment and adoration. Rachel Guinan from the Hardback says it became increasingly uncomfortable for him as his worshipping fans began seeking him out.

"One time a group of tourists from Japan found out River was going to be in here," said Guinan. "River and a friend were just having a beer and this crowd of little girls just came in here and started crying and trying to touch him. It was a weird scenario and it really freaked him out."

Another night Leaf Phoenix overheard some drinkers sitting at the Hardback bar bad-mouthing River and told him about it.

"It was an uncomfortable moment," said Guinan. "River just came over to the bar and started making faces at them and going 'Ah, ah, ah, ah, ah.' He wasn't going to attack them. He wasn't going to tell them to shut up. I mean it was kind of ridiculous to go over there and make faces at them. That made me feel really uncomfortable."

In early 1993 Phoenix contemplated moving out of Gainesville to Athens, Georgia, a thriving music city that had produced bands like R.E.M. and the B-52s. River was close friends with R.E.M.'s charismatic singer Michael Stipe and had often visited Athens to play music.

"River told me it was a hot music area and he wanted to move there," said Coney Island restaurant owner Jim Kesl. "He planned to give the ranch in Micanopy to a charity that helps abused mothers and children."

He also considered moving to Boston or even as far afield as Canada, where he'd heard land was cheap. Now feeling restless in Gainesville, Phoenix hardly ever ventured out in public before dark. When Anthony Campanaro saw his old friend that spring outside the Florida Theater in downtown Gainesville, he seemed to have changed for the better.

"River looked a lot better and a lot cleaner," said Campanaro. "He stopped me in the street and gave me a big hug. He wanted to know all about my life and how I was surviving on my own since my divorce. I didn't want to talk to him because I had my own personal problems so I blew him off and was an asshole to him. I felt bad later because I had the attitude, Why are you interested in me? You have all the money in the world and you have no problems. Little did I know."

When it came to casting the role of the Vampire Lestat in the much anticipated screen adaptation of Anne Rice's best-seller *Interview with the Vampire,* River Phoenix was the author's first choice. She felt that Phoenix, with his mysteriously haunted yet fragile quality was perfect to play the Vampire and fought for him to get the part. It was the first big-budget Hollywood movie for Irish director Neil Jordan, who was just coming off his critically acclaimed *The Crying Game.* Jordan was at the mercy of the studio, who wanted proven box-office star Tom Cruise for the starring role. They agreed to give Phoenix the lesser role of Malloy, the narrator, as a consolation prize.

Rice was furious when Cruise was cast and went public to complain about his being the wrong choice, leading to a public row between the author and the studio before the cameras had even started rolling. The troubled production was originally due to start shooting in April but had to be postponed until October. Phoenix never commented publicly on his rejection for the starring role, and never complained about having to take the much smaller role.

By April, River had fallen off the wagon. At the Dallas Film Festival he turned up at a ceremony to receive a lifetime achievement award on behalf of his friend Richard Harris. At the reception afterward he was near-incoherent and was falling all over the place.

"I've never seen anyone so close to the plate," said festival guest Richard Osterweil, who was sitting at Phoenix's table. "His hair was sweeping through his salad. Then he dropped a piece of chocolate cake on the floor, picked it up and ate it."

For the last months of his life River Phoenix would desperately battle his drug-and-alcohol dependency in a recurring pattern of going on and off the wagon. Turning more and more to the biography of Arthur Rimbaud, *Time of the Assassins,* Phoenix must have seen himself becoming what Henry Miller called "a living suicide."

"In the case of suicide we do not concern ourselves with whether he died a quick or a lingering death," writes Miller about the decline of Rimbaud. "Whether his agony was great or little. It is the *act* that has importance for us, for suddenly we are made to realize that to be and not to be are acts—not intransitive verbs!—which make existence and death synonymous. The act of the suicide always has a detonating effect; it shocks us for a moment into awareness."

## Chapter Twenty-one

# DARK BLOOD

WHEN DUTCH FILM director George Sluizer saw *My Own Private Idaho* he was captivated by River Phoenix's powerful performance. Two years later, after breaking into Hollywood with the American version of his Dutch cult classic *The Vanishing*, starring Kiefer Sutherland and Jeff Bridges, Sluizer was casting an independent new movie project called *Dark Blood*, with a budget of $8 million, and remembered the young actor.

"I saw River standing in the road in *My Own Private Idaho* and I said this is the guy to star in my movie," said Sluizer.

The Dutchman then sent the *Dark Blood* script to Iris Burton, who apparently deemed it unsuitable and told the director that Phoenix was too busy to consider it. A few months later she changed her mind and sent the script to River.

"Once he read it he was very interested and we arranged to meet in San Francisco," said Sluizer.

Arriving at Phoenix's hotel suite an hour late with a raging headache—his plane from Los Angeles had been held up—Sluizer was worried their relationship might be off to a bad start.

"River was wonderful," said Sluizer. "The first thing he did was insist on running downstairs to get me a glass of water and an aspirin. He was a very considerate and helpful young man."

During a three-hour lunch Sluizer told Phoenix about the movie, which was about the harmful, long-lasting effects of nuclear testing. Phoenix passionately identified with the environmental theme of the film and began enthusiastically questioning the middle-aged director about his career. More used to dealing with the superficiality of the movie business, Sluizer was unprepared for Phoenix's genuine interest.

"It amused me," said Sluizer. "At one point he said, 'I respect you.' And I asked why, because we had only been talking two hours and it was the first time we had ever met. River said, 'No. You misunderstand me. I don't respect you because you are good or bad. I respect you because you're much older than I am and so much more experienced in life. I respect older people.'

"River had this unique way of talking. I usually find that young people don't understand the older guys because of the generation gap. I think that he had an open mind because of the education he'd got from his mother."

At one point Sluizer told him how Iris Burton had ignored his calls. Phoenix, who always prided himself on being outside the Hollywood system, admitted that, as with *My Own Private Idaho,* Iris Burton had kept the script from him.

Sluizer said: "I told him, 'River you have an agent, which you have had since you were very small, who doesn't give you the scripts [in order] to protect you from the unknown quantity. You never even know they exist because you don't see them. So whatever you pretend, you are part of the system because you allow your agent to make your decisions.'"

In the delicate negotiations with the film's producers, Phoenix's agents used his charity foundations as a bargaining tool to raise his million-dollar-plus asking fee, arguing he couldn't work for less or his charity work would suffer. Finally terms were agreed on and Phoenix signed on May 24, 1993, to do *Dark Blood.*

George Sluizer says he was aware of the rumors about Phoenix and drugs but wanted to meet him in person before making up his mind.

"I heard the talk," said Sluizer. " 'Oh yeah, you're going to work with River. Is he stoned on coke?' "

At their San Francisco meeting Phoenix seemed perfectly sober but it was a different story the next time they met in Los Angeles in June.

"I would say that it was probable that River had taken something," says Sluizer. "He behaved like someone under the influence. I wasn't too worried, though, as you have to think about drugs and their problems with any actor of a certain age."

Basing himself in a suite at L.A.'s exclusive St. James Club and Hotel, Phoenix dived back into the drug scene. One night he arrived unannounced at the door of a British-born actor to score drugs. The actor, who did not want to be identified and uses the pseudonym Cedric Niles, told People magazine that Phoenix was barefoot and so disheveled that he did not recognize him at first.

"He had all this hair hanging over his face," said Niles. "He was wearing those flared-out hippie pants and one of those hooded Mexican shirts."

Niles said that after freebasing some of the large stash of cocaine Phoenix had brought with him, they hung out together for the next few weeks. Always paranoid that the press would find out about his drug-taking and expose him, Phoenix ordered the receptionist at the St. James Club to put through only callers who used his secret password—Earl Grey.

But according to Niles, it was Phoenix who usually called him when he felt lonely or bored.

"But he'd be too worried to even leave a message," said Niles. "He'd say, 'Hey, is anyone there? Is anyone there? It's . . . it's . . .' And then you'd hear a click. He didn't even want to leave his name on my machine."

Eventually the two were both so burned out they made a pact to sober up and Phoenix flew back to Gainesville to get away from the temptations of Los Angeles.

"I think we both were starting to understand that it was getting out of control," said Niles. "We spent our nights trying to laugh but it wasn't fun for either of us."

Niles began to suspect that River was doing heroin in secret behind closed doors. When Corey Feldman, who co-starred with Phoenix in *Stand By Me,* heard rumors that his old friend was using heroin, he called River.

"He didn't sound very good," said Feldman, who tried to "feel him out" rather than have a direct confrontation. "We talked for a while but he just sounded out of it. My first impression was that there was some validity to the rumors, but he never said that."

A week later Phoenix reached out to his old friend and left a phone message thanking him for his concern and asking to get together as soon as possible.

In mid-July Gus Van Sant and Scott Green flew into Sarasota, Florida, to photograph River and his two sisters, Rain and Summer, as part of the "Individuals of Style" advertising campaign the director was working on for the Gap clothing stores. After the day's shooting Van Sant flew off to Russia but Green, who was working as his photographic assistant, did not have a passport and so couldn't go.

"River and Rain invited me to come and spend a few days with them in Gainesville," said Green. "I'd always intended to, so I went."

During his visit Green stayed at the ranch in Micanopy and saw first-hand how hard Phoenix was trying to kick alcohol and drugs.

"River was always trying to stop completely and for a time he was doing pretty well," said Green. "It was pretty weird. River never fully admitted to me that he was an alcoholic or an addict. It's tough for people.

"River was living very clean. He had a good diet and strong beliefs and it wasn't just an act or a fad or anything. He believed in what he did. He knew his drinking and taking drugs was a contradiction. I mean him living a clean life like that and using drugs just goes to show that addiction is powerful.

"I'm sure River was aware that heroin was bad for him and obviously he wanted to change it. It takes a lot of balls and you've got to want to."

\*    \*    \*

In late July Phoenix flew to Los Angeles to promote *The Thing Called Love*. Receiving journalists at a cabana by the pool at the Art Deco St. James Club, Phoenix, dressed in shorts and T-shirt, sipped herbal tea as he asked writers not to mention his smoking.

"I hope you're not going to write about me smoking," he told James Grant of Detour magazine. "It sets an awful example for your readers, not because I'm an asshole for smoking but I don't want to promote it."

Asked by another writer about his attitude on drugs in Hollywood, Phoenix said: "I've always shied away from the seedy side of Hollywood. I don't do drugs, I get a big enough high from life without trying anything like that. I'm so straight I don't eat meat and even my dogs are vegetarians."

Soon afterward when asked directly if he told the truth in interviews, Phoenix appeared defensive: "I deal with a lot of phonies. I'm not going to give my truth to the phonies. Everything you say they lie and change anyway so maybe if you lie and give them bullshit, it will come out being truthful."

During the series of interviews Phoenix alternated between self-doubt and arrogance.

"I'm a fucking genius when it comes to writing dialogue," he told Mademoiselle, almost in the same breath as saying "I'm a minor, stupid talent."


While in Los Angeles Phoenix visited Abby Rude, who told him she was having problems with her marriage. Phoenix invited her back to Gainesville, offering her Sky Sworski's job as his personal assistant to help her and give himself more freedom at the same time.

"Sky is almost like a cop," said Abby. "He's an ex-New Yorker and he's got a really scary voice. River wanted me to do his phone calls because I had a much more pleasant voice. He led me to believe that I'd be taking over from Sky in a lot of ways.''

Staying at Micanopy, Abby started running Phoenix's life. She'd wake him up in the morning, do his laundry, write his letters and make his phone calls.

"River wanted me to be his voice to the outside world," said Abby. "He didn't want to have to deal with it and he was in a position where he didn't have to."

Heart Phoenix liked Abby immediately and they soon became friends and confidantes.

"Heart is the mother that you wished you always had," said Abby. "She really seems to know what you need in your life. But although she's the mother-figure, Heart's also a young girl. One night we spent five hours talking and giggling about sex."

Abby says that Heart was still trying to cope with the consequences of her son's fame.

"I don't think she realized where this would take her," said Abby. "And what a position she'd be put in. I doubt whether she was prepared for the volume of River's fame and how it affected him."

Phoenix had just one month in Gainesville to finish his CD before he was due on the set of *Dark Blood*. Relaunching the band, Phoenix virtually moved into Pro Media Studios and started recording at an even more frenetic pace than a year before.

"They were working like banshees," said Dave Smadbeck. "They were crazy to finish this album and they would work all night."

River seemed inspired as he recorded an astonishing ninety songs that he had written the music and lyrics to. His band members and the Pro Media staff practically had to drag him out after an eighteen-hour day.

"He was almost on overload," said recording engineer Mark

Pinske. "He was an explosion of creativity. There just weren't enough hours in the day to get it all down."

Even when the other band members dropped from weariness, Phoenix would still be on his feet composing new songs and playing music. He would often keel over and fall asleep in his clothes, hugging his guitar on his lap for a couple of hours before starting all over again.

"He always tried to extend the day much further than a day should be extended," said Bobby Bukowski. "He always felt that he had to fit a lot into the day. At the time when people normally like to sleep, River would get up and say, 'Here are twenty-five songs that I wrote since the last time I saw you.' "

That summer River had a premonition that his days were numbered. He told friends about a recurring dream he was having in which the spirits were coming to take him away. Always superstitious, he was especially concerned with what he considered the bad numerology of turning twenty-three on August 23rd.

"River was saying, 'I feel like I'm going to leave," said Dirk Drake. "He said the spirits were coming to get him and whoever was up there was pulling him away. I never took him too seriously when he said stuff like that. I wish I had."

Suzanne Solgot also had forbodings that River was in danger and tried to warn him.

"A lot of us felt some kind of doom coming," says Solgot. "I would call him and tell him, and he would say, 'Don't be ridiculous. I'm coming up to see you soon.' "

Bassist Sasa Raphael said Phoenix was now working flat out as if time was short.

"River never slowed down," said Raphael. "He was always going full speed. His mind was always turning over and creating. He had all this stuff inside to get out. I think he was prepared for the temporality of life."

John Phoenix, who was in Gainesville to spend some time with his children, made a point of attending every recording session but often found it hard to stay awake.

One day River came back into the studio after a short break to find his father fast asleep on the couch, snoring. As a joke he had Pinske set up a microphone right over his father's mouth to record his snores and turned on the video recorder.

"He started asking his dad all these outrageous questions," said Pinske. "He'd say, 'Well, Dad, what do you think about this?' And he'd just keep on snoring. River and his brother Leaf thought it was hilarious and were just laughing their rear ends off."

When John Phoenix woke up he thought it was funny and insisted on watching and rewatching the video of him snoring. During the sessions father and son became closer than they had ever been and seemed to have, finally, settled their differences.


River's decline was now obvious to all his Gainesville friends. One night his old friend Anthony Campanaro saw him waiting in line at the Covered Dish club and was horrified by his condition:

"He was spiraling down," said Campanaro. "At first I didn't recognize him when he came up to me and started talking. River was really down and he was looking really bad. We talked for a short time and then he turned around to go and started talking to someone else. I just watched him and he looked like shit. Then he came back to me and said, 'I'm sorry. I kinda fucked up.' After that he just walked off."

A few days after his birthday, River, his brother Yoaquin and sisters Rain, Liberty and Summer all flew back to Costa Rica with their father to celebrate the opening of his new vegan restaurant. The restaurant, to be called "Juan's—Nature's Family Restaurant and Cabins," was John's final attempt to woo River and his other kids away from Hollywood by re-creating their favorite Coney Island restaurant in Costa Rica.

John Phoenix had long sat by and quietly watched his son's alarming deterioration from drink and drugs. Now, after their reconciliation and River's vow to stay sober, John wanted to take a firm hand to ensure River did not fall back into his old ways.

"I was shocked later when I learned River had been taking heroin," said John Phoenix as quoted in *Today*. "We always taught him drugs weren't the answer and he wasn't taking it here. He was clean as a whistle. But I realized things were going wrong. I could see Hollywood was eating him up, bleeding him dry.

"I told him I wanted him out of movies. I had seen too many brilliant kids go down and I realized he couldn't buck the system. I thought it was time for him to stop."

John tried to influence River and his other children to stay and help him run the restaurant and pursue the true Phoenix vision away from Hollywood.

"I had opened my place as a vegan restaurant," said John. "Things were buzzing. The idea was for them to spend more time here, helping with the cooking, making music, writing, harvesting the organic fruit and living off the land like we used to."

Finally, River agreed to retire from movies but insisted on fulfilling his contracts with *Dark Blood* and *Interview with the Vampire* and keeping his promise to Bill Richert to star in his remake of *The Man in the Iron Mask*.

"As it turned out that was too many," said John. "Just before he left, I'll always remember, he told me: 'I'll see you after this movie, Dad.' Well, he did. Only he was in a box."

## Chapter Twenty-two

# INTO THE DESERT

On September 6 River Phoenix, Samantha Mathis and Abby Rude flew to the remote village of Torrey, deep in the Utah desert, to start rehearsals for *Dark Blood*. Now almost unrecognizable with his newly shorn hair dyed black, Phoenix was delighted to be working with the English actor Jonathan Pryce, who had starred in his all-time favorite movie, *Brazil*.

Phoenix had kept his vow and had stayed completely sober since his birthday. Physically, he was feeling better than he had for years as he started work on the film. Phoenix's house became a social headquarters, and every night George Sluizer and Jonathan Pryce would arrive for an elaborate vegetarian dinner cooked by Abby Rude.

In the film River plays Boy, a young widower living a hermitlike existence on a desert nuclear-testing site that had already claimed the lives of many Native Americans. He has built himself a holy grotto and waits for the end of the world, making little dolls that have special powers that will allow him to survive the oncoming apocalypse. One day a husband and wife, played by Pryce and actress Judy Davis, are driving from the city through the desert when their car breaks down and Boy comes to their rescue.

Phoenix had more speeches and dialogue to deliver in *Dark Blood* than he had ever had before, and every night Abby Rude

241

would read through the next day's script with him to help him prepare.

"River had me do a lot of research for him," said Abby Rude. "I found out some horrific things about government nuclear testing that made him very angry and fueled his character."

From the first day there was tension between Sluizer and Judy Davis, as she insisted on rewriting the script and challenging his decisions. At one point Davis, who has called Sluizer "an act of the devil," refused to take direction from him. A natural peacemaker, Phoenix found himself continually drawn into the escalating arguments.

"He was very upset by the arguing," said Sluizer. "River preferred not to get involved and he'd go and walk to the door and wait until it was over."

Davis, the Australian star of the acclaimed 1979 film *My Brilliant Career,* decided that some of the dialogue was antifeminist and demanded it be cut from the script.

Sluizer said: "I remember one line Judy opposed was when her character starts flirting with the young man and her husband gets annoyed and says, 'Women of a certain age want to know if they can cut the mustard and are still attractive.' "

Davis claims that Phoenix was having trouble finding his character and Sluizer was making things worse by constantly giving him advice.

"He confused River," Davis told Premiere magazine. "It was a difficult part because it could so easily be absurd. He had most of the dialogue in the film, huge speeches; he kept trying to cut the lines down. Any change freaked this director out. River said to me one day, "Maybe I should give up acting.' "

Sluizer says his working relationship with River was fine until Judy Davis started interfering in their script discussions.

"River had a problem because he was dyslexic," said Sluizer. "He found it hard coping with the long speeches and I agreed to cut down his dialogue. There was never any problems until we started rehearsing with Judy."

As a confidence builder, before going in front of the cameras, Phoenix would often go to his trailer and play tapes of his favorite thrash metal band Fugazi at full volume.

"River would be like rocking really loud," said Abby Rude. "He'd drink a couple of cups of strong coffee and storm around and yell at me. Then he'd just get into character and he'd go out there and do the scene."

Rude was on set the whole time and saw the problems building between Phoenix and Davis.

"She made him mad," said Rude. "River once tried to be friendly and asked her when her family were coming to visit the set. She looked at him and said, 'What is this, frat boy's question time?' "

The building tension upset River so much that he asked Sluizer to delay the love scenes he had to play with Davis as he couldn't face doing them. Eventually Phoenix was let off the hook when it was agreed to use a body double for him in an intimate sex scene.

Their relationship wasn't helped when Davis challenged Phoenix about his using drugs, even though the actor had stayed sober since his birthday.

"I thought he was doing something when I first got there," said Davis. "There was one day when he came in so out of it. River said he'd had too much sodium the night before. Okay, I've never had a sodium overdose. Maybe that's exactly what they're like."

Director Sluizer strongly disagrees and is convinced that Phoenix never touched a thing during the seven-week filming in Utah.

"I never had the impression he was using any drugs whatsoever," said Sluizer. "I would swear to it."

When Samantha Mathis had to fly back to Los Angeles River was so upset that he asked his mother Heart, agent Iris Burton and Ski Sworski to fly to the set to provide additional moral support. For the next week his mother moved into their house and took control, doing her best to calm her son down.

"She was very supportive," said Sluizer. "She spent most of her time watching his dailies and she told me she felt he was doing a good job.''

As shooting progressed there were a chain of natural disasters that Phoenix saw as bad omens. Unseasonably heavy rains turned the set into a mudslide with vehicles skidding out of control. Once Sluizer narrowly escaped with his life when his director's chair slid off the edge of a high cliff only minutes after he had stood up.

"River said, 'Somebody's going to die on this film,' " recalls Jonathan Pryce. "We were on this kind of inexorable journey to some disaster. Every day there was some kind of difficulty. It just seemed as if something had to give."

One day near the end of shooting Phoenix became so miserable that he retreated into his trailer with his DAT recorder to write the lyrics of what would turn out to be his final song. He then had Abby Rude fax it to Josh Greenbaum at Pro Media Studios in Gainesville. Greenbaum was helping to mix their recently recorded tracks.

"It was the scariest thing," said Pinske. "The lyrics were in his own writing and they were about death and passing over to the other side. I think he was trying to give someone a message."

When Phoenix heard that the desert where they were filming was reputed to be a landing site for alien spaceships he felt he was being drawn by some power toward his fate. He became obsessed with the idea of U.F.O.'s, adopting a new catch phrase: "Thanks be to U.F.O. Godmother."

One night in Utah, Heart told Abby Rude a strange story about her son.

"His mom told me that when River was a little boy he used to wake up in the middle of the night and run to her, saying, 'They're trying to take me away. They want me back.'

"And she'd say, 'It's okay. They're good angels. They won't hurt you.' But River would always fight it. Then in Utah he told me, 'I'm not fighting it anymore. I'm going with it and it feels amazing.' "

Cut off from civilization, the actors and crew had to make their own amusement during the long cold desert nights. Every night after eating Phoenix's own special tabbouli, Jonathan Pryce and George Sluizer would discuss the day's shooting, watch videos and listen to River play his new songs.

George Sluizer said that Phoenix never lost his temper with Judy Davis but kept his anger and frustration bottled up.

"River did not have arguments," said Sluizer. "I remember once that he had to whisper to Judy in a close shot. She was behind him and he'd have to say something softly without turning his head to look at her."

According to Sluizer, the actress tried to throw off Phoenix's concentration by being far away when he started speaking and suddenly approaching him at the last possible moment so he couldn't tell where she was.

"River became so disturbed he asked her, 'Can't you be closer, please? I mean, you're in this picture, so why do you have to make it so difficult for me?' Other people might have screamed and shouted but River was introverted and very quiet," says Sluizer.

By the end of shooting Phoenix had been sober two months with no emotional crutch to lean on. Whenever he became overwhelmed by the bad atmosphere on the set he would escape to the telephone and call his friends for reassurance and advice. The one available phone was a party line shared by six local people, and his emotional conversations were continually being interrupted by other calls. One night Bill Richert came home to find a desperate message from Phoenix on his answering machine:

Richert said: "We'd been exchanging calls and I got a message from River saying, 'I'm having a hard time keeping my head above water in this crazy business.' Because he really did feel the intensity of it. The responsibility of it. He wasn't just interested in listening to his agent for advice."

The troubled actor also called his old friend Josh Greenbaum to set things straight over a recent falling-out.

"Every once in a while there's a part of his personality that comes up and hits you," said Greenbaum. "There had been a misunderstanding in our relationship but with his phone call from Utah I didn't feel that at all. It was gone. There was no bullshit and I felt on a new level with the honesty in our friendship."

Scott Green, who got a call from Phoenix in Utah, said his friend seemed calm, as if at peace with himself:

"River could get very moody but he seemed incredibly happy when he called me. He told me how he really loved his friends and family and seemed very positive about everything."

On Saturday, October 23, the production moved to Albuquerque, New Mexico. Phoenix had one day's shooting during which he strained his voice in a scene in which he had to scream. Since he was not needed for a night shoot, Sluizer let him fly back to Los Angeles early on Tuesday, one day ahead of the rest of the cast and crew. The production was due to resume in Los Angeles on Saturday. Before he left, Phoenix went to say goodbye to his director.

"River told me, 'I'm going back to the bad, bad town,'" remembers Sluizer. "There was something childlike about the way he said the word *bad*. I didn't realize at that moment what he meant. I guess he felt he was going to dark places and that L.A. was a bad influence on him. Maybe he disliked the town for things that had happened to him there in the past and was afraid of it."


River Phoenix and Samantha Mathis flew back to Los Angeles on Tuesday and checked into the Hotel Nikko. After seven weeks cooped up in the desert with nothing to do, Phoenix called some friends to go out on the town with him. The heavy tension on the set had had its toll, and Phoenix was easily seduced back into drugs.

"He'd been working hard on location and he'd had a hell of a time," said Bill Richert. "He just wanted to forget everything."

For the next three days Phoenix numbed his pain with drugs as he released himself from the pent-up frustrations of Utah. On

Friday afternoon Sluizer, who had just arrived in Los Angeles to prepare for the next day's filming, telephoned Phoenix to see how he was.

"I was a little anxious about him not getting his voice back in time because he had strained it and he had a cold," said Sluizer. "He told me he was okay and I said I'd see him tomorrow."

On Saturday morning Phoenix took Valium to put him in a fit condition to work but when he rolled up at the studio he looked worn out, as if he'd hardly slept.

"I think he was on something," says George Sluizer. "He was not one hundred percent in control of his body movements. But there was no problem with his acting and so there was no reason for me to interfere."

The morning's shooting went off without a hitch and Phoenix was very steady when he had to light a candle and hold it in an extreme close-up. At lunch he seemed in good spirits as he told Sluizer how he was excited because Jonathan Pryce had arranged for him to meet his hero Terry Gilliam, who had directed *Brazil*.

"River told me that he had loved *Brazil* so much that he had seen it thirteen times," said Sluizer. "He was so happy because he had an appointment to meet Terry Gilliam at two P.M. tomorrow [Sunday] after our ten-thirty A.M. appointment to discuss his scenes for the next week."

After lunch at about four-thirty P.M. Sluizer started preparing his young star for the difficult soliloquy scene to be shot that afternoon.

In the intense scene with Phoenix and Judy Davis, Boy, who has fallen in love with the wife, takes her to a sacred candlelit altar in his cave and gives her peyote. He tells the wife the apocalypse is imminent but his spirit dolls will let them survive to become a sort of Adam and Eve.

Sluizer said: "It was a scene where his character had to go to the very depths of his being and to play it River had to reach into his own depths. Obviously it asks a lot of the actor and in that sense I'm sure that River had to go quite deep to get to some essential truth of life. In the scene he is meditating about what life is about and the energy.''

The scene was uncannily parallel to his own parents' idealistic hippie search for truth so many years earlier.

Sluizer said: ''In the nineteen-sixties hippies went to Nepal and asked questions like, 'What shall I do with my life? Do I want to be like my father in the Establishment or do I want to be a guru or some Buddha? Maybe people took that very seriously and it affected them strongly in their inner selves.

''You can imagine when someone has to play something where his character is asked to convey, not only to himself but to the audience: 'Listen to me because this is the most important thing I can tell you about life.' Then you have to take that somewhere to make it believable on the screen and deeply believe in it yourself.''

With hindsight, the lines that River Phoenix had to deliver to Judy Davis are chilling: ''It took a few thousand years just to invent the alphabet and it's all going to be flushed down the john, the entire civilization. You see I see things and I know things.''

The wife tells Boy he's crazy and that they'll only have to pass on a small part of human knowledge.

''Don't you want to know?'' says Phoenix's character. ''Don't you realize? *I don't want to die. I don't want to die.*''

He then shows her one of his dolls, saying, ''They are my army of spirits. Can you feel them? This is forever.''

When Sluizer said ''cut'' after the tenth take, cameraman Ed Lachman forgot to turn off his camera. He finally realized but when he pressed the button it jammed and went on running until the film ran out.

''For ten seconds River was in front of the camera,'' said Lachman. ''Just a silhouette lit by ambient light. It was . . . eerie. For me as a cameraman, I find that strange, the last take. Why I didn't turn the camera off, why there was just enough light in the room to make him a silhouette, why he stood in front of the camera for ten seconds.''

George Sluizer said he couldn't account for what happened with the camera.

"It was creepy," said the director. "You could see River walking away into the darkness for maybe a whole minute before he finally disappeared."

## Chapter Twenty-three

# THE VIPER ROOM

AFTER LEAVING THE *Dark Blood* set at about seven P.M., River Phoenix took the studio limousine back to his $350-a-night suite at the Hotel Nikko in West Hollywood, where Samantha Mathis was waiting for him. When he arrived at Room 328 there was a family reunion, Rain and Leaf having just flown in from Florida to audition for parts in John Boorman's upcoming film *Safe Passage,* which River had now committed to doing.

An impromptu party began in the suite as the actor had a couple of drinks and began with marijuana and cocaine. Soon afterward, when the Rudes arrived at the room, Phoenix checked his upcoming schedule with Abby and asked her to set up a lunch with Iris Burton for the following week. He decided against going to a second birthday party for the son of his friend Bradley Gregg, who had played his elder brother in *Stand By Me,* and telephoned to say he was tired.

Then the partying began in earnest. Later police would find a variety of drugs in the room. After almost two months of sobriety in the desert Phoenix was ready to let off some steam in Los Angeles. It was Saturday night and Halloween Eve and he planned to see his friends, the Red Hot Chili Peppers, who were to play an unannounced set at actor Johnny Depp's new club, the Viper Room. It would be something of a reunion, the Chili Peppers were to be joined on stage by John Frusciante, the young guitarist who had quit the band mid-tour the year before and had lately become very close to the actor.

At 8:30 P.M. Phoenix called room service and sent Abby Rude out for a twenty-dollar bottle of champagne from a nearby liquor store. When the room-service waiter arrived with the vegetarian snacks they had ordered, the music was so loud they could hardly hear him knocking at the door. As the waiter wheeled in the snacks he saw Phoenix dancing by himself in the middle of the room.

At about ten P.M. Phoenix called for a car to be brought 'round to the front of the hotel to take them to the Viper Room.

"As River left he asked me something," remembered Abby Rude. "I saw something in his eyes that I'd never seen before. He had this intense look in his eyes which was really calm and peaceful. It was the last time I ever saw him alive."

Leaving the Rudes behind in the room to wait for some friends who were to join them later, Phoenix, Samantha, Rain and Leaf trooped out of the hotel just as George Sluizer was arriving in his car.

"I saw River in the car with Samantha and some other people," said Sluizer. "I shouted, 'Have a good time,' but I don't think he could hear me."

By the time they arrived at the Viper Room just after midnight, the Halloween party was in full swing. At the door Phoenix had a small red star stamped on his right hand as proof of entry. The tiny all-black room, dimly lit by Art Deco green wall lamps, was packed with people in Halloween costumes. Phoenix went in to find Flea and John Frusciante and was soon drawn into the action. Few recognized him, dressed in black jeans and Converse All-Star sneakers and with his short dark brown hair.

After chatting to Frusciante and Flea near owner Johnny Depp's private booth, which was separated from the main club area by a two-way mirror, Phoenix and his party were given a table toward the back of the club. The actor was approached by drug dealers who offered him a taste of their wares. He disappeared into the men's room with them. At 12:45 A.M. a musician friend of Phoenix offered him some high-grade Persian Brown. "Try this, it'll make you feel fabulous."

As soon as Phoenix snorted it he started trembling and shaking in front of the sink. He screamed at his friend, "What did you give me? What the fuck is in it?" After he vomited in the men's room someone tried to help him by splashing cold water over his face and he was given some Valium to calm him down. As he staggered back to the long bar across from the stage, where Mathis and Rain were waiting for him, a loud stage jam had started with actor Johnny Depp, Gibby Haynes of the Butthole Surfers, Flea and Al Jourgensen of Ministry.

Phoenix complained that he couldn't breathe and briefly passed out. When he came to he asked Mathis to take him outside. Not knowing what to do, and perhaps afraid of calling for medical help with drugs involved, she telephoned the Rudes back at the hotel for help.

"Sam called and said she was really scared," said Abby. She said River had just keeled over and Leaf was there with him at the club. We said we'd be right over to help."

Mathis and Leaf helped Phoenix past the stage to the back door of the Viper Room, which opens directly onto Sunset Boulevard. As soon as they got him outside he collapsed on the sidewalk. Just after one A.M. Phoenix went into a seizure under the canopy of the Viper Room, just four traffic lights down the road from the Chateau Marmont where comedian John Belushi had overdosed from a heroin-and-cocaine speedball more than a decade earlier.

Celebrity photographer Ron Davis and a fellow photographer, Miranda, were just finishing their regular late-night round of clubs checking for celebrities when they saw River Phoenix collapsed on the sidewalk. They walked up to help and were standing directly over him trying to see who he was.

As Phoenix came out of the first seizure he saw Davis and Miranda towering over him, their four cameras hanging down from their shoulders. He looked up, appearing trapped and terrified that the game was finally up and he would now be captured on film for the whole world to see. He turned to Mathis and Leaf and gasped his last words: "No paparazzi. I want anonymity." And sank back into unconsciousness.

Ed, the Viper Room doorman, saw him collapse again and yelled for someone to call an ambulance. Leaf Phoenix kept saying, "He'll be all right, he's fine." Still trying to respect his brother's wishes.

As River went into a second seizure his sister Rain suddenly came out of the club. When she saw him shaking uncontrollably she threw herself on top of him to stop him. She tried to give her brother mouth-to-mouth resuscitation as he flailed on the ground. At the third seizure, Ron Davis, who never attempted to take a photograph, ran into Turner's liquor store on the corner of Larabie and Sunset Boulevard and dialed 911. When he came out, Leaf had also dialed for an ambulance at 1:10 A.M.

"My brother's having seizures," screamed Leaf as his sister still lay over River and an hysterical Mathis paced up and down the sidewalk where River was lying. "You must get over here, *please. You must get over here, please,*" he pleaded. When the dispatcher attempted to calm him down, telling him to "take it easy," Leaf said, "Now I'm thinking he's had Valium or something. You must get here, please, because he's dying."

While Phoenix was going in and out of seizures, the late-night Halloween partyers walked up and down Sunset, gazing down at his body, staring. At one point two girls walked by in Halloween witches costumes, saw the dying River Phoenix and one said, "Oh, God. Gross."

Christina Applegate, from the television show "Married . . . with Children," came out of the Viper Room, looked down at River and then walked over to the corner, where she burst into tears.

After making his 911 call, Leaf put his arm around River and desperately started to try to reassure his elder brother that he was going to be all right. At one point he angrily snapped at Mathis when she asked him a question.

"He was like a fish out of water, flapping around the sidewalk like a guppy," said Ron Davis. "It was almost like his body was possessed. His legs and arms were all over the place while his knuckles and the back of his head kept hitting the sidewalk hard."

The seizures lasted fifteen to twenty seconds each and after each one there would be a terrible silence. Davis found himself praying for the next seizure because at least it would show that Phoenix was still alive. Finally, after eight minutes of seizures, which seemed an eternity, River Phoenix lay still. Terrified that his brother had died, Leaf shouted, "Oh my God, he's not breathing."

By the time the paramedics arrived at 1:14 A.M. River Phoenix had gone into cardiac arrest with no signs of a pulse or blood pressure. Paramedic Ray Ribar of the Los Angeles County Fire Department began to administer CPR and was told by someone at the scene that the actor had been "speedballing." Mathis, Rain and Leaf would later deny any knowledge of Phoenix using drugs, with Samantha claiming that someone had given him Valium in the club to calm him down because he had been acting strangely.

Soon after the ambulance came, Abby and Dickie Rude arrived at the Viper Room to find River lying motionless on the sidewalk with the paramedics still working on him. Finally word of what was going on filtered into the Viper Room to Flea, who immediately ran outside to help his friend as he was being lifted into the ambulance.

"I'm going with him!" the bassist yelled, and tried to jump into the back but was told if he wanted to go he had to travel in the front. Finally the ambulance drove off on the two-mile journey to Cedars-Sinai Medical Center, leaving Mathis and Rain waiting helplessly on the sidewalk and Leaf banging his head against a wall.

By the time he arrived at Cedars-Sinai, River's skin was dark blue but his body was still warm. Emergency room physicians battled to revive him, even inserting a pacemaker to stimulate his heart. But it was too late. At 1:51 on the morning of Halloween, River Phoenix was pronounced dead by Dr. Paul Silka.

Word spread fast. Within minutes Iris Burton and Sky Sworski were at the hospital to start taking care of matters. As soon as Heart Phoenix heard she jumped in a car and drove straight to Gainesville Airport to get the first connecting flight to Los Angeles. A profoundly distraught John Phoenix and his fifteen-year-old daughter Summer were also on their way from Costa Rica to join the rest of the family.

When news of River's death reached the wire services, TV stations and newspapers, it caused an explosion. City editors were in no doubt that his death had all the ingredients of the biggest Hollywood tragedy in years. They dispatched crews to the hospital and to Gainesville for the beginning of a month-long media feeding frenzy.

When Samantha Mathis turned up at the hospital and demanded to see River's body, a nurse took her to the emergency room to view it. But by the time L.A. homicide Detective Sergeant Mike Lee arrived at Cedars-Sinai, River's friends and family had all gone and were on their way back to Gainesville. They would later decline to furnish any further information about what had happened at the Viper Room.

River's body was taken to the morgue for an autopsy later that Sunday. Heart Phoenix arrived and demanded possession of her son's body to take back to Florida. After being told that was not possible until after the autopsy, she left.

The next day Heart made it clear through her attorney, Eric Greenspan, that the family did not want to see anyone prosecuted for supplying River with drugs.

"The bottom line was the family didn't want anyone to go to jail who was participating with River in ingesting the drugs," said Detective Sergeant Lee. "They said that if it was an overdose of drugs then so be it."

John Phoenix said that he did initially consider turning in the musician who had given River the deadly speedball but decided against it:

"What good would it serve?" he said nine months after his son's death, as reported in the British newspaper *Today*. "It would have meant going through maybe two years of litigation in another media-hyped court case. We didn't want that, and River wouldn't have wanted it either."

Heart's public-relations person, Susan Patricola, issued a statement not mentioning drugs. But it was too late. When reporters, puzzled about how a healthy twenty-three-year-old could just collapse and die on the sidewalk, caught up with paramedic Ray Ribar he revealed:

"It was the classic cocaine overreaction," Captain Ribar told reporters, as carried in the New York *Daily News*. "It just nails some people and stops the heart. We had been told by the people with him that he had been taking drugs."

Within a few hours of his death all possible witnesses were back in Micanopy and refusing to answer questions from homicide detectives. When Detective Sergeant Lee contacted them he was told firmly but politely that the family would appreciate time to grieve before talking to police.

Less than two hours after River's death a tearful Iris Burton started dealing with the catastrophic effects of Phoenix's death on the film he was making. She telephoned George Sluizer at 3:00 A.M. to give him the news and asked for the home phone numbers of the other *Dark Blood* producers.

"I thought I was having a nightmare," said Sluizer. "Iris was quite short on the phone and she was crying. It was the most shocking and horrible thing I had ever heard. I broke down crying."

Months later, director Bill Richert would describe River Phoenix's death as "mysterious" as his life.

"River died in front of the Viper Club on Halloween under a full moon. Those are dark circumstances."

## Chapter Twenty-four

# FALLOUT

IF RIVER PHOENIX had spent his off-screen life trying to keep out of the spotlight and avoid publicity, his death provided the ultimate irony. On Monday, November 1, the tabloid and the mainstream press converged to give massive coverage of the young actor's still-unexplained death. The death of legendary Italian director Federico Fellini, who had passed away the same day as Phoenix after a long time in a coma, went largely unnoticed, the huge banner headlines devoted to Phoenix.

Leaf Phoenix's 911 call was played and replayed on almost every news show around the world. In the hours following Phoenix's collapse on "this cold Hollywood sidewalk"—as it was described by Los Angeles' KNBC-TV on Monday—came a wave of media coverage that would anoint River Phoenix as the "James Dean of his time." There were endless images of distraught fans, flowers, candles and cards. The sidewalk outside the Viper Room became an instant shrine as River's young fans camped out there to show solidarity in their grief. There had not been such a display of grief in Hollywood since the death of Rudolph Valentino nearly seventy years earlier.

The *Variety* columnist Army Archerd, attempting to put River's death into some perspective, wrote: "There hasn't been anything this catastrophic since . . . James Dean, Natalie Wood."

The Phoenix family issued a statement: "Our heartfelt thanks

258

goes out to all of you who have been a friend and support to our darling son, brother, grandson and lover, River, who lives on in all of our lives. His beauty, gentleness, compassion, vulnerability and love is a gift for all eternity.''

And River's publicist Susan Patricola told reporters: ''It comes as a total shock that this extraordinarily talented young man's life would end so abruptly. It's just tragic.''

From the beginning there was speculation in the media that Phoenix had overdosed. Phoenix's clean-cut image began to unravel. Leaf Phoenix's 911 mention of Valium and L.A. County Sheriff's Department spokeswoman Diane Hecht's comment that River had been ''acting strange'' fueled the fire.

That River Phoenix was such a well-publicized figure of clean-living vegetarianism and an environmentalist only made it a bigger story—the classic case of a pure soul being corrupted by the Sodom of Hollywood. At first the rumors that Phoenix had been taking drugs were contemptuously dismissed by friends and business associates. When questioned about drugs playing a part in Phoenix's death Patricola replied: ''We don't have any comment.'' A little later she released a second statement, saying: ''We've heard these last few days many theories and much speculation surrounding the death of River Phoenix. We may never know why we have lost this extraordinary young talent. We, his family and friends, would like to remember him as he was: giving, caring, hoping and forever.''

On Monday night the syndicated tabloid show ''Hard Copy'' reported, after obtaining Cedars-Sinai Emergency Room reports, that Phoenix had died from a drug overdose. This was immediately denied by the hospital. The same night ''A Current Affair'' played Leaf's five-minute 911 call. From then on it was open season. In Los Angeles, Channel Nine started linking River's death with the new designer drug gamma hydroxybutyric acid, popularly known as GHB, which had become the ''in'' drug for the Hollywood nightclub scene.

Closing down the Viper Room until further notice out of respect for the dead star, Johnny Depp, who had not known Phoenix well, issued a statement: "This is a tragedy—I feel deep sympathy for his family and friends."

On Monday, after a two-hour autopsy proved "inconclusive," the L.A. coroner's office said it could be up to six weeks before the results of drug- and alcohol-screening tests would be known.

By Tuesday Phoenix's death was being seen in a broader light and many newspapers printed appreciations of his work. The New York *Times* devoted four columns to the young actor's death with a story titled "Death of River Phoenix Jolts the Movie Industry." The producers of *Dark Blood* announced that the project had been abandoned since it was impossible to complete without River, and many actors started calling the producers of *Interview with the Vampire* to check about the auditions for Phoenix's role.

In the days following his death people hotly debated whether the actor often called Mr. Granola could really have been a junkie. Right-wing radio talk-show host Rush Limbaugh commented: "From the moment his death was discovered, you would have thought the President of the United States has been assassinated here . . . that we've lost some great contributor to the social and human condition. This guy . . . look at his name. River Phoenix. He's the son of a couple of whacked-out hippies."

His female fans went into mourning, and the gay movement felt it had lost an icon. Millions of people felt disbelief that the cleanest-cut star in Hollywood could have been dabbling with the very drugs he so often preached against. In America there was an immediate run on the Blockbuster chain of video stores for all of Phoenix's videos, and across the Atlantic, Serena Gilbert, a pupil of Cheney School, Oxford, England, told the *Sunday Times* that her classmates had taken their idol's death very hard indeed:

"Some feel as though a lover has been taken away from them," she said. "Phoenix was the boy most girls wanted to have as a boyfriend."

In the tabloid press on both sides of the Atlantic the "tarnished star" was being built up as the next James Dean, whose films

Phoenix had never seen and comparison with whom he rejected. Wrote the London *Sun:* "In an eerie parallel with James Dean— the young 'rebel without a cause,' who died in 1955 aged just twenty-four—River's life and untimely death have captured the imagination of America's youth. The similarities between River's death and that of James Dean are impossible to miss. Both lived life in the fast lane and died young. Both shared the same dark, brooding intensity. Both were tragically cut down in the prime of life."

When the cast and crew of *Dark Blood* reported to the set the Monday after Phoenix's death, an emotional George Sluizer asked them to form a large circle around him so he could pay tribute. Many of River's colleagues were near tears as Jonathan Pryce asked them to join hands to wish River's spirit a happy journey.

"I felt very uncomfortable with all that," Judy Davis told reporters in Premiere magazine in October, 1994. "I didn't want to hold hands, I don't believe in spirits passing. But I didn't have a choice, so I wished that I'd not gone into the studio. I don't like to be forced to be dishonest. I think it has to be remembered in the midst of all this that he was twenty-three and he made the choice. He thought he was immune, I think. There's something about stardom and the way it empowers people, the way people give these stars such power."

Back in Gainesville, Phoenix's family and friends tried to make sense out of his death. For the first few days there was a lot of reminiscing as friends visited Micanopy to pay their respects to the family. A few nights after Phoenix's death, soon after his body had been released by the L.A. coroner's office to make its journey home to Micanopy, his parents and their closest friends held their own wake. Some of those closest to River, including Bobby Bukowski and Sue Solgot, were seated around the kitchen table to remember River over a bottle of John Phoenix's favorite Gentleman Jack whiskey. Suddenly in the midst of their laughter a glass tumbler shattered for no reason. A little later, while Solgot was doing the washing up, three more tumblers shattered simultaneously, convincing everyone that it was River the joker having the last laugh.

"When he died I was surprised—but not *really* surprised," said Solgot. "It was like I knew it would happen. I just felt it. I'm sure it wasn't suicide or anything like that. He had so much to live for, there was so much he wanted to do.

"He had just finished filming and he got to L.A. and everyone around him was crazy. Having been so good and healthy, he thought he would go wild."

Another night Heart told Abby Rude about a vision she had a couple of nights after his death in which River had bargained with God about being born.

"We were upset," said Abby. "We were thinking that when his soul entered his body he made a deal with God that he'd be here for a certain amount of years and then he'd go. Because he didn't really want to come here in the first place. He told God that he would rather remain up there with him. River finally agreed to come here, do as much good as he could, and then go. And God said, 'Right, you go for fifty years.' And River's like, 'No way. I'm going for ten.' God then asked him for thirty years. Eventually they agreed on twenty-three because there are twenty-three chromosomes in the body."

On their return to Gainesville the family refused to talk to the press. As the world clamored for an explanation of what had happened to River Phoenix, they locked themselves away in Micanopy to grieve. The only family member who did initially speak to the press was Phoenix's grandmother Margaret Dunetz, who was then silenced.

"He was such a terrific kid, sweet and lovable," said Ms. Dunetz. "He's natural. He watches his weight. He watches what he eats. He doesn't eat meat. He's gentle. It's a mystery."

Friends who knew Phoenix as a tireless campaigner for the environment and a serious musician who often performed at charity benefits could not believe the junkie image of him that was now being painted by the media.

"The hardest drink I ever saw him drink was carrot juice," said Dan Mathews, director of international campaigns for PETA.

Jim Kesl of the Coney Island restaurant said he found it hard to believe what happened:

"I knew River as a vegetarian trying to take care of his body," said Kesl. "The tabloids just focused on the drug culture and I found that really frustrating, there was so much more to him. The people who really knew him, not as a Hollywood star but as a person, were very hurt by the distorted coverage.

"River was not in the gutter and there had to be some event that pushed him too far. He was an incredibly sensitive man with all this stuff churning about inside. There was so much sensitivity that it had to blow sometime. Like a steam valve, it's got to be released."

The family's grief and coming to terms with his death was not made easier by the unrelenting glare of the world's media. Packs of reporters descended on Gainesville looking for stories to feed public curiosity. Anyone who was even slightly acquainted with River Phoenix was grist for the news mill. There was also bad feeling among his friends when some peddled their "exclusive" stories for cash.

The night before Phoenix's cremation, according to Dirk Drake, someone with access to the Milam Funeral Home, where the body was lying, sneaked in and rearranged the corpse in a chilling pose before taking a photograph that was sold to the *National Enquirer* for $5,000.

As more facts about the life of River Phoenix were revealed, John and Heart Phoenix's deep distrust of the press seemed to be confirmed. Overnight all River Phoenix's philanthropic work and deeply held beliefs were forgotten as their son became a sensationalized Hollywood drug casualty. In a media savaging, River

Phoenix, who had once publicly endorsed Nancy Reagan's "Just Say No" antidrug campaign, was now branded a hypocrite and a junkie.

Many writers played amateur analyst as they attempted to discover how Phoenix had become what England's *Mail on Sunday* called "a Cocaine Zombie." In the article, River's tutor Dirk Drake came to his defense, observing, "Before Hollywood took him away he was known as a deeply concerned and passionate young man. He spoke out against drugs and lectured to our local school drama group. Drugs were never any part of his scene."

Josh Greenbaum almost lost control when he saw the tabloids in Orlando airport. "I was this close to setting the newsstand on fire," said Greenbaum. "There was a lot of misinformation and bullshit. The media thrives on that."

Over the next few weeks hundreds of heartbroken fans made the pilgrimage to Gainesville to visit the Hardback and the Coney Island.

"It was weird," said barmaid Rachel Guinan. "People wanted to come in and look at this place with all the ripped couches and mismatched chairs like it was some glorious tribute to River."

Phoenix's body, dressed in his blue Aleka's Attic T-shirt, lay in a blue coffin. His favorite necklaces and beads hung around his neck, and his long hair, which had been cut for *Dark Blood,* was placed next to his head in a ponytail. Sixty relatives and friends attended a final viewing before the cremation. The ashes were placed in an urn and returned to Micanopy.

It was a clear sunny day in the seventies when more than two hundred fifty guests trooped to Micanopy for the memorial service held under a large oak tree in the garden the Thursday following his death. Some, like his show-business friends Dan Aykroyd and Keanu Reeves, came down the tree-lined country road in limousines; others came in beat-up pick-ups; still others walked from neighboring farms, weeping openly as they arrived.

There were music friends Flea and Michael Stipe, singer of the group R.E.M., and the three young women in Phoenix's life—Martha Plimpton, Sue Solgot and Samantha Mathis. Other long-time friends of the family arrived with tents, pitching them alongside the house and staying for weeks after the service.

Heart had tried to keep the memorial service private, but word of Dan Aykroyd's arrival at Gainesville Airport alerted the media, which converged on the house.

When Bill DeYoung of the Gainesville *Sun* called the house he was surprised to be put straight through to Heart Phoenix.

"She was incredibly strong," said DeYoung. "She told me that River had been chosen by the greatest director of all—the Creator."

Heart gave DeYoung a ten-minute taped interview on the condition that she could edit her final quotes for the story. When DeYoung called back later he kept getting a taped message, saying, "Pray for us. We're out under the tree."

Finally, with his deadline fast approaching, DeYoung managed to reach Cindy, the Phoenixes' housekeeper, who summoned Heart to the phone.

Said DeYoung, "I could hear people in the background. I started reading Heart her quotes and she immediately stopped me, saying, 'I really sound stupid.' Then she put me on the speakerphone and it felt like the whole family was listening. It was spooky. When I got to the part of their childhood and I mentioned Children of God, Heart stopped me. 'We don't want our name anywhere near the Children of God,' she said. Then she [added], 'Oh no, we don't want that. Take it out.' "

At the service Heart told the mourners, who were gathered around her in a large circle, that her son was "a very spiritual young man."

"He was born very privately in a log cabin near Grizzly Mountain, Oregon, without even a doctor, without anyone even touching him but me and my husband.

"When he left they didn't even let me near him. They had him in a morgue. I couldn't even see him until he got to Gainesville. I couldn't even see him. I'm his mother. I think we have the right to hold him . . . the way he was held by me and my husband.''

Heart finished by telling the mourners that she still felt connected to his energy.

"When the wind blows I see River," she said. "When the sun shines I see River, when I look in someone's eyes and make a connection I see River. To have death transformed into another way to look at life is his huge gift.''

One by one the members of the extended Phoenix family and his friends stood up to pay tribute to him. "He was my brother and I loved him a great deal,'' said Michael Stipe. "It was just an awful, awful mistake. We fed off each other and learned a lot from each other.''

"Everyone was talking about River and his life and what the family had meant to them,'' said Kenny Greenbaum. "When it came my turn I felt like I had eaten a magic mushroom. I was watching the family across the circle. I thought of what my mother used to say to me as a youngster, that blood is thicker than water. In other words, your loyalty should be to your family before your friends. And looking at them made me realize you can love your friends even more than you love your family. And to me love is thicker than blood. And that's what I said.''

Many eulogized the dead actor by representing his horrible death as nothing less than the divine progression of a pure soul, too perfect for this sordid world, to a higher plane. And many of his friends felt a deep guilt that they had not been able to save him from himself.

"He's already being made into a martyr,'' his first love Martha Plimpton told writer Tad Friend. "He's become a metaphor for a fallen angel, a messiah. He wasn't. He was just a boy, a very good-hearted boy who was very fucked up and had no idea how to implement his good intentions. I don't want to be comforted by his death. I think it's right that I'm angry about it, angry at the people who helped him stay sick, and angry at River.''

One week later, on November 12, the coroner's report was released showing Phoenix had ingested eight times the lethal dose of cocaine; four times the lethal dose of heroin as well as traces of marijuana, Valium and ephedrine, the last an over-the-counter cold medication. Scott Carrier of the L.A. coroner's office gave the cause of death as "acute multiple drug intoxication," and ruled it accidental. No needle marks were found on the body and the sheriff's department closed the book on the investigation.

But if River Phoenix's friends, who had supplied him with the heroin and cocaine that night, thought they could breathe more easily, they were mistaken. Detective Sergeant Mike Lee said that murder charges could still be brought if the supplier was ever found—even if River had taken the drugs voluntarily.

"It will be a matter if people come forward and do the right thing," said Lee. "But for some reason in these situations, people who know often turn around and defend the person who supplied it. Because they just want it to go away."

The following day's newspapers carried headlines like "Phoenix Died of 'Belushi' O.D." and "River Mixed Belushi Recipe," drawing the obvious parallels to comedian John Belushi's death in 1982. With Phoenix's drug use now documented, those close to him could no longer deny the facts and tried to put his death into some kind of meaningful perspective.

"Hopefully, it's a wake-up call to the world," said Susan Patricola. "It leaves you to question why young people are compelled to do this. I could only surmise what everyone else could surmise. People talk about him having such a clean life. I think that's not right . . . He didn't die from carrot juice."

Iris Burton commented on the "Hollywood forces that tempt—occasionally destroy—someone so beautiful. I don't know what changes them," said the agent. "Even I wasn't aware. Do you think I didn't love this boy? I thought he was acting funny, but I thought that was part of being an actor." Adding that she did not want to "glorify" his death, she added: "I'm in the same amount of pain no matter how he died. We're all really in enough pain that he passed away.''

Almost as soon as the coroner's court released its results, accusatory fingers began to be pointed both inside and outside the Phoenix family. One of the first to be blamed was Abby Rude, who had been his close friend and confidante as well as secretary during the final two months of his life. Soon after the memorial service, Heart gave Abby a one-way ticket to England.

"After River's death the relationship between Heart and myself was different,'' said Rude, who strongly denies ever giving drugs to Phoenix. "There were people who sought to blame me and thought I could have done something. They were putting pressure on her [Heart] to get rid of me. We sat down and Heart said that I'd better go away because she was under pressure that I was still here.''

John Phoenix, who had seen tragedy coming for so long, was also held responsible for his son's death by many around the family who blamed his drinking for leading River down the path to destruction.

"Sure,'' says John Phoenix. "We all feel guilt. Everyone who knew River. Not a day goes by when I don't think long and hard about River's death and ask myself why.''

Dirk Drake says that John Phoenix was perhaps the hardest hit by his son's death and was unfairly singled out for blame.

"A lot of people would like to blame John but I can't,'' says Drake. "John's drinking has been exaggerated and used to pinpoint River's strong passions. His passion to live fully he inherited from his father but did that lead to uncontrollable substance abuse? In a minor way, yeah. In a major way there's more to it than that to explain the extreme indulgence that led to his death outside the Viper Room.

"I think fame and pressure were to blame. He wasn't built for it at all. There were others who were extremely savvy that allowed his progress in the industry to take place."

Director Gus Van Sant was also blamed after it was reported that Phoenix had first tried heroin during the making of *My Own Private Idaho*. Still staunchly denying any knowledge of drugs on *Idaho*, Van Sant said River's death was an unfortunate mistake.

"River had been working hard on *Dark Blood* and there were a lot of politics and ego-clashing happening on the set that really got to him," said Van Sant. "Though he wasn't new to wild partying, I really don't think the overdose was a result of addiction. It was an isolated incident, like at a frat party when someone goes overboard."

River's lifelong friend from the Children of God, Jonathan Sherman, has no doubt where the ultimate blame for his death lay.

"I saw River coming to grief," said Sherman. "Anybody that does drugs has pain and I think River had a lot of stuff from his days in the Children of God that surfaced later on. He had a lot of pain and he was searching for happiness which was why he was so involved in drugs."

Sherman's mother and Heart Phoenix's friend, Bithia Sherman, tells of how she arrived home a few years ago to find another son had overdosed and was close to death.

"He was in a coma," said Bithia. "The doctors had to zap him three times to get a heartbeat. The doctors said he was very close to suffering irreversible brain damage."

Her son, who survived and made a complete recovery, later told Bithia why he had wanted to die.

"It all went back to the Children of God," said Bithia. "His pain was so great, his distress so overwhelming, that he just could not see a way out."

## Chapter Twenty-five

# SMELLS LIKE TEEN SPIRIT

ON WEDNESDAY, NOVEMBER 24, the Los Angeles *Times* printed an intimate letter from Heart Phoenix to the public to explain her son's death from the family's perspective. After almost a month-long barrage of bad publicity she felt it was time to state her case.

Headed "A Mother's Note on her Son's Life and Death by Heart Phoenix," it read:

> I think people want to know if River ran his course or if he was taken from the world prematurely.
>
> River was my first born. He introduced me to motherhood and has been the strongest influence on my life. I feel blessed to have been the woman who held him deep within my being as he grew from a tiny seed. I birthed him at home, suckled him to a chubby two-year-old and then held him in love and awe until his safe passage on October 31.
>
> It was incredible to watch River grow. From the beginning, he was a soul filled with passion and a sense of service for others. At a young age he took on the responsibility of sharing the wonderful gifts that were given to him. He diligently taught himself guitar at four, sang on the streets from Venezuela to Westwood, Calif., and wrote music and lyrics seeking to open hearts in a new way.
>
> Many of you have been able to experience his openness,

gentleness, beauty and vulnerability on the screen. He chose characters that reached inside the souls of the audience, awakening long-forgotten feelings. With River's passing, people the world over have been touched by the loss and once again their deep feelings have surfaced.

The coroner's report states that drugs were the cause of death. His friends, co-workers and the rest of our family know that River was not a regular drug user. He lived at home in Florida with us and was almost never a part of the club scene in Los Angeles. He had just arrived in L.A. from the pristine beauty and quietness of Utah, where he was filming for six weeks. We feel that the excitement and energy of the Halloween nightclub and party scene were way beyond his usual experience and control. How many other beautiful young souls, who remain anonymous to us, have died by using drugs recreationally? It is my prayer that River's leaving in this way will focus the attention of the world on how painfully the spirits of his generation are being worn down.

They are growing up with polluted air, toxic earth and food, and undrinkable water. We are destroying our forests, the ozone layer is being depleted, and AIDS and other diseases are epidemic. The world is a very confusing place for most people and we need to address that. Drug abuse is a symptom of an unfeeling, materialistic, success-oriented world where the feelings and creativity of young people are not seen as important. Drugs, including alcohol, are used to soften the pain of feeling separated from ourselves, each other and love. We can't just say "Just Say No"—it's ridiculous—we need to offer our children something they can say "yes" to.

I have been trying to make sense out of the chaos in relation to the world situation for many years, and with River's passing I feel more clear than ever before. I feel the answer to our destructive nature, which manifests itself in many forms and our inability to love and care for one another, is based on our disconnection from every natural part of who we are. The universe and the earth is a magnificent system of oceans, tributaries and streams; of electrons, atoms, microorganisms, plants and animals; of plankton, moss and trees. And we, the humans, believe we can stand apart from this living system and say we are the masters. We act as if all of this was put here for us to use, abuse and profit from. We have separated ourselves from the very essence of life in order to raise ourselves up as the ultimate divine expression on Earth.

River made such a big impression during his life on Earth. He found his voice and found his place. And even River, who had the whole world at his fingertips to listen, felt deep frustration that no one heard. What is it going to take? Chernobyl wasn't enough. *Exxon Valdez* wasn't enough. A bloody war over oil wasn't enough. If River's passing opens our global heart, then I say, thanks dear, beloved son, for yet another gift to all of us.

The day after Heart Phoenix's letter appeared, 150 people gathered at a screening room at Paramount Studios for the Hollywood memorial service for her son. This second memorial service was for River Phoenix's friends in the business: fellow actors, directors, crew members.

Actress Christine Lahti, who played his mother in *Running on Empty*, was overcome by emotion, and veteran actor Sidney Poitier was visibly shaken as he described his young friend as "incandescent." Rob Reiner, the director who had given Phoenix his big break in *Stand By Me*, urged Hollywood to start facing up to its responsibilities to ensure that child actors and their families were better counselled on how to handle the dangers of stardom.

With the audience on the verge of despair, Heart Phoenix walked to the stage and like a mother telling a story, beckoned the mourners to come nearer. Reiner grasped Heart's hand in support as she began to speak.

"We believed we could use the mass media to help change the

world,'' she told the mourners. ''And that River would be our missionary.''

She then recounted her vision of how God had bargained with River to spend twenty-three years on Earth. Her performance was spellbinding and when she finished the audience remained seated in stunned silence. Later, film director Alan Moyle's wife Diana Moran, who had lost her own mother when she was twelve, came over to Heart to embrace her and said: ''You know, you are the mother I wish I could have had.'' Without missing a beat, Heart turned to her and replied, ''Diana, I am your mother.''

''I was moved to tears,'' said Alan Moyle. ''Heart made that moment work.''

During the emotional testimonials in which his friends and associates spoke of him like a gallant hero fallen in battle, British director John Boorman, who was sitting at the corner of the stage, was getting restless that no one was quite facing the reality of the actor's tragic death. At one point Boorman could no longer contain his frustration and shouted out: ''Is there anybody here who can tell us why River took all those drugs?''

There was an embarrassing silence that was punctuated by Liberty and Summer Phoenix running out of the room. Even before Heart could answer, Phoenix's girlfriend, Samantha Mathis, who had been with him when he died, bravely stood up in the front row to try to explain.

''River was so sensitive,'' she began. ''He had so much compassion for everyone and everything that he had a weight on his heart. He was obsessive. When he wanted to eat artichokes he would eat ten at a time. He did everything to that degree.''

Casting director Mali Finn, who had never known River Phoenix and had come as a friend of Iris Burton, also felt compelled to speak.

''Hollywood is such an unreal world,'' she said. ''There's a danger. On a set you're living in other worlds and in this town one movie can change a lifestyle. Children lose their childhood if they live in this city because adults have them acting like little adults going to auditions. A child's world in theater should be one of play. It shouldn't be one of business. I think they are pushed too fast into adulthood and they can't cope with all the things that are thrown at them so early on.''

Finn, who spent fifteen years as a teacher before entering the film industry, says making those vital transitions from child star to teen star and then on to adult star are freighted with pressures and insecurities.

"I think escapes are the obvious outlet,'' she said. "Young people think they're invulnerable and nothing is going to happen to them. There's almost that attitude that you've got to experience life. You get into drugs to feel that artistic vision.''

A few months later Heart Phoenix would answer Boorman's poignant question, telling writer Tad Friend that the director had raised a valid point.

"It's what everyone was thinking,'' said Heart. "Why, when you're living this dream, when you can have any car, any house, any girl, you're so famous—why? The only understanding I can come to is that River knew the Earth was dying and that he was ready to give his passing as a sign.''

Heart Phoenix's attempts to portray her son as a martyr were ridiculed by many in Hollywood who saw her as a naïve throwback to the hippie sixties. Her letter was greeted with derision by such as syndicated conservative journalist Mona Charen, who criticized Heart in a tough, some might say mean-spirited, commentary printed in the New York *Post:*

"We are all accustomed to the bereaved families of drug abusers finding meaning in the deaths of their loved ones by dedicating themselves to the fight against drug abuse,'' wrote Charen.

"At first, it looked as though Heart Phoenix was headed in that direction. But then Ms. Phoenix veered immediately into the Never-Never Land of left-wing kookiness.''

After recounting Heart's list of human and environmental tragedies, Charen wrote: "Oh dear. So that's how it is. Young people in Hollywood night clubs are not indulging in drugs because they lack self-control. They aren't drowning their poor self-esteem in a bath of hallucinogens. No, they are making a statement about ozone depletion.''

Charen rounded off her comment with: ''The notion that large forces like global warming and pollution are responsible for individual actions is exactly the kind of thinking that unhinged this country during the 1960s. River Phoenix was an adult, responsible for his actions. Leave aside the stupid ozone hole. Phoenix did a terrible, ghastly thing by polluting his own brain with chemicals— to say nothing of the example he set.''

River Phoenix's death catapulted him into the unwitting figurehead for Generation X—the new media tag for the children of the sixties baby-boomer parents. The grunged-out existential Generation X, it is said, has few expectations of the world, seeing it as a bleak place awash with rampant crime, pollution and AIDS. Where the hippies, like the Phoenix parents, had indulged themselves to celebrate life, their children took drugs to get ''blunted'' and numb themselves from the horrors around them.

John Phoenix blames the death of his son on the Hollywood groupies and hangers-on who use drugs as a means to get near the young stars.

''River was a very brilliant, beautiful child who would do no harm to anyone,'' says John. ''But he was rather gullible. He wanted to please everyone. Okay, River was an adult, and he should have known what he was doing. But he was an innocent among some of the Hollywood sewer rats.

''And it was, 'River can I get you this? River, try that. Let's drive there, do this crazy thing.' Don't get me wrong, he had a crazy side, too, but these people were something else. It started to take him over. There are so many assholes who cater for your every need. There were times when people should have said, 'No, River, actually it's late, I'm tired and so are you.' ''

John Phoenix bitterly regrets that he had not gone to Los Angeles to make sure River stayed sober after leaving Utah.

''If I'd been in Hollywood with him last October, he would

never have died,'' John told *Today*. ''He would never have even gone to that club. I'm not saying I could have run his life—he was twenty-three, his own man—but he listened to what I had to say and respected it.''

River Phoenix's terrible death now thrust him into the very Hollywood fast lane he had detested. Entertainment Weekly featured him in an issue investigating ''Drugs and Young Hollywood.''

''River Phoenix may have been unlucky but he wasn't unusual,'' began the article, which started on the cover with his picture. ''In clubs and in cars, at home and at work, young stars are doing drugs like there's no tomorrow. Heroin. Cocaine. Marijuana, LSD. Valium. GHB. Ecstasy. Here's a hard look at the underside of the high life.''

River Phoenix's dramatic death soon became glamorized as disillusioned young people the world over made him their hero.

But although ''River may have been a role model for Generation X he wasn't a player in that crowd,'' said Abby Rude. ''He was definitely not into the club scene and was not part of that Hollywood fast set.''

In the wake of his death reporters converged on the Sunset Strip to discover, as People magazine did, that ''Despite River Phoenix's death, the party goes on.''

Viper Room owner Johnny Depp bore the brunt of the accusations that his club, which took its name from 1920s slang for smoking marijuana, was a center of the drug trade. Depp defended his club, saying: ''It's a ridiculous accusation. I was there and it happened at the club, or outside the club, yes,'' said Depp to the New York *Post*. ''But as far as the drugs and the unfortunate death of River Phoenix, and that nightclub, they aren't connected, even remotely.''

The spot where Phoenix died outside the Viper Club became something of a shrine to his memory. ''Since River died everybody wants to come here,'' says Adam Khan, who manages Turner's liquor store next to the Viper Room. "People were coming and staying all night for weeks after he died."

Among the loving tributes to Phoenix scrawled on the wall outside the Viper Room was one saying, "River. Thanks for opening my eyes. Dreams will never die. We love you River. You'll be missed." Another read: "River, we pray for God to take you to heaven where the Lord will take care of you forever." And a third one: "River, I love you. Don't do drugs in heaven. Love Sara."

Six months after River Phoenix's death, Kurt Cobain, the charismatic frontman of the grunge band Nirvana, killed himself with a shotgun in his Seattle mansion. Samantha Mathis, who was a friend of the young musician, was with Dirk Drake in Los Angeles when she heard the news.

"It reminded her of River," said Drake. "She took it very hard and people were very concerned for her.

Although River Phoenix had never met Kurt Cobain they did move in the same circles and shared many of the same friends. R.E.M. singer Michael Stipe was very close to both of them and has dedicated an album, *Monster,* to River's memory. Butthole Surfers member Gibby Haynes had been in rehab with Cobain a few months prior to his death and should have jammed on stage at the Viper Room with Phoenix on that fateful night.

A year after River's death the Phoenix family have picked up the pieces of their lives in Micanopy. Heart Phoenix and Iris Burton still oversee the film careers of Rain and Leaf, who are attempting to become stars, if in the shadow of their famous brother. In early 1994 Rain starred in Gus Van Sant's movie *Even Cowgirls Sing the Blues.* Leaf, who is starring in Van Sant's next film and is considered the family's main hope of approaching River's success, already seems to be feeling the pressure of the movie business. When Leaf met River's friend Mike Parker on the *Cowgirls* set soon after his death, the nineteen-year-old seemed despondent about his acting career.

"He said he found it hard seeing himself getting any work in the shadow of his brother's success," said Parker. "Leaf seemed very worried about whether he was going to get work because of River or because of his own talent."

Since his son's death John Phoenix has stayed in his Costa Rica hideaway to grieve alone. Having seen his worst fears realized, John withdrew into himself. Concerned friends worried for him as he felt the full impact of his beloved son's death descend upon him.

John Phoenix, one might say, has seen his family's twenty-five-year-old saga come full circle, confiding that it might even be best if the family got out of the pressure-cooker of Hollywood and once again were innocently panhandling on the streets of Westwood, true to their ideals and beliefs.

# FILMOGRAPHY

*Television*

**Seven Brides for Seven Brothers** (MGM/UA Entertainment Ltd. and David Gerber, 1982–1983) Television adaption of the 1954 MGM musical broadcast on NBC from September 19, 1982 to March 23, 1983.

|  |  |
|---|---|
| Guthrie | River Phoenix |
| Hannah | Terri Treas |
| Adam | Richard Dean Anderson |
| Daniel | Roger Wilson |

**Celebrity** (NBC, 1984) Screenplay by William Hanley, directed by Paul Wendkos, produced by Rosilyn Heller and Richard L. O'Connor, director of photography, Philip Lathrop.

|  |  |
|---|---|
| Mac Crawford | Joseph Bottoms |
| Calvin Sledge | Hal Holbrook |
| T. J. Lowther | Michael Beck |
| Jeffie (aged 11) | River Phoenix |

**It's Your Move** (NBC, 1984) River Phoenix briefly appeared as Brian with just one line of dialogue in this TV pilot.

**Hotel** (ABC) River Phoenix appeared in one episode of the series starring James Brolin.

**Backwards: The Riddle of Dyslexia** (1984 after-school educational TV special)

|  |  |
|---|---|
| Brian Ellsworth | River Phoenix |

**Robert Kennedy and His Times** (CBS, 1985) Played Robert Kennedy as a boy in this three-part TV drama.

|  |  |
|---|---|
| Robert Kennedy | Brad Davis |
| Ethel Kennedy | Veronica Cartwright |
| Joseph Kennedy, Sr. | Jack Warden |
| Kathleen | Shannon Doherty |
| Robert Kennedy as a boy | River Phoenix |

**Family Ties** (NBC, 1985) River Phoenix appeared as Eugene Forbes in one episode of the long-running show.

**Surviving: A Family In Crisis** (ABC, 1985). Screenplay by Joyce Eliason, directed by Waris Hussein.

|  |  |
|---|---|
| Tina Brogan | Ellen Burstyn |
| David Brogan | Len Cariou |
| Rick Brogan | Zach Galligan |
| Lonnie | Molly Ringwald |
| Lois | Marsha Mason |
| Philip Brogan | River Phoenix |
| Sarah Brogan | Heather O'Rourke |

*Feature Films*

**Explorers** (Paramount Pictures, 1985). Screenplay by Eric Luke, directed by Joe Dante.

|  |  |
|---|---|
| Ben Crandall | Ethan Hawke |
| Darren Woods | Jason Presson |

|                 |                  |
|-----------------|------------------|
| Wolfgang Muller | River Phoenix    |
| Lori Swenson    | Amanda Petersen  |

**Stand By Me** (Columbia Pictures, 1986). Based on a short story by Stephen King called "The Body." Screenplay by Raynold Gideon and Bruce A. Evans, directed by Rob Reiner.

|                  |                    |
|------------------|--------------------|
| Gordie Lachance  | Wil Wheaton        |
| Teddy Duchamp    | Corey Feldman      |
| Chris Chambers   | River Phoenix      |
|                  | Jerry O'Connell    |
| Ace Merrill      | Kiefer Sutherland  |
| The Writer       | Richard Dreyfuss   |

**The Mosquito Coast** (Saul Zaentz, 1986). Screenplay by Paul Schrader, directed by Peter Weir.

|                  |                    |
|------------------|--------------------|
| Allie Fox        | Harrison Ford      |
| Mother           | Helen Mirren       |
| Charlie Fox      | River Phoenix      |
| Jerry Fox        | Jadrien Steele     |
| Emily Spellgood  | Martha Plimpton    |

**A Night in the Life of Jimmy Reardon** (Island Pictures, 1988). Screenplay and directed by William Richert from his novel *Aren't You Even Gonna Kiss Me Goodbye*.

|                   |                    |
|-------------------|--------------------|
| Jimmy Reardon     | River Phoenix      |
| Joyce Fickett     | Ann Magnuson       |
| Lisa Bentwright   | Meredith Salenger  |
| Denise Hunter     | Ione Skye          |
| Faye Hallaren     | Jane Reardon       |

**Little Nikita** (Columbia Pictures, 1988). Screenplay by John Hill and Bo Goldman, directed by Richard Benjamin.

|                 |                  |
|-----------------|------------------|
| Roy Parmenter   | Sidney Poitier   |
| Jeff Grant      | River Phoenix    |

Richard Grant    Richard Jenkins
Konstantin Karpov    Richard Bradford
Verna McLaughlin    Loretta Devine

**Running on Empty** (Lorimar Film Entertainment, 1988). Screenplay by Naomi Foner, directed by Sidney Lumet.

Arthur Pope    Judd Hirsch
Danny Pope    River Phoenix
Annie Pope    Christine Lahti
Lorna Phillips    Martha Plimpton
Harry Pope    Jonas Abry

**Indiana Jones and the Last Crusade** (Lucasfilm for Paramount Pictures, 1989). Screenplay by Jeffrey Boam, directed by Steven Spielberg.

Indiana Jones    Harrison Ford
Dr. Henry Jones    Sean Connery
Marcus Brody    Denholm Elliott
Young Indy    River Phoenix

**I Love You To Death** (Tristar Pictures, 1990). Screenplay by John Kostmayor, directed by Lawrence Kasdan.

Joey Boca    Kevin Kline
Rosalie Boca    Tracey Ullman
Devo Wod    River Phoenix
Harlan James    William Hurt
Marlon James    Keanu Reeves
Nadja    Joan Plowright

**Dogfight** (Warner Bros., 1991). Screenplay by Bob Comfort, directed by Nancy Savoca.

Birdlace    River Phoenix
Rose    Lili Taylor

| | |
|---|---|
| Berzine | Richard Panebranco |
| Oxie | Anthony Clark |
| Rose Sr. | Holly Near |

**My Own Private Idaho** (New Line Cinema, 1991). Screenplay and directed by Gus Van Sant.

| | |
|---|---|
| Mike Waters | River Phoenix |
| Scott Favor | Keanu Reeves |
| Bob Pigeon | William Richert |
| Gary | Rodney Harvey |
| Digger | Mike Parker |
| Bud | Flea |
| Alena | Grace Zabriskie |
| Richard Waters | James Russo |
| German john | Udo Kier |

**Sneakers** (Universal Pictures, 1992). Screenplay by Phil Alden Robinson, Walter F. Parkes and Lawrence Lasker, directed by Phil Alden Robinson.

| | |
|---|---|
| Martin Bishop | Robert Redford |
| "Mother" | Dan Aykroyd |
| Carl | River Phoenix |
| Cosmo | Ben Kingsley |
| Crease | Sidney Poitier |

**Silent Tongue** (Bebo Films/Alive films, 1993). Screenplay and directed by Sam Shepard.

| | |
|---|---|
| Prescott Roe | Richard Harris |
| Awbonnie | Sheila Tousey |
| Eamon McCree | Alan Bates |
| Talbot Roe | River Phoenix |
| Reeves McCree | Dermot Mulroney |
| Silent Tongue | Tantoo Cardinal |

**The Thing Called Love** (Paramount Pictures, 1993). Directed by Peter Bogdanovich.

| | |
|---:|:---|
| James Wright | River Phoenix |
| Miranda Presley | Samantha Mathis |
| Kyle | Dermot Mulroney |

**Dark Blood** (Uncompleted) Directed by George Sluizer.

| | |
|---:|:---|
| Boy | River Phoenix |
| Wife | Judy Davis |
| Husband | Jonathan Pryce |

# CHAPTER NOTES

The following chapter notes are designed to inform the reader of the sources used in preparing *Lost In Hollywood: The Fast Times and Short Life of River Phoenix.*

**Chapter One**

The author interviewed for this chapter: Frances Beck, Lala Delude, Dirk Drake, Margaret Dunetz, Josh Greenbaum, Kenny Greenbaum, Judy Knapp, Roy Nance.

St. Petersburg *Times* (May 19, 1979)
Premiere magazine (April 1988)
People magazine (September 29, 1988).

Grace Catalano, *River Phoenix: Hero and Heartthrob*, Bantam, 1986.

**Chapter Two**

Author interviewed: Dr. Sam Ajamian, Deborah Berg, Priscilla Coates, Jonathan Sherman and Hap Wotilla.

Time magazine (August 22, 1977)
Los Angeles *Times* (March 22, 1993)
New York *Times* (October 14, 1974 and January 5, 1989)
Movieline (September 1991)
St. Petersburg *Times* (May 19, 1979)

Details (July 23, 1991)
US magazine (October 17, 1988)
Premiere magazine (April 1988)
Chicago *Sun-Times* (September 28, 1988)
The Face (July 1989)
*The Coping Show*—Charter Hospital, California
Anti-COG filmed lecture by Bithia Sherman
Flirty Fishing Handbook #383

Grace Catalano, *River Phoenix: Hero and Heartthrob,* Bantam Books, 1986.


**Chapter Three**

The following were interviewed for this chapter: Frances Beck, Dirk Drake and Wade Evans.

Chicago *Sun-Times* (September 25, 1988)
*Daily News* magazine (August 16, 1987)
New York *Times* (January 5, 1991, September 29, 1991)
Los Angeles *Herald-Examiner* (September 11, 1988)
San Francisco *Chronicle* (December 29, 1988)
St. Petersburg *Times* (May 19, 1979)
Interview magazine (March 1987)
Movieline (September 1991)
Time magazine (November 12, 1984)
US magazine (October 17, 1988)

Grace Catalano, *River Phoenix: Hero and Heartthrob,* Bantam Books, 1986.


**Chapter Four**

For this chapter the author interviewed: Frances Beck, Joe Dante, David Gerber, Waris Hussein, Jonathan Sherman and Terri Treas.

The Advocate (September 24, 1991)
Chicago *Sun-Times* (September 28, 1988)
Premiere magazine (March 1994)
St. Petersburg *Times* (February 5, 1983)

Grace Catalano, *River Phoenix: Hero and Heartthrob,* Bantam Books, 1986.

**Chapter Five**

The author interviewed for this chapter: Joe Dante and Pat Brewer.

Orange County *Register* (June 1987)
Philadelphia *Inquirer* (August 31, 1986)
Chicago *Sun-Times* (September 28, 1988)
New York *Times* (September 16, 1986)
Details (1989)
Premiere magazine (March 1994)
Movieline (September 1991)
US magazine (October 17, 1988)
People magazine (September 29, 1986)
Interview magazine (March 1987)
Life magazine (August 1987)

Grace Catalano, *River Phoenix: Hero and Heartthrob,* Bantam Books, 1986.

**Chapter Six**

The author interviewed for this chapter: Pat Brewer, Bill DeYoung and Dirk Drake.

Philadelphia *Inquirer* magazine (January 25, 1987)
*USA Today* (January 8, 1987)
Los Angeles *Times* (September 7, 1988)
*Hollywood Reporter* (July 1988)
US magazine (October 17, 1988)
Elle magazine (February 1994)
Starlog (October 1989)
People magazine (September 29, 1986)
Premiere magazine (March 1994)
Life magazine (August 1987)
Playgirl (August 1988)
Esquire (March 1994)
Interview (March 1987)

Grace Catalano, *River Phoenix: Hero and Heartthrob,* Bantam Books, 1986.

## Chapter Seven

The author interviewed for this chapter: Jim Dobson, Dirk Drake, Josh Greenbaum, Nick Richert and William Richert.

Premiere magazine (April 1988 and March 1994)
New York *Times* (March 23, 1988)
New York *Post* (March 28, 1988)
*Hollywood Reporter* (July 1988)
Playgirl (August 1988)
River Phoenix's unpublished taped interview with Bill DeYoung (March 1989)
The Mail on Sunday (September 1988).

Grace Catalano, *River Phoenix: Hero and Heartthrob*, Bantam Books, 1986.

## Chapter Eight

In this chapter the following were interviewed by the author: Pat Brewer, Jim Dobson, Dirk Drake, Josh Greenbaum, Jim Kesl and Nick Richert.

*Associated Press* (October 10, 1988)
New York *Post* (November 18, 1986 and March 28, 1988)
Boston *Herald* (March 23, 1988 and September 30, 1988)
*USA Today* (April 4, 1988)
Los Angeles *Times* (September 7, 1988)
*Village View* (September 9–15, 1988)
San Francisco *Chronicle* (December 29, 1988)
Premiere magazine (April 1988 and March 1994)
Esquire (March 1994)
US magazine (October 17, 1988)
Playgirl (August 1988)
London *Guardian* (July 1989)

Grace Catalano, *River Phoenix: Hero and Heartthrob*, Bantam Books, 1986.

## Chapter Nine

For this chapter the author interviewed: Frances Beck, Anthony Campanaro, Dirk Drake, Josh Greenbaum, Kenny Greenbaum and Charlie Scales.

Gainesville *Sun* (January 28, 1994)
Los Angeles *Times* (September 7, 1988)
New York *Daily News* (March 17, 1988)
New York *Times* (March 18, 1988)
The Face (July 1989)
Premiere magazine (April 1988)
Movieline (September 1991)
Details (July 23, 1991)

Grace Catalano, *River Phoenix: Hero and Heartthrob,* Bantam Books, 1986.

## Chapter Ten

For this chapter the author interviewed: Anthony Campanaro, Dirk Drake, Josh Greenbaum, Kenny Greenbaum, Rachel Guinan, Holly Jensen, Heidi Lopez, Abby Rude.

Los Angeles *Herald-Examiner* (September 11, 1988)
New York *Daily News* (January 16, 1989)
San Francisco *Chronicle* (December 29, 1988)
*Today* (London) (September 5, 1994)
New York *Times* (January 5, 1989)
Boston *Herald* (September 30, 1988)
*Hollywood Reporter* (July 1988 and September 19, 1988)
Playgirl (August 1988)
Premiere magazine (April 1988)
Esquire (March 1994)
Movieline (September 1991)
Starlog (October 1989)

**Chapter Eleven**

The author interviewed for this chapter: Anthony Campanaro, Bill De-Young, Jim Dobson, Dirk Drake, Josh Greenbaum, Kenny Greenbaum, Rachel Guinan, Bill Perry, Charlie Scales, Steven Ward.

Washington *Post* (February 24, 1989)
Boston *Globe* (February 21, 1994)
*Village View* (September 9–15, 1988)
Gainesville *Sun* (March 20, 1989)
Esquire (March 1984)
Starlog (October 1989)
Premiere magazine (March 1994)
River Phoenix's unpublished taped interview with Bill DeYoung (March 1989)

**Chapter Twelve**

For this chapter the author interviewed: Melanie Barr, Anthony Campanaro, Bill DeYoung, Dirk Drake, Wade Evans, Scott Green, Josh Greenbaum, Jim Kesl, Mike Parker, William Richert, Steven Ward.

Sunday Mirror (London) (January 1994)
Gainesville *Sun* (July 13, 1990)
Boston *Herald* (April 18, 1990)
Starlog (October 1989)
Premiere magazine (March 1994)
Esquire (March 1994)
US magazine (November 1991)
River Phoenix's unpublished taped interview with Bill DeYoung (March 1989)
Today (London) (March 1994)

**Chapter Thirteen**

In this chapter the author interviewed: Anthony Campanaro, Dirk Drake, Margaret Dunetz, Wade Evans, Josh Greenbaum, Kenny Greenbaum, Holly Jensen, Jim Kesl, William Richert.

Toronto *Star* (December 22, 1989)
*Today* (London) (September 5, 1994)
San Francisco *Chronicle* (July 22, 1990)
New York *Daily News* (September 12, 1990)
Boston *Globe* (October 1, 1990)
Boston *Herald* (October 21, 1991)
People magazine (April 1990)
Vogue magazine (May 1990)
Esquire (March 1994)


## Chapter Fourteen

The author interviewed for this chapter: Dirk Drake, Scott Green, Conrad "Bud" Montgomery, Mike Parker, Bob Pitchlynn and William Richert.

Mademoiselle (March 1993)
Willamette *Weekly* (October 21, 1993)
New York *Times* (September 29, 1991)
*Women's Wear Daily* (September 25, 1991)
Philadelphia *Inquirer* (October 13, 1991)
Esquire (March 1994)
US magazine (September 1991 and November 1991)
Details (July 23, 1991)
Interview magazine (November 1991)


## Chapter Fifteen

The following were interviewed by the author for this chapter: Wade Evans, Scott Green, Conrad "Bud" Montgomery, Mike Parker, Bob Pitchlynn, Nick Richert, William Richert, Lannie Swerdlow.

New York *Daily News* (September 12, 1991)
Philadelphia *Inquirer* (October 13, 1991)
The Paper (October 1991)
Interview magazine (September 1990 and November 1991)
Premiere (March 1994)
Esquire (March 1994)

The Advocate (September 24, 1991)
US magazine (November 1991)


**Chapter Sixteen**

The author interviewed for this chapter: Melanie Barr, Bill DeYoung, Joe Dolce, Dirk Drake, Wade Evans, Josh Greenbaum, Kenny Greenbaum, Jim Kesl, Nick Richert, Abby Rude, Jonathan Sherman.

Gainesville *Sun* (January 28, 1994)
New York *Post* (January 4, 1991 and March 14, 1991)
Chicago *Sun-Times* (April 19, 1991)
*Newsday* (March 7, 1991)
Star magazine (January 22, 1991)
Globe (February 1991)
Premiere (March 1994)
Sassy (June 1991)
US magazine (September 1991)
Movieline (September 1991)
Empire (April 1992)
Esquire (March 1994)
Out magazine (February/March 1994)
Details (July 23, 1991)


**Chapter Seventeen**

For this chapter the author interviewed: Bill DeYoung, Jim Dobson, Dirk Drake, Josh Greenbaum, Conrad "Bud" Montgomery, Mike Parker, Mark Pinske, Bob Pitchlynn, William Richert, Abby Rude and Steven Ward.

Gainesville *Sun* (January 28, 1994)
Boston *Herald* (October 21, 1991)
New York *Daily News* (September 12, 1991)
New York *Post* (September 14, 1991 and October 3, 1991)
*Today* (London) (September 7, 1994)
*USA Today* (October 18, 1991)
*Women's Wear Daily* (September 25, 1991)

Philadelphia *Inquirer* (October 3, 1991 and October 13, 1991)
Detour (July 1993)
Newsweek (June 13, 1994)
People (January 17, 1994)
Esquire (March 1994)
Movieline (September 1991)
Spin (December 1993)
*Hollywood Reporter* (September 19, 1988)
Rolling Stone (October 17, 1991)
Premiere (October 1992 and March 1994)
The Paper (October 1991)


## Chapter Eighteen

For this chapter the author interviewed: Dirk Drake, Josh Greenbaum, Nick Richert and William Richert.

Los Angeles *Times* (November 1993)
New York *Post* (February 25, 1994)
Premiere (March 1994)
Esquire (March 1994)


## Chapter Nineteen

For this chapter the author interviewed Dirk Drake and Alan Moyle.

Chicago *Sun-Times* (January 21, 1994)
*Mail on Sunday* (London) (November 14, 1993)
Premiere (March 1994)
US magazine (October 1993 and January 1994)
Detour (July 1993)
Seventeen (August 1993)
Entertainment Weekly (November 12, 1993)

**Chapter Twenty**

The author interviewed for this chapter: Melanie Barr, Rachel Guinan, Josh Greenbaum, Kenny Greenbaum, Jim Kesl, Paul Petersen, Mark Pinske, Nick Richert, William Richert, Abby Rude, Dave Smadbeck.

Gainesville *Sun* (January 28, 1994)
New York *Post* (April 30, 1993 and November 11, 1994)
Esquire (March 1994)
Detour (July 1993)
Premiere (March 1994)
People (November 15, 1993)

**Chapter Twenty-one**

For this chapter the author interviewed: Dirk Drake, Scott Green, Mark Pinske, Sasa Raphael, Abby Rude, Dave Smadbeck and George Sluizer.

Los Angeles *Times* (November 3, 1991)
*Sun* (London) (November 1, 1994)
*Today* (London) (September 5 and 7, 1994)
Gainesville *Sun* (July 1994)
Mademoiselle (August 1993)
People (January 17, 1994)
Detour (July 1993)
Premiere (March 1994)

**Chapter Twenty-two**

The author interviewed the following for this chapter: Dirk Drake, Scott Green, Josh Greenbaum, Mark Pinske, William Richert, Abby Rude and George Sluizer.

Premiere (March 1994 and October 1994)
Esquire (March 1994)

**Chapter Twenty-three**

For this chapter the author interviewed the following: Ron Davis, Dirk Drake, Detective Sergeant Mike Lee, William Richert, Abby Rude and George Sluizer.

Los Angeles *Times* (November 2, 1993)
*Today* (London) (September 7, 1994)
New York *Daily News* (November 1, 1993)
Esquire (March 1994)


**Chapter Twenty-four**

For this chapter the author interviewed: Bill DeYoung, Dirk Drake, Josh Greenbaum, Kenny Greenbaum, Rachel Guinan, Holly Jensen, Jim Kesl, Pat Koch and Jonathan Sherman.

*Associated Press* (November 1 and 2, 1993)
Willamette Week (December 16–22, 1993)
Washington *Post* (November 2 and 13, 1993)
New York *Times* (November 2, 1993)
Los Angeles *Times* (November 2 and 4, 1993)
*Sun* (London) (November 2, 1993)
*Today* (London) (September 5 and 7, 1993)
Chicago *Sun-Times* (November 14, 1993)
New York *Post* (November 13, 1993)
New York *Daily News* (November 13, 1993)
Gainesville *Sun* (November 13, 1993)
*Hollywood Reporter* (November 15, 1993)
Premiere (October 1994)
Esquire (March 1993)
KCAL-TV (November 1, 1993)
*Variety* (November 1, 1993)
New York *Post* (November 11, 1994)

Bithia Sherman, filmed Anti-COG lecture

## Chapter Twenty-five

For this chapter the author interviewed: Dirk Drake, Mali Finn, Scott Green, Adam Khan, Alan Moyle, Mike Parker, William Richert and Abby Rude.

Los Angeles *Times* (November 24, 1993)
New York *Post* (November 11 and December 8, 1993)
*Today* (London) (September 5 and 6, 1993)
Esquire (March 1993)
People (January 17, 1994)
Entertainment Weekly (January 1994)